Optimizing Human Capital
with a Strategic Project Office

CENTER FOR BUSINESS PRACTICES

Editor
James S. Pennypacker
Director
Center for Business Practices
Havertown, Pennsylvania

The Superior Project Organization: Global Competency Standards and Best Practices, Frank Toney

The Superior Project Manager: Global Competency Standards and Best Practices, Frank Toney

PM Practices

The Strategic Project Office: A Guide to Improving Organizational Performance, J. Kent Crawford

Project Management Maturity Model: Providing a Proven Path to Project Management Excellence, J. Kent Crawford

Managing Multiple Projects: Planning, Scheduling, and Allocating Resources for Competitive Advantage, James S. Pennypacker and Lowell Dye

ADDITIONAL VOLUMES IN PREPARATION

Optimizing Human Capital
with a Strategic Project Office

*Select, Train, Measure, and Reward
People for Organization Success*

J. Kent Crawford
Jeannette Cabanis-Brewin

Auerbach Publications
Taylor & Francis Group
Boca Raton   New York

Published in 2006 by
Auerbach Publications
Taylor & Francis Group
6000 Broken Sound Parkway NW, Suite 300
Boca Raton, FL 33487-2742

© 2006 by Taylor & Francis Group, LLC
Auerbach is an imprint of Taylor & Francis Group

No claim to original U.S. Government works
Printed in the United States of America on acid-free paper
10 9 8 7 6 5 4 3 2 1

International Standard Book Number-10: 0-8493-5410-2 (Hardcover)
International Standard Book Number-13: 978-0-8493-5410-6 (Hardcover)
Library of Congress Card Number 2005048101

Library of Congress Cataloging-in-Publication Data

Crawford, J. Kent.
   Optimizing human capital with a strategic project office : select, train, measure, and reward people for organization success / J. Kent Crawford with Jeanette Cabanis-Brewin.
       p. cm. -- (Center for business practices)
   Includes bibliographical references and index.
   ISBN 0-8493-5410-2 (alk. paper)
   1. Project management. 2. Human capital. 3. Organizational effectiveness. I. Cabanis-Brewin, Jeanette. II. Title. III. Center for business practices (Series) (Boca Raton, Fla.)

HD69.P75C723 2005
658.3--dc22
                                                  2005048101

Taylor & Francis Group
is the Academic Division of T&F Informa plc.

Visit the Taylor & Francis Web site at
http://www.taylorandfrancis.com

and the Auerbach Publications Web site at
http://www.auerbach-publications.com

Contents

SECTION II: MANAGING PEOPLE AS THOUGH PROJECTS REALLY MATTER: BEST PRACTICES FOR CAPITALIZING ON PROJECT PERSONNEL

Preface

People and Projects: The Keys to a "Living Company"

A living thing is distinguished from a dead thing by the multi-
plicity of the changes at any moment taking place in it.

—Herbert Spencer, *Principles of Biology*, 1865

These words of a great British scientist provide a shorthand explanation
for why companies should pay close attention to the work being accomplished in the form of projects.

Learning to do a thing well may be a company's entrée to success,
but merely doing that thing well over and over again — the realm of
operational management — leads in time to irrelevance. In his study of
long-lived companies, Royal Dutch Shell strategist Arie de Geus saw that
companies that survived for decades (even, in some cases, centuries) were
in a constant state of renewing themselves, changing strategies, even
changing the core business entirely over time. These he called "living
companies."

How do living companies change and renew? How are new products
developed and launched? How are new processes put in place? How are
new markets explored?

Projects are the answer.

Any change in an organization takes the form of a project, whether
formally or informally. There is a vision of what needs to change, a path
toward it, a group that carries out the tasks along the way; money is
spent, and — as organizations move from the informal to the formal in
managing projects — deadlines are set, schedules are developed, and

closure is defined. "Projects," once considered to be the province of construction, defense, or, more recently, IT, are now understood as the lifeblood of organizations, taking place all over the organization, creating the change that characterizes a living, growing business.

Over the past 30 years, much attention has focused on developing and refining the tools and techniques of project management. We have moved from paper-and-pencil systems of scheduling to sophisticated software solutions; from flipcharts to Web-based applications for collaborative work. But despite the increasing variety and functionality of software for managing projects, certain problems have remained intractable. Tools alone, apparently, are not the "silver bullet" that assures successful project management.

Again and again, as academic and professional research focuses on project management failure and success, the problems they define and the prescriptions they recommend circle around a single theme. What is the common thread in the following research-based statements?

- "Most problems in projects are not technical in nature; they are communication problems." (This conclusion, reached in some of the earliest project management research by Barry Posner, has been proven true in countless studies.)
- "The single most important factor in project success is a professional project manager." (From *The Superior Project Manager*, by Frank Toney, research based on seven years of Top 500 Project Management Benchmarking Forums.)
- "All project failures are political." (Jim Johnson, chairman of software development research firm The Standish Group, in a 1997 interview in *PM Network*.)

You got it: *people*. This should not surprise anyone, in the age of knowledge management, knowledge workers, and intellectual capital. Over the past decade, research in human resource development and related fields has underlined the value and importance of investing in the "human capital" of the organization. The strategic importance of human capital has grown exponentially as the workforce has changed from "strong backs and capable hands" to "flexible and creative minds." Today, for the companies that generate most of society's wealth — technology, biomedical, and financial services organizations — human capital and business success are inseparable.

As these two realities of the modern marketplace converge — projects as the engines of growth and people as the engine of projects — one finds the traditional methods of dealing with human resource issues becoming dated. The old economy view of "employees as a cost center to be rigidly contained" is incompatible with the knowledge economy. What can replace it?

We do not claim to be experts in human resource development. However, 30 years of experience on projects has shown us that:

1. Management by projects has the potential to be a winning strategy for most, if not all, organizations, *but*
2. The ability of project managers and team members to do their best is often constrained by organizational models and structures not suited to the project environment.

Yet management alternatives do exist, and one of these is the enterprise-level Project Office: an organizational center that promotes excellence in the practice of project management.

Project Office is a term that is loosely defined and can mean different things in different companies, from a discrete organizational unit that simply manages one mega-project, to an "office" of one person who mentors project managers throughout a company. But we have a vision — not a fantasy, for these types of Project Offices do exist and function in many successful companies — of a Project Office that takes on the responsibility for making sure that, across an enterprise, the promise of project management can unfold without being cramped by bureaucratic barriers. This "Strategic Project Office" (or SPO) was the subject of an award-winning book in which we discussed the process necessary to set up such an organizational entity in some detail.[1]

This book expands on one aspect of the SPO: its potential to transform an enterprise by making the most of people. We have made an exhaustive review of the literature available on pressing topics such as the hiring, retention, measurement, training, and professional development of knowledge workers. The chapters that follow summarize current thinking on these topics and offer a model of how the best aspirations of people can be made a reality through the medium of the SPO. The authors share best practices of project-savvy organizations and give detailed information on their own company's working models for assessing and developing competency, building inspired teams, and providing people with a work environment where their intrinsic motivation can flower.

It is the authors' hope that this book will become a blueprint for the creation of "living companies."

Acknowledgments

If you steal from one author, it's plagiarism; if you steal from many, it's research.

—Wilson Mizner, *U.S. dramatist*, 1953

I am so pleased to put many years of life's experiences to paper with the publishing of this book. To my knowledge, no text has captured the information portrayed in these writings. I have scoured my memory banks from government areas in the Air Force aeronautical systems offices, the Department of Energy, NASA, as well as commerce in information technology, product development, pharmaceuticals, research and development, marketing, and operations to develop these concepts. Our research has stretched our investigation to areas where "none have gone before." I am very proud to publish this work, which I believe will shape the course of many careers in project management.

My greatest appreciation is lavished on Jeannette Cabanis-Brewin; researcher, writer, and investigator extraordinaire. Jeannette worked countless hours to develop wonderfully powerful research to support and develop the direction we took with this book. Jeannette's work has been well known through the Project Management Institute, the Center for Business Practices, and countless publications both in print and online. We relied heavily on Jeannette's background in human resource management and organizational change, as well as on her previous writings on project management, for much of the research conducted for this book. Thank you, Jeannette!

Many thanks go to the staff of Project Management Solutions, PM College, and the Center for Business Practices. Your brilliant work for our many clients provides creative insight into the many new concepts and approaches developed within these pages. So many times you have served as the "test bed" for these concepts and patiently retried new ideas until we found the one that worked. Thank you for sticking with me through those challenging times. Particular thanks go to those associates who have helped develop our competency, career pathing, and professional development processes: Deborah Bigelow, Jimmie West, Karen R.J. White, and Meredith McNichol, as well as our partners at Caliper, Inc.

My deepest love and affection to those who make it all worthwhile. Thank you to my children; Janelle, Jordan and Tiffany, Matt and Rebecca, and Jason and Jenny. A special "I love you" to my grandchildren, Jonah, Tyler, Anna, and Silas.

Finally, thanks to you, the reader. You are part of the fastest-growing profession of the 21st century — project management. I hope you will apply the concepts contained in these chapters to build your career and the careers of those around you. I also hope you will take what you learn, share it with others, and build your organizations to levels of dynamic performance.

— **J. Kent Crawford, PMP**®
June 2004

Introduction

People, Projects, and Knowledge:
Change Drivers for Today

> We estimate the wisdom of nations by seeing what they did
> with their surplus capital.
>
> **—Ralph Waldo Emerson, *Wealth,* 1856**

Measuring corporate performance used to be easy. Assets, in particular, were simple to evaluate: buildings, machinery, orders for widgets, materials to make them … these concrete things had agreed-upon dollar values. Divvy up time into neat fiscal years, apply a formula, and … voila!

Then came the knowledge economy. In a shift that has been compared to the Industrial Revolution in terms of its far-reaching consequences, the majority of workers, from entry-level service jobs to professionals, have moved from concrete tasks based on *making things*, to more abstract work based on *thinking problems through* and designing solutions. This paradigm shift changes everything, and business is still grappling with the fallout. How to educate, recruit, reward, manage, and retain the knowledge worker is a subject that fills volumes. Concepts such as self-managing teams, the community of practice, pay-for-performance, intangible rewards, and intrinsic motivation are all outgrowths of our economy's shift from what has been termed a "make-and-sell" orientation to a "sense-and-respond" model. Make-and-sell, an industrial-age model based on capital assets and mass production, contrasts sharply with the sense-and-respond information- and service-age model, which emphasizes relationships and intellectual assets.

Business Week magazine, in a feature about 21st-century organizations, has warned:

> "If you've worked as a manager for at least a decade, you can forget much of what you've learned so far. The vast changes reshaping the world's business terrain are that far-reaching, that fundamental, that profound."

Failure as a Signal of Change

As we study the business press these days, it is difficult to escape the sinking feeling that the majority of enterprises are measuring the wrong things, managing the wrong way, and engaging primarily in unproductive exercises. Author Gary Hamel has noted that "we are living in a world so complex and so uncertain that authoritarian, control-oriented companies are bound to fail."[2] The signs of this failure are everywhere. To briefly catalog a few examples:

Failure of Strategy

Fortune magazine has reported that nine out of ten corporate strategies devised on the executive level never come to fruition.[3] One clue to the reason for this is found in a survey conducted by the Society for Human Resource Management and the Balanced Scorecard Collaborative: 73 percent of polled organizations said they had a clearly articulated strategic direction, but only 44 percent of them communicated that strategy well to the employees who must implement it. These companies "are like a body whose brain is unable to tell it what to do."[4]

Perhaps out of frustration with these failures, many companies are spending less time on strategy; research has shown that 60 percent do not link strategy and budgeting and 85 percent of management teams spend less than an hour a month discussing strategy.[5]

One traditional strategy for boosting profits and securing customers is the merger or acquisition, the rate of which has skyrocketed in the past decade. Two assumptions underlie this craze: (1) that shareholder value will increase significantly because the performance of the merged organizations will be at a higher level, and (2) that managers' skills are sufficient to integrate two organizations. Both assumptions are apparently wrong. About 70 percent of mergers and acquisitions fail to deliver the expected financial benefits. One problem is that mergers break up intact communities of people in marketing, R&D, IT, and other knowledge-intensive pockets of the organizations. When these groups break up, the important work that they support is at risk. The most difficult asset to identify and capture during a merger is "tacit knowledge," those intellectual assets that exist in the minds of people. When the human element of a sweeping organizational change such as a merger is mishandled — as it often is — the tacit intellectual assets often walk out the door.[6]

Project management research has shown that most companies, far from having a coherent model for managing the projects under way and planned as a "portfolio," have at best a vague idea of how many projects they have in the pipeline, how much they will cost, how they will be staffed, or who is qualified to run them, thus making strategic planning an exercise in fantasy.[7] Studies of the failure of customer relationship management systems confirm that lack of knowledge about one's own company is a primary reason for project failure. Companies that do not know their starting position build future corporate plans not on a solid foundation, but on shifting sand. Furthermore, their leadership does not even understand what is wrong, or how to distinguish what needs fixing. In more than 100 assessments of customer management ability, the companies that were worst at dealing with customers had the highest opinion of themselves.[8]

Failure of Measurement Models

In a 1998 *CFO Europe* survey, 88 percent of respondents said they were dissatisfied with the budgeting model, and that its value had diminished because the mechanics of the budgeting process are inefficient; budgets are prepared in isolation from, and not aligned to, company strategy and goals; the focus is on financial outputs and excludes other performance measures; and employee goals and appraisals are not linked to business objectives. At the same time, budgeting has become even more expensive: a KPMG study showed that budgeting consumes 20 to 30 percent of senior executives' time.[9]

Conventional performance evaluation is based on current financial measures, which are well accepted — and backward looking. To identify processes and activities that generate value over the long term, attention to historic financial data is not enough. When managers concentrate strictly on improving financial reporting indicators, they miss opportunities to develop the company's intangible assets. The balanced scorecard is a relatively new model for integrating financial and nonfinancial measures to monitor organizational performance.[10] It is a model well-suited to the "new economy" of knowledge and service work. Yet, according to the Centre for Business Performance at Cranfield School of Management, the balanced scorecard is rarely implemented properly. According to one study, around half of all large firms had adopted this performance measurement technique but up to 70 percent of implementations had failed.[11,12]

Failure of Technology Solutions

Recent developments in information technology have led many companies to attempt to leverage knowledge. However, most companies quickly find that leveraging knowledge is very difficult to achieve. They typically focus on information systems — identifying what information to capture, constructing taxonomies for organizing information, determining access, etc. These knowledge management (KM) systems projects, according to one KM expert, have been "a train wreck,"[13] expensive failures that simply create what KM guru Richard McDermott has called "information junkyards." KM systems are not the only failures. Customer relationship management systems fail more than 70 percent of the time. Human resource management systems, ERP systems, and other enterprise "solutions" display equally dismal outcomes: 92 percent of companies are dissatisfied with results achieved to date from ERP implementations, and HRIS systems implementations create such chaos that HR executives cannot even provide any figures to researchers on success or failure. A qualitative evaluation, however, was provided by one survey respondent: "The implementation has been extremely painful and costly to the organization."[14] Although a Gartner Group study suggests that companies that use technology effectively to manage the human resource function will have a tremendous advantage over those that do not, less than 20 percent of the human resource managers in a survey conducted by Deloitte & Touche/Lawson Software said that their organization has the technology to provide human resource information for business planning.[15]

Failure of Human Systems

A 1998 McKinsey report, *The War for Talent*, pointed out that big companies are finding it difficult to attract and retain good people. Since then, despite mass layoffs and high unemployment, companies still complain of a shortage of the right skills, and of problems attracting qualified people. Meanwhile, downsizing, short-term contracts, and higher productivity demands are pushing workers to the verge of nervous breakdowns. A recent report from the International Labor Organization, *Mental Health in the Workplace*, stated: "Workers worldwide confront, as never before, an array of new organizational structures and processes … For employers, the costs are felt in terms of low productivity, reduced profits, high rates of staff turnover, and increased costs of recruiting and training replacement staff."[16] Table 1 displays research that shows what today's CEOs are most concerned about: human capital issues.

Respondents to a survey sponsored by *Chief Executive* magazine and the consulting firm Accenture chorused that "People are the key to success

TABLE 1   What Matters Today

CEOs say the greatest challenges in the new economy are...	
Finding/retaining good people	47 percent
Strategy and planning	21 percent
Business partnering/alliances	10 percent
Compared to three years ago, people issues are...	
More important	84 percent
Equally important	14 percent
Less important	2 percent
CEOs see top people issues as...	
Attracting the best talent	39 percent
Retaining/motivating key staff	26 percent
Managing the process of change	17 percent
Will developing current talent become more important than training?	
Agree	62 percent
Equal importance	34 percent
Disagree	4 percent

Source: Robert S. Benchley, The Value of Human Capital, *The Chief Executive,* February 2001.

in the new economy." However, their responses to questions showed that only a minority of companies have made significant changes to their HR strategies. Although 74 percent of senior execs say that people-related issues are more important to a company's success than they were a year ago, only one in four believes that most of its employees have the skills to execute their jobs effectively. However, 57 percent said their companies never or rarely measure the impact of HR investments on employee satisfaction.[17]

In 1996, the Olsten Corporation released a study showing that, after the rush to resize, two-thirds of American companies were understaffed. Industries from high-tech to finance were unable to meet deadlines because they did not have enough people. And, 80 percent of them said that the people they had lacked the right skills — a tacit admission that they had gotten rid of top performers in their enthusiasm for short-term cost-cutting.[18] Today we are beginning to see the same issues arise. Except, this time, the repercussions will be more severe. We have the knowledge economy to thank for that.

Researchers who began a study with the assumption that CIOs want to retain scarce IT professionals found that, in fact, many organizations do not seek long-term relationships with these knowledge workers, despite the fact that they are expensive to replace, with each new hire costing thousands — some studies show costs of 100 percent to 300 percent of the position's annual salary.[19] They prefer a maximum productivity strategy that author James R. Lucas has called "burning all your resources to build a bigger short-term fire."[20]

Meanwhile, about a third of new hires in some industries consist of temporary contract jobs. In some workplaces, workers recruited through temp agencies or consulting firms have become the "core," not just in the sense that they are quantitatively larger than the permanent workforce, but also in that their presence at the workplace changes its culture and dynamics, often in unintended ways.[21]

In fact, change initiatives of every kind experience high rates of failure; large companies are especially at risk. In the Accenture Business Results study, although 71 percent of CEOs saw their company as better than existing competitors at dealing with change. But when comparing themselves to emerging competition, only 50 percent felt they were better and 19 percent said they were much worse.[22] Often, failures of change initiatives occur because companies attempt to apply knowledge-economy solutions to industrial-era organizational structures. The fit is not good and the Band-Aid is not likely to stick.

Yes, the old precepts of scientific management have been turned on their heads in the past few decades. It is not that we do not have any new models and structures to replace them, but the status quo structures and policies of organizations lag behind the ideas held by many of the people that comprise them. In many companies, knowledge workers — the majority of them also project team members — continue to be managed and rewarded as though they were units of labor on an assembly line. Companies continue to try to measure the value of knowledge work as though it were the same as widget manufacture. They use industrial-era models to measure corporate performance. They devise strategy in a top-down fashion and forecast as though the world and the marketplace were static. They focus on tweaking operations and "automating the cowpath" while ignoring the breakthrough projects and new competencies that are central to their future success. And when these antiquated policies fail, companies still act as though labor were nothing but a cost center, and try to downsize their way to greatness.

There must be a better way, and we think it has a lot to do with the ideas and practices inherent in project management.

What We Know ...

Three interconnected features characterize the Knowledge Economy: people, change, and projects. It is impossible to talk about knowledge management without addressing all three topics. Change initiatives are always projects; projects almost always create change. "Change agents" are people — not technologies. And *human capital* is the key to the knowledge-intensive work carried out in projects. This should not surprise us, because the Latin root of the word *capital* itself is *caput* — "head."

... About Knowledge

"Knowing is a human act," says Richard McDermott, a leading expert on knowledge management. The only way we create value out of information is through people thinking about it. Knowledge workers turn information into solutions. To solve problems, they piece information together, reflect on their experience, generate insights, and use those insights to solve problems. And, they rarely do this all alone. People learn by participating in communities — workplaces, teams, disciplines, professions — where they receive and share accumulated wisdom.

Not only that, but new knowledge — the kind of most value in today's business climate — comes from thinking outside the bounds of those communities. Just as disruptive technology is often developed by small companies at the edge of a marketplace, and scientists are most productive when they switch from one specialty to another, people create new knowledge from information by looking at it from startling angles. This truth fits very uncomfortably in the traditional, functionally organized company where accountants sit beside accountants and practice accounting tasks using accounting language, while HR people and project management people are segregated elsewhere in the building.

Even companies that are aware of these precepts about knowledge mistakenly have relied on technology to overcome the boundaries between thinkers. The knowledge revolution is inspired by new information systems, but it takes human systems to realize it. The most natural way to do this is to build communities that cross disciplines, time, space, and business units.[23] If this sounds a lot like modern project management to you, you are right on track.

Despite these difficult challenges, organizations are beginning to view knowledge as their most valuable strategic resource and bringing knowledge to bear on problems and opportunities as their most important capability. To remain competitive, businesses must manage their intellectual resources mindfully — not on the automatic pilot installed in the industrial era. The knowledge-enabled organization uses *all employees'* knowledge and skills, regardless of level, function, or location, and provides tools and opportunities for all employees to share their knowledge with each other. As a "learning organization," it also provides opportunities for learning so that employees can access a wide variety of knowledge resources; and it is risk-tolerant in ways that allow employees to create new knowledge without fear of being punished for making mistakes or taking initiative.[24]

... About Human and Intellectual Capital

The focus on human performance now reaches across all industries and from the front lines of customer service to the highest executive ranks. The statistics in Table 1 are evidence of this shift. This emphasis necessitates fundamental shifts in employer–employee relationships; and for those companies that succeed in creating an environment friendly to knowledge sharing and transfer, where people feel they can reach their potential, they now have quantifiable proof of a sizable return. Research by Accenture, Jac Fitz-Enz, Watson Wyatt, and others has shown that even a modest improvement can have a significant bottom-line impact, strengthening the link between workforce–management practices and financial results.[25,26]

Offering a challenging environment is crucial to engaging and keeping the right people, but an organization with top-heavy bureaucracy, memos and directives, and detailed rules and procedures undermines such an environment. Talented people today are much more demanding about their future employers; one study showed that the top reasons why managers chose one firm over another were "values and culture" (58 percent), "freedom and autonomy" (56 percent), and "exciting challenge" (51 percent). The new assumption is that performance improvement is more likely to come from giving capable people control over decisions than from simply adopting new or more stringent measures. Cultural and structural change must accompany — if not precede — changes in technology and performance measurement in the knowledge economy era.[27]

... About Strategy and Performance Measurement

"What gets measured gets managed" is the traditional view of performance measurement, and it is a strong argument for the collection of metrics, provided that they are the right metrics and that they are used in helpful ways. Yet, at a project management conference, we have heard metrics described as "that bundle of sticks that I collect and give my manager to beat me with" — a comment that reflects a lack of respect for human capital is inherent in common performance measurement practices. Franklin Becker of Cornell University has further observed that "what gets measured is eloquent of the real motives of management." These motives may be clearer to the people victimized by inappropriate metrics collection and use than they are to executives, thus causing morale problems rather than performance improvement.

Drivers of business change have historically been primarily economic and reactive. Companies act to save money or ward off threats. Today, however, change is required for other motives. Change projects are often initiated to support new business strategies; to sustain organizational development and human relations initiatives; to attract, nurture, and empower human capital; to incubate process reinvention and product innovation; to reinforce technological systems reengineering; to stimulate information and knowledge management sharing; or to catalyze culture shifts and corporate identity change. These types of change projects are notoriously difficult to carry out, yet until we master the organizational art of helping people to do their best work in an environment characterized by many overlapping change projects, much of our investment in workplace improvement will continue to be wasted.[28]

The difficulty in leading organizations through change, with populations of knowledge workers, is often blamed on individual employees' resistance to change. But according to David J. Armstrong, of Personnel Decisions International, many of the problems companies face as they change are systemic and derive from the existing organizational structure. For example:

■ "The more you change, the more you stay the same. Sources of cost inefficiencies and strategic misalignment often rooted in the culture of the organization and its leaders. Therefore, their solutions 'carry the seeds of the same weaknesses they seek to correct.'"
■ "Companies are quick to cut costs by reducing their workforce. While [this] may allow the company to limit short-term losses, it rarely creates competitive advantage. The most successful changes combine strategic refocus with organizational realignment in roles, processes, and structure."
■ "Organizations are often blind to their own talent. The talent needed most during change is often found in the middle levels; in disciplines that may not be considered, and comes ... from different angles and experiences than those that shaped the last generation."[29]

Our bias is that, often, the "talent needed most" is *project* talent. In both IT and in R&D, significant amounts of research scholarship exist to show the importance of both human factors and project-based work in the management of knowledge professionals. Scientists and engineers solve problems, find information, and discover relationships among phenomena that may lead to the development of new products, services, and processes; in addition, today's business environment has meant that time-to-market is more critical than before, so project cycle-time reduction is critical; intellectual capital development is increasingly being treated as a core competency; teamwork has become widespread; and the emphasis has changed from commanding and controlling people to leading them. About 75 percent of R&D laboratories now rely on cross-functional teams for new product development; one advantage of these teams is that "they increase quality of work life."[30]

If businesses are to survive the complexities and uncertainties of the Knowledge Economy, they must align their business processes, their corporate strategies, their human capital, and their core technologies.[31,32] Table 2 offers advice from organizational development expert James Lucas on aligning strategy and action. But there is one more organizational tool that acts powerfully to focus and align efforts, but which Lucas does not mention — although he alludes to it in his last few bullet points when he mentions decentralizing, people who want to remain mobile, ways to make a quick impact on the organization, and growing leaders.

The Project Connection

At the same time that all this chaos has emerged — and this is no coincidence — the idea of "managing by projects" has been taking hold in many industries.[33] High tech, health care, pharmaceuticals, services such as banking and telecom: these industries are the engine of the Knowledge Economy. They are also, increasingly, industries that rely on projects and project management for competitive success.

Most accounting measures of performance are based on the assumption that a business firm's efficiency of *operations* is the best way to assess goal attainment. The criteria for performance in this case is how much the company obtains as returns from the amount invested on its operations.[34] This is a logical and widely held assumption, which also happens to be wrong. Robert A. Neiman explains why managing by projects helps relieve many of the persistent people and performance problems that business faces today:

> The key to sustained improvement is to use breakthrough projects …. The extraordinary performance achieved by organizations in response to a crisis is well known. In times of crises, some companies have managed to show a threefold increase in unit output, a tenfold increase in speed, a sevenfold increase in productivity. The urgency … of crisis events evokes performance and innovation well beyond the norm.[35]

TABLE 2 The Way Forward

Tips from James Lucas, author of *The Passionate Organization,* for aligning people and strategy for high performance:

Prepare the company for long-term success by nurturing the growth of individuals and the culture. Do not burn all your resources to build a bigger short-term fire.

Involve everyone in strategy formation. The selection and development of strategy cannot be the province of a select few at the top. Get every potentially useful thought into your strategic thinking.

Work for seamless integration. The natural course of organizations is to build barriers, both horizontally between functions and vertically between layers of management.

Ensure that employees' values are not violated. Saying "People are our most important asset" and then mercilessly downsizing is a blatant contradiction. It is in the day-to-day that values and ethics are formed or dismembered.

Do not waste people. Burnout comes from being wasted and imbalanced, not from being stretched and worked hard. Your people are at least as important as shareholders because they are investing their lives.

Speak the truth and eliminate barriers to hearing it. Often, reports and ideas slowly work their way up and get modified by each person along the way. That is why "most organizations are, to one degree or another, reality-impaired."

Power is a means, not an end. Share it.

Go beyond the learning organization to be a teaching organization, where everyone shares what he or she knows and helps others grow. Everyone can participate in this process, middle [managers] can become mentors, coaches and resources rather than babysitters and passive channels of information and direction up and down the organization.

Centralize around vision, not structure. Then decentralize thinking and contributing.

Build mutual trust. Without it, leaders will waste time limiting and controlling others, and followers will resist those limits and controls.

Give people who want to make a difference — but also remain mobile — the opportunity to make an impact more quickly, as well as mentoring and nurturing systems to keep them going.

Help new leaders develop leadership skills, maximize their impact on people and projects, and create broader definitions of success.

The "zest factors" that evoke such high performance, says Neiman, include:

- A clear challenge with a specific goal
- Urgency that requires immediate action and stirs emotion and commitment
- A sense of teamwork and cooperative action that crosses boundaries
- The pressure of necessity and a flexibility in work arrangements that creates innovation and new leaders

These "zest factors" that produce extraordinary performance are part and parcel of projects but are often absent in day-to-day work life (operations). Outside of crises (or projects), performance goes back to "normal." Goals proliferate and become fuzzy. Urgency dissipates and unproductive routines reassert themselves.

Organizing work into short-term initiatives (projects) with goals, deadlines, and achievable visions keeps the "zest factor" in place. Because projects are performed by teams, it also facilitates knowledge creation and transfer. When project managers and teams work within an organizational system that supports the project paradigm, the resulting work environment is one that energizes people, achieves goals, and promotes flexible responses to organizational challenges and opportunities. A recent article on project management in an HR publication said that "projects actually make things happen. Put simply, project management is defining and executing the series of actions required to bring about a result. ... [It] outlines a new way of thinking and performing ... When effectively applied within any job, department or organizational level, project management will promote change in the way a company organizes and allocates work. It helps ... enable employees to work on projects they perceive as important and accomplish organizational goals."[36]

Elements of project management turn up everywhere in business today. Recent studies of customer loyalty show that rotating customer service people through various roles on different teams is an important strategy for keeping a vendor firm's relationship with the customer strong. In customer service, rotation lessens the impact of losing any specific key contact employee, while respondents in consulting, advertising, and technology systems use rotating key contact employees as a strategy to bring fresh, unbiased perspectives to customers. When cross-functional teams are used to sell and service customers, even when individual team members change, the team knowledge about the customer remains.[37]

Projects are "unique endeavors" by definition, and their uniqueness makes any project-driven organization a knowledge-management nightmare — or treasure trove, depending on how the people and processes are managed. Because project work calls for people to think on their feet and apply lessons from seemingly unrelated projects to new problems, project personnel carry around a huge amount of valuable knowledge in their heads. This "tacit knowledge" is difficult to nail down, difficult to collect, and difficult to warehouse in any effective way. Some KM experts have given up on the whole idea of trying to warehouse intellectual capital. Speaking at the Project Leadership Conference in March 2002, David Gilmour of Tacit Knowledge Systems explained that it is far more efficient to simply connect those who need knowledge with those who want to share it.[38]

However, the free flow of knowledge between interconnected personnel requires a lot more than a network and a skills database. It requires people who trust others in their organization enough to ask questions ... and others who feel comfortable sharing what they know. This kind of organizational climate does not happen by accident, but new research into best practices in human capital management contains specific pointers for how to get the most — and the best — out of people. Many of these pointers lead straight into project management territory.

Managing by Projects: An HR Best Practice

HR research firm Watson Wyatt's "Human Capital Index" (HCI) has established a solid link between a company's human capital practices and corporate profitability. The practices with the strongest links to financial success fall under what the report terms "Communications Integrity and Value Creation." These include easy access to technologies for communicating and employee input into how work gets done. Other high-payoff practices are those that create a "collegial, flexible workplace." In this area, project-oriented organizations have the advantage because the management of projects is founded on some of the high-value practices noted in the HCI, such as a culture that encourages teamwork.[39] Other research has identified project-friendly HR practices within the research and development field (see Table 3).

Some surprising, not-so-obvious HR and business effects can result from project management activities. For example, consider the role of project management leaders in communicating the costs of IT to top management. Where project management activities are performed well, the workload is better balanced among IT professionals, resulting in a greater sense of equity; there is also a greater sense of accomplishment, and better morale leads to more open communication with management, a key issue in the formation of trust. Because trust between IT and senior leadership plays a role in the accuracy of estimates and the rationality of resource allocation, the costs of

**TABLE 3   HR Practices to Build Long-Term Relationships
with Knowledge Workers**

Notice that a "management-by-projects" theme runs through these tips.
Design work arrangements to provide sustained opportunities for interesting work; for example, through job rotation.
Provide training and development to build new competencies or to broaden business knowledge or managerial skills.
Employ HR practices that reflect concern for individual employees such as employee participation, community building, and lifestyle accommodations.
In recruiting, focus on influencing the "joining behavior" of knowledge professionals, who prefer collegial, team-based workplaces.
Pay close attention to the management of important relationships, throughout the organization and beyond.

Source: Ritu Agarwal, Crafting an HR strategy to meet the needs for IT workers, *Communications of the ACM,* July 2001.

IT are communicated better and projects are either funded at appropriate levels or the demand for IT services are better matched with available resources. Thus, the stress level within the IT workforce is less likely to lead to burnout — and its expensive twin, turnover.[40,41]

The transition to a team-based work environment requires the integration of team processes and the organization's current management systems and structures. That is not simple, but the rewards are great: in one study, 15 percent of organizations surveyed reported a reduced number of engineering change notices, 13 percent indicated improved customer relations, 24 percent reported increased collaboration between stakeholders in the process, and 20 percent saw an increase in the quality of communication.[42]

Empowerment — that human capital buzzword — means making people more powerful. One way to make people more powerful is to remove the barriers that keep them from succeeding. These barriers are generally structural: functional silos, chains of command, restrictive job descriptions, cultures that hoard information and power rather than sharing it, and incentives that inadvertently reward the wrong behaviors.[43] In the project management field, these barriers are more visible than they perhaps are to people working in more operational jobs within functional areas because project managers and teams are, by nature, "boundary spanners" who operate outside the usual organizational hierarchy. In this, project management is a natural ally with HR. After all, people reside everywhere in the organization ... and so do projects.

How to Use This Book

Section I (Introduction through Chapter 2) focuses on the business case behind reorganizing companies around the managing-by-projects model, and on the roles that executives can play in implementing project management change initiatives. In particular, the focus is on the organizational changes required to create an environment suited to the "care and feeding" of project managers and team members. This section should be of particular interest to executives and organizational development specialists, and to high-ranking members of the project-management community who are seeking both the business rationale and suggested steps for creating a project-friendly work environment.

Section II (Chapters 3 through 7) covers the nuts-and-bolts topics of project personnel management: competency, recruiting, rewards, development, retention, performance measurement, etc. Much of this research is drawn from fields allied to project management: the management of scientists, engineers, and other technical yet creative personnel. But many of the tools offered are original to Project Management Solutions, Inc. and its training and education division, the PM College. This section should be useful to "managers of project managers," to the project managers themselves, to human resource professionals in project-oriented companies, and to the executives responsible for oversight of project management offices.

Section III (Chapter 8) scans the present developments and trends in business and in project management and identifies those "people management" issues and trends that are likely to bring the greatest organizational changes in the immediate future. Forward-looking companies will be interested in considering how the growing interest in virtual work, remote project management, outsourcing, communities of practice, and the like might affect their own workforce planning.

The appendices (A through K) provide several examples of tools for establishing project-friendly human resource practices under the auspices of a Strategic Project Office, including role descriptions for many project-management positions, sample assessment questions from a project manager competency tool, and a maturity assessment for project-related human resource management.

This is not an academic book: we are not professors. It is meant to be a handbook for organizational change. If you want to change the way your company does projects, first change the way you deal with project people. With the right people working at the right tasks — and being managed in the right way — project management excellence is in your future. Good luck!

Notes

1. J. Kent Crawford, *The Strategic Project Office: A Guide to Improving Organizational Performance,* Marcel Dekker, 2001.
2. Gary Hamel, *Leading the Revolution,* Plume, 2002.
3. Jeannette Cabanis-Brewin, Interview with Richard Russell of the Balanced Scorecard Collaborative, *Project Management Best Practices Report,* September 2000.
4. Joe Mullich, Human Resources' Goals Work Best When They're Tied to Company Success, *Workforce Management,* December 2003.
5. Jeremy Hope and Robin Fraser, Figures of hate: traditional budgets hold companies back, restrict staff creativity and prevent them from responding to customers, *Financial Management,* February 2001.
6. Gene Slowinski, Zia Rafii, John Tao, Lawrence Gollob, Matthew Sagal, and Krish Krishnamurthy, After the acquisition: managing paranoid people in schizophrenic organizations, *Research Technology Management,* May–June 2002. Other resources: Maslow, A., *Motivation and Personality,* Harper & Row, New York, 1954; Nonaka, I., A Dynamic Theory of Organizational Knowledge, *Organizational Science,* Vol. 5, No. 1, February 1994; Feldman, M. L. and Spratt, M.F., Post-Merger Integration, pp. 409–417 in Rock, M.L., Rock, R.H., and Sikora, M., *The Mergers and Acquisitions Handbook,* 2nd edition, McGraw-Hill, New York, 1994.
7. Jeannette Cabanis-Brewin, Fooling with tools: project portfolio management: what it isn't, *Project Management Best Practices Report Executive Briefing,* Winter 2003.
8. Michael Starkey and Neil Woodcock, 'I wouldn't start from here': finding a way in CRM projects, *Journal of Database Marketing,* Sept. 2001; also Taylor, A., IT projects: sink or swim, *Computer Bulletin,* January 2000.
9. Jeremy Hope and Robin Fraser, ibid.; also Russ Banham, Revolution in planning, *CFO Magazine,* August 1999; Corporate strategic planning suffers from inefficiencies, PR Newswire, 25 Oct. 1999.
10. The Balanced Scorecard, briefly, allows companies to assess the knowledge, skills, and systems that employees have or will need to innovate and build the right strategic capabilities and efficiencies (the internal processes) that deliver specific value to customers, which will eventually lead to higher shareholder value (the financials). For more about applying the scorecard concept to project management, see Chapter 8.
11. Mike Bourne, Patience charter, *Financial Management,* March 2002.
12. Jason Oliveira, The Balanced Scorecard: an integrative approach to performance evaluation, *Healthcare Financial Management,* May 1, 2001. Also Kaplan, Robert S. and Norton, David P., *The Balanced Scorecard: Translating Strategy into Action,* Harvard Business School Press, Boston, MA, 1996.
13. David Gilmour, presentation at the *Project Leadership Conference,* March 2002.
14. Michael Starkey and Neil Woodcock, presentation at the *Project Leadership Conference,* March 2002.

15. Breaking HR's vicious cycle, *Canadian HR Reporter,* December 3, 2001, www.hrreporter.com, article #1448.
16. Gopika Kannan and K.B. Akhilesh, Human capital knowledge value added: a case study in infotech, *Journal of Intellectual Capital,* 2002.
17. From an Accenture study of 200 CEOs, COOs, CFOs, CIOs, and others in the United States, Europe, and Australia, cited in *Workforce Magazine,* August 2003.
18. Jeannette Cabanis-Brewin, Your career: project of a lifetime, *PM Network,* April 1996.
19. Ritu Agarwal, Crafting an HR strategy to meet the need for IT workers, *Communications of the ACM,* July 2001. Also Becker, B. and Gerhart, B., The impact of human resource management on organizational performance: progress and prospects, *Academy of Management Executive,* Aug. 1996, p. 779–801; Ferratt, T. and Short, L., Are information systems people different: an investigation of motivational differences, *MIS Quarterly,* Dec. 1986, 377–387; Pfeffer, J., *Competitive Advantage through People,* Harvard Business School Publishing, Boston, MA, 1994; see also Pfeffer, J., Hatano, T., and Santalainen, T., Producing sustainable competitive advantage through the effective management of people, *Academy of Management Executive,* Feb. 1995, 55–72; U.S. Department of Commerce, *America's New Deficit: The Shortage of Information Technology Workers,* Office of Technology Policy, Washington, D.C., Sept. 29, 1997; and Walton, R., From control to commitment in the workplace, *Harvard Business Review,* March 1985, p. 77–84.
20. James R. Lucas, *The Passionate Organization: Igniting the Fire of Employee Commitment,* AMACOM, 2001.
21. Kevin Ward, Damian Grimshaw, Jill Rubery, and Huw Beynon, Dilemmas in the management of temporary work agency staff, *Human Resource Management Journal,* 2001.
22. From an Accenture study of 200 CEOs, COOs, CFOs, CIOs, and others in the United States, Europe, and Australia, cited in *Workforce Magazine,* August 2003.
23. Richard McDermott, Ph.D., Knowing is a human act: how information technology inspired, but cannot deliver knowledge management, *California Management Review,* Summer 1999. Also Jolene Galegher, Robert Kraut, and Carmen Egido, 1990, Intellectual Teamwork, New Jersey: Lawrence Erlbaum Associates; Majchrzak, J. and Q. Wang, 1996, Breaking the functional mindset in process organizations, *Harvard Business Review,* 74,5; Wenger, Etienne, *Communities of Practice,* Cambridge University Press, 1998.
24. Gopika Kannan and K.B. Akhilesh, Human capital knowledge value added: a case study in infotech, *Journal of Intellectual Capital,* 2002.
25. Accenture study, ibid.
26. Jac Fitz-Enz, The ROI of Human Capital, *AMACOM,* 2000; Watson Wyatt, The Human Capital Index, www.watsonwyatt.com.
27. Jeremy Hope and Robin Fraser, ibid.

28. Stephen J. Bradley, What's working? Briefing and evaluating workplace performance improvement, *Journal of Corporate Real Estate,* April 2002. Also a reading list on workplace innovation and measurement can be found on www.spaceforbiz.com; Becker, E.D., New Measures for New Ways of Working', *IWSP News,* Cornell University, December, 1997; Vischer, J.C., *Workspace Strategies: Environment as a Tool for Work,* Chapman & Hall, 1996; Cornell International Workplace Studies Program, pp. 129ff; Meyer, C., How the right measures help teams excel, *Harvard Business Review,* Vol. 72, No. 3, pp. 95–10, 1994; Kadzis, R., Measuring Workplace Performance in the Information Age, Site Selection, August–September, 1998.

29. What You Need for a Strategic HR Plan, Workforce, October 1, 2001.

30. George F. Farris and Rene Cordero, Leading your scientists and engineers, *Research Technology Management,* Nov.–Dec. 2002. Also Badawy, M.K., what we have learned about managing human resources, *Research Technology Management,* September–October 1988, pp. 19–35; James, W.M., Best HR practices for today's innovation management, Research Technology Management, January–February 2002, pp. 57–60; Amabile, T.M., How to kill creativity, *Harvard Business Review,* October 1998, pp. 77–87; Kochanski, J. and Ledford, G., How to keep me — Retaining technical professionals, *Research Technology Management,* May–June 2001, pp. 31–38; Petroni, A., Myths and misconceptions in current engineers' management practices, *Team Performance Management,* 6, 2000, pp. 15–24; Cooper, R.G., Developing new products on time, in time, *Research — Technology Management,* Sept.–Oct. 1995, pp. 49–57; Ransley, D.L. and Rogers, J.L., A Consensus on best R&D practices, Research — *Technology Management,* Mar.–Apr. 1994, pp. 19–26; Thompson, P.H. and Dalton, G.W., Are R&D organizations obsolete?, *Harvard Business Review,* November–December 1976, pp. 105–116; Cordero, R., Farris, G.F., and DiTomaso, N., Technical professionals in cross-functional teams: their quality of work life, *Journal of Product Innovation Management,* 15, 1998, pp. 550–563; Reynes, R., Training to manage across silos, *Research Technology Management,* September–October 1999, pp. 20–24; and Wageman, R., critical success factors for creating superb self managing teams, *Organizational Dynamics,* Summer 1997, pp. 49–61.

31. Dennis Comninos and Anton Verwey, Business Focused Project Management, Management Services, January 2002. Other resources on this topic: Tyrell, B., 1998, Customer futures: implications for relationship marketing, *The International Journal of Customer Relationship Management,* Vol. 1, No. 2.; Graham, R.J. and Englund, R.L., *Creating an Environment for Successful Projects,* Jossey-Bass, 1997; and Nicholas J.M., *Managing Business & Engineering Projects — Concepts and Implementation,* Prentice Hall, 1990.

32. Cristiano Busco, Angelo Riccaboni is professor of accounting, Robert Scapens, Culture vultures, *Financial Management,* March 2001.

33. We distinguish between "managing by projects" and "project management." The latter is the application of standards and skills to bring an individual project to a successful outcome. "Managing by projects" is project management raised to an enterprise, or business level. It is applying systems thinking to organizational life, recognizing that much of the activity within the organization is happening within projects, and managing the organization therefore as a collection, or portfolio, of projects.

34. Esmeralda Garbi, Alternative measures of performance for e-companies: a comparison of approaches, *Journal of Business Strategies,* March 22, 2002.

35. Robert A. Neiman, Breakthrough capability, *Executive Excellence,* April 2002.

36. Betty E. Reed, Making things happen (better) with project management, *AFP Exchange,* May–June, 2001.

37. Neeli Bendapudi and Robert P. Leone, Managing business-to-business customer relationships following key contact employee turnover in a vendor firm, *Journal of Marketing,* Spring 2002.

38. Jeannette Cabanis-Brewin, Knowledge creation and projects: haven't you learned your lesson yet?, *Project Management Best Practices Report,* March 2003.

39. Watson Wyatt, Human Capital Index, www.watsonwyatt.com/hci.

40. Ritu Agarwal, ibid.

41. Jeannette Cabanis-Brewin, Managing to estimate, People on Projects: The Project Management Best Practices Report, October 2003.

42. Paul J. Componation, Dawn R. Utley, RE., and James J. Swain, Using risk reduction to measure team performance, *Engineering Management Journal,* December 2001.

43. Francis J. Quinn, Making change happen: an interview with John Kotter, *Supply Chain Management Review,* Nov./Dec. 2002.

THE NEW PROJECT MANAGEMENT

Chapter 1

The Strategic Project Office: A Catalyst for Organizational Change

> What is there that does not appear marvelous when it comes
> to our knowledge for the first time? How many things, too, are
> looked upon as quite impossible until they have been actually
> effected?
>
> **—Pliny the Elder, ca. 70 AD**

At first glance, it might seem folly to propose project management as a
solution to organizational problems, given the discipline's reputation for
project failures. The most often-cited research on project management is
that of the Standish Group International, Inc., a research firm in Dennis,
Massachusetts,[1] whose aptly named *CHAOS Report*, first published in 1994,
has detailed high rates of software project failures. These failures, in a
single industry, have somewhat tainted the name of project management
for those executives with only a passing familiarity with the discipline.
(Table 1.1 offers a quick overview of project management for those who
may not be familiar with the discipline).

No wonder companies have become enchanted by Six Sigma and other
apparent "silver bullets." No wonder that, in many cases, after establishing
project offices and implementing project management (PM) practices, these
same initiatives have been defunded or underemphasized as time passed.[2]

However, a primary contributor to the sense of failure surrounding PM
lies in the inability of organizations to integrate projects with strategy and

TABLE 1.1   Project Management Quick Study

Projects are:

Temporary endeavors undertaken to create a unique product or service[a]
Activities organized to deliver something of value to a customer (and therefore to your organization)
The building blocks in the design and execution of your organization's strategies

Project management is:

The application of knowledge, skills, tools and techniques to project activities in order to meet or exceed stakeholder needs and expectations of a project. Meeting or exceeding stakeholder needs and expectations invariably involves balancing competing demands.[a] These demands include scope, time, quality and cost; identified requirements (needs) and unidentified requirements (expectations).

Management by projects or enterprise project management is:

A system that integrates all the project activity within an organization and links it to organization-wide strategies, priorities, and resource pools. The most common infrastructure to support management by projects is the Project Office.

What value can an organization expect to derive from implementing a Project Office?

Research shows that establishing a Project Office is predictive of success in IT projects: the Gartner Group states that companies with a PO will experience half the delayed and cancelled projects as compared to companies without a PO.

What challenges will the organization face?

Changes in organizational culture, including new information systems, altered communications channels, and new performance measurement strategies.

[a]   Project Management Institute, A Guide to the Project Management Body of Knowledge, PMI, 2000.

in a lack of will to manage project management effectively. Project management implemented half-heartedly within an organizational structure that is unfriendly to it is often set up to fail. Nevertheless, "lessons learned" are an important part of project management discipline, and the lessons of failure have improved the practice of project management and helped develop a body of knowledge about how *not* to manage project-oriented enterprises.

Failure: Wake-Up Call and Teacher

We now have weighty evidence of the most persistent management problems with projects. A survey of project managers conducted in 1999 by Robbins-Gioia, Inc., found that 90 percent often underestimate project size and complexity. Nearly half (44 percent) had cost overruns of 10 to 40 percent, and only 16 percent consistently met scheduled due dates.[3] IT software development projects as presently managed are often 170 percent to 180 percent over budget.[4]

In the consulting field, several industry giants became targets of lawsuits in the late 1990s by companies furious about ERP and HR system implementations that had dragged on for years, run millions of dollars over budget, and created a culture of dependency on the consulting firm.[5,6]

What is the solution? One of The Gartner Group's "Strategic Planning Assumptions" for companies, through 2004, is that organizations should establish enterprise standards for project management, *including a Project Office with suitable governance [italics ours]*. Companies that follow the IT research firm's advice will experience half as many major project cost overruns, delays, and cancellations as those that fail to do so.[7]

Why is project management and, in particular, the project management office, so important? The reason is that most of the value-adding activities that companies do come in the form of projects. Think of operations as interest on capital already amassed; think of projects as the entrepreneurs who create new wealth. New products, new marketing initiatives, new facilities, new organizational processes implemented, mergers and acquisitions: all of these are projects. Think of time as money: if a project is late for an amount of time equal to 10 percent of the projected life of the project, it loses about 30 percent of its potential profits.[8] A study by McKinsey and Company has shown that high-tech products lose 33 percent of after-tax profits when they are late to market, but lose only 4 percent when they are on time — even if they are 50 percent over budget.[9]

In the past decade, there has been a trend toward improvement in our ability to pull off projects. Project slippage and failure rates are falling, at least in those application areas that attract research interest, such as software development and pharmaceutical R&D.[10] Cost and time overruns are down. Large companies have made the most dramatic improvement. In 1994, the chance of a Fortune 500 company's project coming in on time and on budget was 9 percent; its average cost was $2.3 million. In 1998, that same project's chances of success had risen to 24 percent, while the average project cost fell to $1.2 million.

Three factors explain these encouraging results:

1. A trend toward smaller projects that are more successful because they are less complex
2. Better project management
3. Greater use of "standard infrastructures," such as those instituted through a Project Office. (Large companies show up as more

successful in the Standish Group study for one simple reason, in our view large companies lead the pack in the establishment of enterprise-level or Strategic Project Offices.)[11]

The Project Office can also take credit for the implementation of better project management because it is only under the auspices of this organizational home for project management that some of the persistent management problems that plague projects can be ameliorated, including:

- Project managers who lack enterprise-wide multiproject planning, control, and tracking tools often find it impossible to comprehend the system as a whole.[12] Such tools are rarely effectively implemented, trained for, or utilized except under the auspices of a project office. Buying a tool addresses the software issue; and the "peopleware" issues must be addressed by a management entity that specializes in projects.
- Poor project management/managers. Most of the reasons technology projects fail are management related rather than technical. Technical ability is a poor indicator of project management ability, yet many enterprises have no processes in place to ensure that project managers are appropriately trained and evaluated.[13] Does the average corporate HR department possess the knowledge to appropriately hire, train, supervise, and evaluate project management specialists? No; but a Strategic Project Office does.
- There is a high correlation between lack of clear project sponsorship and failure. Executive support for and understanding of projects is lacking in many organizations.[14] When project management gains a seat at the executive level, via the implementation of a Strategic Project Office, the chasm between projects and executives closes.
- Accurate project resource tracking is imperative to successful project management, but many organizations are hampered by awkward or antiquated time-tracking processes.[15] Most companies' time-tracking processes are owned by and originate in the HR department; and most HR departments are still using an employment model developed in the early Industrial Age. Project-based work requires new processes for reporting work progress and level of effort.

Many of the best practices for preventing failures are also directly related to Project Offices, including:

- Enterprises that hold post-implementation reviews harvest best practices and lessons learned, and identify reuse opportunities are laying the necessary groundwork for future successes.[16]
- A Project Office shines as the repository for best practices in planning, estimating, risk assessment, scope containment, skills tracking, time and project reporting, maintaining and supporting methods and standards, and supporting the project manager.
- Sound project plans are realistic, up-to-date, and frequently reviewed; reviews focus not just on what has been done, but look forward to identifying risks and opportunities.
- Project metrics and milestones are defined, measured, and reported.[17]
- Experienced sponsors and project managers develop and maintain a "go/no-go" cancellation strategy. They do not hesitate to kill a project that becomes a liability — and do not indulge in blame and punishment.[18]
- Monitoring critical dates is imperative, and enterprise time-tracking software — usually Web-based for ease of use — has become a necessity for larger projects, multiproject environments, and dispersed project teams.[19]

However, the greatest area of promise for the Project Office lies in its effect on the management of project personnel. Competent and experienced project managers are not accidental: they are grown in an environment that trains, mentors, and rewards them based on performance in projects — a topic that most HR departments know very little about. Benefits of having a good project manager include reduced project expense, higher morale, and quicker time to market. The skills most executives cite as desirable in a project manager include technology and business knowledge, negotiation, good communications (including writing ability), organization, diplomacy, and time management. Understanding the business is more important than understanding technology. They must be able to define requirements, estimate resources and schedule their delivery, budget and manage costs, motivate teams, resolve conflicts, negotiate external resources, manage contracts, assess and reduce risks, and adhere to a standard methodology and quality processes. Obviously, there is a growing body of knowledge about who makes the best project managers, how to develop their skills, and what kinds of rewards motivate them. That body of knowledge has an organizational home in the Project Office.[20] More facts and trends associated with the Project Office are noted in Table 1.2.

TABLE 1.2 Project Management Offices in the News

Research studies are accumulating on the value of the project management office. Some findings:

Senior-level sponsorship and visibility are keys to a successful project management office.

67 percent of companies today have project management offices, but only a fraction of these have enterprise-level SPOs. However, those companies that have a senior-level executive who oversees the PMO reported greater project success rates (projects completed on time, on budget and with all the original specifications) than those without.

SPOs at a corporate level that establish processes for the entire company are taking on a greater number of the company's projects, and the projects managed are larger in terms of dollars invested.

The higher the PMO resides in the organization, the fewer the problems reported.

A project office is a communication tool, maintaining a consistent flow of communication to senior executives and reporting both successes and problem areas.[a]

Problems resolved by project offices include: projects not supported by senior executives, lack of authority, conflict over project ownership, difficulty of cross-functional interface with projects, project prioritization and selection, development of project manager and project team capabilities, and knowledge management issues.[b]

[a] Lorraine Cosgrove Ware, By the Numbers, *CIO Magazine*, July 1, 2003.
[b] Dennis Comninos and Anton Verwey, Business focused project management, *Management Services*, January 2002.

Let us examine two big issues facing companies today — strategy execution and productivity of resources — and how the Strategic Project Office addresses each of them.

Integrating Strategy and Action: Managing the Project Portfolio

Let us go back for a moment to the statistic cited in the Introduction: 80 to 90 percent of strategic plans are never carried out. Just a decade ago, project failure rates were also in the 80 to 90 percent range. Is there a connection? Could strategies be failing because they are not put in place through coordinated projects? Could projects be failing for lack of strategic focus?

Project management writers and researchers see a definite connection. For a decade, experts in the discipline have been predicting that, when executives become more informed about project management and project management wins a voice at the strategy table, the issues we have experienced with project failure will ameliorate.[21] Already in some industries such as IT, this seems to be happening. One helpful trend is that project managers are moving up the ladder. Speaking at the Top 500 Project Management Benchmarking Forum in 2002, Dr. Frank Toney of the University of Phoenix's Executive Initiative Institute noted that "As professionalism increases ... [p]eople who know projects are pointing out to executives that projects are the value-creation engine of business."[22] He also noted that, as with many other business opportunities, portfolio management is a hot topic partly because the tools now exist to facilitate it: "In order to make sound decisions on a portfolio level, decision makers must have sound information on the project and program level." Recent improvements in project management methodology and software support that need for information. With this visibility and understanding has come a drive toward managing the entire enterprise as a portfolio of projects.

Project Portfolio Management: An Overview

A frequent refrain in the business press is that projects must develop more of a business focus. The same might be said of business: that is, a project focus is required. Without a project focus at the highest level of the business, projects seem to pop up at will across the organization, generating confusion. There is a lack of clarity as to how projects align and link to organizational strategy; often there is no business process for selecting projects, and senior management is unaware of the number, scope, or benefits of projects being undertaken. As a result, people both on projects and on the business side feel they are working at cross-purposes with each other.

Giving projects a strategic focus goes a long way toward resolving these concerns. Combining a strategic focus with a business process for selecting and prioritizing projects is an important step in creating an environment for successful projects. In the project-focused business, business-focused projects are driven by results and objectives more than by internal activities. Performance measures are outcome focused and include things such as contribution to organizational goals, objectives and strategies, and stakeholder satisfaction with process and results.[23]

In the past, a focus on managing individual projects well sufficed organizations because most projects were large-scale, long-duration, tangible items: an airplane or a legacy computer system. With the shift to short-term projects and more intangible deliverables, a disconnect has developed between companies' ability to manage projects on the project level and their ability to manage them collectively on the organizational level. Project portfolio management brings order to this situation in two important ways: (1) it brings realism to an organization's planning processes by aligning what an organization *wants* to do with the resources — the money, hours, people, time, and equipment — required to *get it done*; and (2) it brings rationality in the allocation of resources, both human and financial.

While there still are some instances in which a company is almost entirely focused on one or two major projects at a time — small software development firms or capital construction firms — the reality in most businesses is that dozens of projects exist throughout the company in various stages of completion (or, more commonly, of disarray). It would not be at all uncommon for a company to have several new product development projects in process, along with a process reengineering effort, a TQM initiative, a new marketing program in the works, and a fledgling E-business unit. Widen the scope of thought to take in facilities, logistics, manufacturing, and public relations and one begins to understand why most companies have no idea how many projects they have going at one time. And, when one considers that technology plays a role in almost all changes to organizations these days, and that technology projects have an abysmal record of failure,[24] the light begins to dawn: unless all the projects that a company engages in are conceptualized, planned, executed, closed out, and archived in a systematic manner — that is, using the proven methodologies of project management — it will be impossible for an organization to keep a handle on what activities add value and which drain the resources.

You cannot manage what you cannot measure, as the old saying goes; and unless all the projects on the table can be held up to the light and compared to each other, a company has no way of managing them strategically, no way of making intelligent resource allocation decisions, no way of knowing what to delete and what to add. And the only way to have a global sense of how a company's projects are doing is to have some sort of project focus point.

We call this center of organizational focus on projects the Strategic Project Office; but whatever you name it, a home base for project managers and project management is a must for organizations to move from doing a less-than-adequate job of managing projects on an individual basis, to creating the organizational synergy around projects that adds value, dependably and repeatably, to the entire portfolio.

Project managers take a lot of heat when project management does not deliver organizational nirvana, but the truth is that the business of selecting which project to invest in must be carried out at the executive level — at the level of *managing by projects* rather than of *project management*.[25]

And project portfolio management should be an easy sell: Research by Cooper, Edgett, and Klienschmidt reveals that, for R&D portfolios, the top 20 percent of companies had an explicit, established method of portfolio management, consistently applied across the organization. The same research showed that even rudimentary portfolio management processes created a spike of benefits almost immediately. But there are a few basic issues that must be addressed in order to do portfolio management, and all of them are best addressed through the auspices of the Project Office. An organization that is sufficiently mature to do portfolio management must have certain basic organizational attributes and infrastructure in place, including the following attributes.

Attribute: The Organization Knows How To Manage Projects

Trying to implement portfolio management before mastering the basics of managing individual projects is putting the cart before the invention of the wheel. Without project management methodology and practices in place, one does not have the most basic data with which to work. Bad project management means cost and schedule estimates that are exercises in fantasy. How can one implement project management methodology without a Project Office?

Attribute: Projects Are Inventoried

What is in the portfolio? Most companies do not know. Whether the "portfolio" consists of departmental or divisional projects alone, or a more ambitious portfolio of projects from across the enterprise, a complete list of all the initiatives competing for resources is a baseline requirement to even begin portfolio management. Counting projects is a first step toward deriving value from portfolio management because certain realities are quickly revealed: if one schedules 130 percent of project human resources to projects, for example, a lot of things will not get done (and valuable people will quit or go crazy). Some companies list only projects that surpass a predetermined threshold number: a schedule of 30+ days or 100+ hours; or a budget of at least $50,000, for example. Who will be the census-taker, if not the Project Office?

Part of the inventory process should be, literally, counting heads. The organization must know who is available to work on projects, and when. How many project managers and project team members do you have? What is each one doing, right now? When will he be finished with it? What are his areas of particular expertise? The recent trend toward improved resource tracking and leveling functionality in project management software is a great boon to the portfolio manager. In fact, without a system for knowing what each person in the pool of potential project personnel is capable of, and when they will be available, one cannot really be said to manage a portfolio. After all, *people do projects*; and without them, all one has is a plan. Who are the project managers? Again, many large companies do not know. "Project manager" may not be among the role descriptions codified by HR. For some companies, therefore, the scarcest resource is not money, but project managers. When it comes to identifying existing and prospective project managers, an organizational entity devoted to project management does it best.

Attribute: Projects Are Fully Described

Once the parameters of the list are decided, each project on it must be described. Details such as technologies required; estimates of time, cost, and personnel required; and a basic risk/reward calculation give portfolio managers the data they need to compare and contrast projects. Companies skilled at opportunity identification on one hand, and at tracking existing projects on the other, have a significant advantage at this stage. Their lists will be more complete and their estimates more meaningful. Many questions must be answered in detail before one can begin to select and prioritize the projects in the inventory, and some of the answers will not come easily. Which projects make the most money? Which have the lowest risk? Which have subjective value, in terms of community image or internal morale? Which are not optional — projects dictated by regulatory requirements, for example? In the information-gathering process, a second level of shakedown will naturally evolve. Some projects will be backburnered because human resources are not available, some because the technology is immature, some due to looming external risks. Much, if not all, of the information necessary to populate the database about projects in the inventory is generated by the steps in the project management process: scope definition, risk management, scheduling. The software and peopleware required to generate, analyze, and deliver this information should not be scattered all over the organization, but unified under the flag of the SPO.

One cannot make good decisions based on bad information. This is where the enterprise-level project management tools with portfolio management capabilities really earn their keep. Being able to view the most salient information on each and every project in thumbnail-sketch form allows executives to compare apples to apples … and weigh the relative benefits of apples versus oranges. What is less certain is organizational willingness to use these features and train appropriately for them. Who will drive the effort to derive benefit from project management software if not those who are passionate about project management ... and whose appropriate organizational home is the SPO?

Attribute: Projects Are Selected, Prioritized, and the Portfolio Is Balanced

The process used to balance the portfolio must be designed to optimize the portfolio, not just the individual projects, and must take into account the interrelationships between projects. Criteria for project selection, prioritization, and balance are as individual as the companies that use them. No matter what criteria are used, however, it is imperative that some organizational entity owns the process of portfolio selection.[26]

Attribute: A Strategic Project Office Is in Place

If an enterprise-level project management office does not own the process of project inventory, prioritization, and selection, it cannot be done well. The META Group recommends this strategy, and those companies that have put enterprisewide project portfolio management in place, such as Cabelas and Northwestern Mutual Life, have relied on it. In fact, while intradepartmental portfolios may perhaps be selected and balanced without involvement of a project management office, it is doubtful that anything on a wider scale can succeed ... and one cannot optimize the system by balancing only parts of it.[27] This is undoubtedly why the Gartner Group has predicted that, through 2004, companies that fail to establish a project office will experience twice as many major project delays, overruns, and cancellations as companies with an SPO in place.[28]

Productivity of Resources: How a Strategic Project Office Builds Human Capital

Project management is now widely recognized as a way to "get things done": a set of practices that make it possible to systematically solve problems and create solutions, within constraints of time and money. But there is another face to project management: the organizational and human face.

Over decades of project management experience, we have come to recognize that the project environment holds promise for today's organizations far beyond the mere appropriate management of individual projects. The team-based, cross-disciplinary, and milestone-oriented environment of projects, as discussed in the Introduction, has the potential to fill organizations with "zest factors" and bring the kind of engagement and productivity usually only seen in crises, into everyday organizational life.

A project office is good news for project managers and team members, as it focuses attention on the training, rewards, and career path of the project professional.[29] But it is also good news for the bottom line because it translates the improved capabilities of individuals into better project management … better portfolio management … and strategies that are executed.

At the same time, it resolves many of the issues of motivation and retention that bedevil human resources managers. For a decade or more, writers in the HR and organizational development fields have been telling us that today's workers are changing — becoming more achievement oriented, less motivated by the "hygiene factors" of money, benefits, and safety, and more driven by the need for what Abraham Maslow called "self-actualizing" work. Project work, because of its time-limited and cross-disciplinary nature, offers people the "zest" of a sense of urgency, continuous learning, contacts with a wide variety of colleagues within and outside their specialty areas, and repeated new challenges. On the organizational level, it makes possible the "flattening" and streamlining of management, reducing bureaucracy, facilitating the development of intellectual capital, and helping the organization stay focused on strategic goals.

Of course, companies cannot reinvent themselves as project-based entities overnight. The path is long, and the first steps lead through a Project Office. But until recently, the history of project management, and the Project Office, has been a difficult one. Many companies have implemented project management initiatives without realizing the hoped-for benefits. What went wrong? And how can companies do it right?

History Lesson: An Evolving Structure

The concept of the project as an organizing principle and a management specialty — with its own techniques, tools, and vocabulary — had its beginnings in the 20th-century military. These military origins help explain why the initial focus in projects was on planning and controlling. In fact, control might be considered the *raison d'être* for project management: control of schedules, costs, and scope on endeavors that otherwise might career over budget, over time, or fail to meet specifications.[30]

At the same time, despite the focus on control, projects have tended to feel "out of control" … and frequently to run amok in fact as well as feeling. This "out-of-control" feeling stems from the way projects were superimposed on existing bureaucratic structures, with their bulky communications mechanisms. Obeying the strictures inherent in the hierarchy and at the same time acting for the best interest of the project has been difficult at best — and often downright impossible. But this is the model we began from in project management. No wonder projects felt uncontrolled, mysterious; no wonder project management developed a reputation as both science and an art.

Inside the Matrix

When project management's early tools — Gantt charts, network diagrams, PERT — began being used in private industry, the new project managers faced a hurdle: business was also fashioned on the command-and-control model. Putting together an interdisciplinary team was a process fraught with bureaucratic roadblocks. The earliest uses of project management — in capital construction, civil engineering, and R&D — imposed the idea of the project schedule, project objectives, and project team on an existing organizational structure that was very rigid. Without a departmental home or a functional silo of its own, a project was the organizational stepchild — although it may have been, in terms of dollars or prestige, the most important thing going on. Thus was born the concept of the "matrix organization," a stopgap way of defining how projects were supposed to get done within an organizational structure unsuitable to project work. It was a "patch," to use a software development term, not a new version of the organization.

In the matrix organization, if a project is lucky to have a "project office," it may be nothing more than a "war room" with some Gantt charts on the walls and perhaps a scheduler or two. This simple single-project control office is what we call a Level 1 Project Office; Figure 1.1 graphically depicts the roles and organizational placement of the project office models discussed in this section.

Up the Steps to Maturity

A Level 2, or the "divisional level," Project Office may still provide support for individual projects, but its primary challenge is to integrate multiple projects of varying sizes within a division from small, short-term initiatives to multimonth or multiyear initiatives that require dozens of resources and complex integration of technologies. With a Level 2 PO, an organization can, for the first time, integrate resources effectively, at least over a set of related projects. (We should note that, while the Level 2 PO is most often an IT office, organizing around projects is not "an IT thing." Project offices have arisen first in IT because of the competitive pressure to make IT projects work. IT is one of our primary drivers of economic prosperity; the United States spends over $200 billion annually on software development

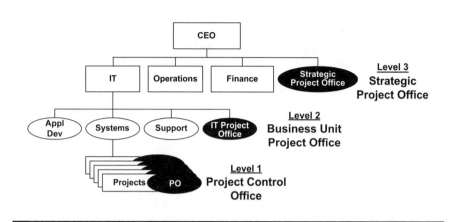

FIGURE 1.1 Types of project office. A project office can be integrated into the organizational structure at the single-project level, at the divisional or business-unit level, or at the enterprise level. Some companies have project offices with appropriate ranges of responsibility at each level.

projects, many of which fail. That IT project offices have been proven to reduce waste, bring projects in on time, and improve morale should be a wake-up call for all areas of the corporation, and in all industries.[31])

For an organization without any repeatable processes in place, which is at the first, or Initial level, on a Project Management Maturity Model,[32] these levels of Project Office organization are beneficial. At Level 1 or the individual project level, applying the discipline of project management creates significant value for the project because it begins to define basic processes that can later be applied to other projects within the organization. At Level 2 and higher, the project office not only focuses on project success, but also migrates processes to other projects and divisions, thus providing a much higher level of efficiency in managing resources across projects. A Level 2 PO allows an organization to determine when resource shortages exist and to have enough information at their fingertips to make decisions on whether to hire or contract additional resources. And at Level 3, the Strategic Project Office applies processes, resource management, prioritization, and systems thinking across the entire organization.[33,34]

The Power of Level 3

Although admittedly many companies today still struggle to implement even Level 2 POs, the primary focus of this book is on the Level 3 Strategic Project Office (SPO). Why? Because that is where organizations can get more bang for their buck — and help realize organizational and personal dreams at the same time. Like the matrix organization, lower-level project offices are a waystation: a stage between the old-style organization and the new, project-based enterprise.

At the corporate level, the SPO serves as a repository for the standards, processes, and methodologies that improve individual project performance in all divisions. It also serves to mitigate conflicts in the competition for resources, and identify areas where there may be common resources that could be used across the enterprise. More importantly, a corporate SPO allows the organization to manage its entire collection of projects as one or more interrelated portfolios. Executive management can get the big picture of all project activity across the enterprise from a central source — the Project Office; project priority can be judged according to a standard set of criteria, and projects can at last fulfill their promise as agents of enterprise strategy.

The Gartner Group has identified several key roles for a Project Office,[35] all of which are most effectively carried out at Level 3 and all of which include important implications for "people management," not only within the project office, but across the enterprise:

- As developer, documenter, and repository of a standard methodology (a consistent set of tools and processes for projects), the SPO provides a common language and set of practices. This methodology boosts productivity and individual capability, and takes a great deal of the frustration out of project work. Research by the Center for Business Practices revealed that more than 68 percent of companies that implemented basic methodology experienced increased productivity, and 37 percent reported improvement in employee satisfaction. One manager noted, "If the organization values project management, that translates into very specific policies and behaviors — policies and behaviors that affect the lives of individuals. What is it that keeps people working for a company? It's being valued."[36]
- As a center for the collection of data about project human resources, and tools for evaluating and scheduling them, based on experience from previous projects, the SPO can validate business assumptions about projects as to people, costs, and time; it is also a source of information on cross-functional project resource conflicts or synergies. The human capital implications of rational allocation of human effort are immense; we discuss these in a separate section of this chapter (see "Realistic Plans; Rational Workloads.")
- As a project management consulting center, the SPO provides a seat of governing responsibility for project management and acts as a consultant and mentor to the entire organization, staffing projects with project managers or deploying them as consultants

or mentors. As a center for the development of expertise, the SPO makes possible a systematic, integrated professional development path and ties training to real project needs as well as rewarding project teams in ways that reflect and reinforce success on projects. This is quite different from the reward and training systems presently in place in most organizations, which tend to focus on functional areas and ignore project work in evaluation, training, and rewards.

■ As a "competency center" for project management, the SPO provides a knowledge management locus not only for project management knowledge, but also for knowledge about the content of the organization's projects. With a "library" of business cases, plans, budgets, schedules, reports, lessons learned, and histories, as well as a formal and informal network of people who have worked on a variety of projects, the SPO is a knowledge management center that maximizes and creates new intellectual capital. Knowledge is best created and transferred in a social network or community, and the SPO provides just that. Through mentoring both within the SPO among project managers, and across the enterprise to people in all specialty areas, knowledge transfer about how to get things done on deadline and within budget is facilitated.[37]

Thus, more than a place or a set of people, the Project Office is "a shared competency" designed to integrate project management within an enterprise. A Level 3 PO can promote enterprise competency in project analysis, design, management, and review. And, says Gartner, "given the appropriate governance, it can improve communication, establish an enterprise standard for project management and help reduce the disastrous effect of failed development projects on enterprise effectiveness and productivity." The SPO facilitates the management of projects on one level, and improves management of the entire enterprise via project portfolio management and linking projects to corporate strategy on another level. More than establishing an office and creating reports, it infuses cultural change throughout the organization.

Such change does not come easy. To take it out of the management context and put it in political terms, reorganizing a company's work around projects is the equivalent of moving from a feudal system to a participatory democracy. Many times, organizations misjudge the magnitude of the change they are about to undergo. Nevertheless, there are two areas in which implementing project management enterprisewide under the auspices of a Strategic Project Office creates such value that it makes all the pain of change worthwhile. Those areas are: the development of human capital and the maturation of organizational capability to manage projects.

Human Capital: Empowerment and Streamlining

Multidisciplinary, team-based endeavors are now recognized as the only way to stay adaptive and flexible enough to succeed in a changing marketplace.[38] Many organizations that host projects now take a different tack: rather than forcing projects to fit within a bureaucratic structure, they embrace projects as an organizing principle.[39] Projects are no longer "something extra" — they are the way work gets done in an increasing number of companies, from small start-ups to the likes of Hewlett-Packard, IBM, USWest, Motorola, ABB, and many others. Organizing around projects has the effect of "flattening" the organization: erasing boundaries between functional silos and thinning the barriers between decision makers and those who carry out the work. This trend is driven by both market imperatives and by the seamless communication made possible by modern communications technology.

The Role of Technology

The use of enterprise project management (EPM) software as a force for organizational change cannot be underestimated. EPM software, which puts top executives more or less directly in touch with activities within projects, erases many layers of boundaries in an organization and allows a fluidity of contact and communication across functional boundaries and up and down the bureaucratic levels that is unprecedented. The time-tracking functions of the software also serve to make people working on projects more self-managing.

PM software pioneer Joel Koppelman has noted that our relationship to computers has changed as software has become more sophisticated. "In mainframe days, people structured their work around the limitations of the machine. They did their jobs thinking 'what's the best way to get this stuff into the computer so I can get it back out?' If you made a mistake you were dead, so everything was done for the ease of computer use." Technological advancement has meant that now the machine is adapted to human needs; "ease of use" means ease for the user. This shift in software design from tinkering with algorithms to facilitating communication Koppelman characterizes as "radical." New EPM tools not only facilitate communication, he adds, but promote "ease of understanding." As whole organizations move toward managing by projects, he says, project management will not be limited to people with a technical background, and EPM software is moving toward a transparency that helps everyone do project tasks without feeling intimidated by a lot of specialized language. "If you need to know what the software has to tell you, you'll be told; you don't have to learn the technology," he says. "The system can collect very, very simple information: Did you do it? When did you start?

When did you finish? You say, 'yeah,' and everyone who needs to know about that will know it. It's actually getting more people involved in the process, but not by teaching them arcane techniques."[40]

Microsoft Project executive Kathleen Hebert predicted in 1998 that we would see "project data linking more tightly into other business systems. Project data is critical data; people are just beginning to realize how critical. Having access to it means people being able to manage themselves better." Her prediction has proven correct; today's EPM and portfolio management tools do just this.

A key focus of today's project management software design is making sure that project coordination and communication works smoothly: making sure the right people are talking to each other, that people do not have inappropriate access to information, but have what they need, getting more decision-quality information to people, without overwhelming them. This is not strictly a technical question. Instead, it goes to the heart of how organizations are managed: who holds the information, who wields the power. Viewed as a cultural change, the trend toward enterprise project management systems, putting information at the fingertips of every contributor, causes a tremor in the foundation of the pyramid-shaped organizational chart. A company buys software to make people more productive by taking out routine, mindless things and presenting them with a process that makes it easy for them to do the right thing. In the process, it makes work more rewarding for individuals and breaks down structural barriers that are inappropriate to a flexible, competitive organization. Decision making moves out to the people who are closer to the situation. Says Koppelman, "It doesn't mean you get all right answers ... it means you get broader, more sensitive input, and it happens faster so companies can move faster. There's some chicken-and-egg thing that happens between people and technology. Change in technology influences how people work, which influences the growth of technology ... through technology, we are constantly reinventing ourselves."[41]

Leadership from the Bottom Up

In part as a result of this technology, the change instituted by project management has begun to "trickle up" from department-level project offices. IT project offices, in particular, have been thrown into the spotlight because of the research studies into failure and success factors, and by high-profile projects like Y2K and the Euro conversion. With a tremendous amount of pressure on IT and other technology development projects to improve performance, all eyes have been on IT projects. Project performance has become a significant driver for people's careers and even for the existence of some internal IT departments. They must bring the organization to a position where it is actually delivering projects on time and within budget and with the quality that is desired by the customer. When they are successful, their methods become highly desirable to the rest of the organization.

So, unlike most organizational change projects of the past, we see the initiative to formalize project management begin on the department level, even on the project level. As technology efforts begin to show results, two things happen: (1) all the other business units begin to come into the project teams as stakeholders of the organization, and (2) those business units see improved delivery performance on technology projects and ask themselves, *What can we do to improve our own performance? What are they doing right that we can adapt to our own projects?*

It is a grassroots change process quite different from anything traditional companies are used to. And when change comes from the grassroots instead of being imposed from above, the usual problems of resistance are minimized. As our Center for Business Practices research showed, the implementation of systems that promote rationality in planning, resource allocation, and rewards has a profound effect on morale, on the sense of ownership felt by stakeholders, and ultimately on productivity. At the individual level, this sense of empowerment builds trust in the organization and satisfies the intrinsic motivational needs of project personnel.

A Systems-Thinking Perspective

To effectively deploy project management throughout an organization, all the players must be on board. Everyone from the project team member on up to the executive sponsors of projects must understand what is happening with project management. This translates to an organizational setting in which virtually everyone who is touched by a project is impacted by what happens with the project management initiative. Ultimately this impact sweeps across the entire corporation. That is why effective organizations have project offices located at the corporate level, providing data on total corporate funding for projects, the resources utilized across all corporate projects, capital requirements for projects at the corporate level, materials impact, supplies impact, the procurement chain impacts. A fully mature organization may actually have project offices at each of the levels described in Figure 1.1: at the corporate level to deal with enterprise (cross-divisional) programs/projects, corporate reporting, corporate portfolio management, etc.; a divisional Project Office to deal with divisional programs/projects, divisional resource management, divisional portfolios, and the division's contribution (technology, labor, etc.) to corporate programs/projects. And, there may be one or more Level 1 Project Offices within a divisional PO dealing with major projects.

When corporate executives can effectively prioritize projects and make fact-based decisions about initiation, funding, and resources, they will be in a position to apply systems theory to their organization: to optimize the system (corporation) as a whole, rather than just tinkering with the parts (projects and departments).

Realistic Planning; Rational Workload

Some of the clearest thinking about how human resource planning and management affects business outcomes has been done by project management software developers. In the 1990s, a handful of companies writing software for project management began to attack the problem of better project performance from a different angle: the human angle. As PlanView's Patrick Durbin said in a 1998 interview, "Our belief is that resources drive work. If you don't know the resources you don't know that project. Just having a name is no big thing. What skills does that name have?"

Steve Cook, vice president and co-founder of Welcom, agreed. "People used to assume that they could just go out and grab whatever resources they needed, and if not, just throw money at it and make those resources appear. So planning was task-oriented. Now everyone's trying to reduce cycle time, reduce cost; resources have become much more important because they can create real crunch problems. Understanding where the resources are coming from gives a project a much better chance of succeeding."[42]

Enterprisewide Systems

Today, having common corporate data on resource projections means that planning can be accomplished in a common database, resource projections summarized at the project level, then at the organizational level, on up to the corporate level. In this way, EPM software allows us to understand the impacts of individual projects or new programs on the overall corporate resource pool. This resource-based approach to planning is an integral part of portfolio management, and key to the rational allocation of resources, both human and financial.

Maturity: Growing Human Capital and Organizational Capability

Maturity in the practice of projects cannot be measured in an institutional vacuum; it would be meaningless to say that a company had superior project management when it is going bankrupt due to misapplied resources and misaligned priorities. Individual capability and organizational capability must grow together and reinforce one another, just as project management and strategic planning, under the portfolio management paradigm reinforce one another.

Knowledge management (KM) is a "chicken-and-egg" component of project management maturity. Merely "installing" a KM system does not induce knowledge capture or transfer to take place. A whole new set of procedures and standards must be established, along with a common mechanism for storing and sharing that information. In addition to this, a training process and data collection must be established to get information into this database before knowledge transfer can take place.

Few organizations have kept a history of lessons learned on projects done in-house, or possess standards for data collection of this kind. So most organizations are very new to this business of project management and are unable to rapidly develop this complex, integrated system that is necessary for accurate data collection and reporting.

Yet without good data, decisions are going to be poor. So the organization is faced with a very complex integrated system and process that they have little knowledge how to deploy. That is why the Gartner Group recommends incorporating a contractor or consultant in the implementation strategy.[43] The Strategic Project Office, equipped with experienced senior project managers, is capable of acting as an "internal consultant" for projects of this type. Since much of the most valuable data is generated on projects, a KM system centered in the project office offers the best chance for comprehensive collection and dissemination of shared knowledge.

Learning — and Learned — Project Organizations

If your company has a system in place for educating, mentoring, and evaluating project personnel, you are in the minority. Many companies do not even know how many people they have who are capable of managing projects. This has led to the unfortunate phenomenon of the "accidental project manager." We would not think of dumping major accounting responsibilities on whoever happened to be available, even though they had no background in accounting. Yet this is routinely done even with major projects, even though the skill set and knowledge one needs to effectively deploy a project management initiative rivals the knowledge set of an MBA in terms of complexity and integration. This skill set is becoming more readily available as part of college- and university-level degrees, but is still relatively rare compared with other management specialties. And for project management to reach its potential, learning must take place enterprisewide — not on one team or in one department. Who will be in charge of such learning? Only an enterprise-level project office has the expertise to make appropriate training decisions for project management. (The SPO can identify necessary training and coordinate its conduct but may not provide trainers, who usually come from, or are coordinated by, the training department.)

Open Communication

Communication — a sticky issue even within project teams — must become free flowing, not just within but between projects and up and down the organizational levels. Why is this so important? Because 80 percent of what we call the "art" of project management is just communication and all the traits that good communicators display: trust, integrity, and honesty. Through new channels of communication set up by the Strategic Project Office, it will become possible for the entire organizational culture, from chief executives all the way through project teams, to communicate in a common language and work together to understand the issues surrounding how projects are faring and how the issues on one project affect other projects and, ultimately, the organization.[44]

The Strategic Project Office approach to building organizational and individual maturity is to move forward quickly: show results on specific projects within six months, really begin changing the culture within the first year, and begin showing corporate results within a two-year time frame. But be prepared — this is no quick fix. It will take anywhere up to five years to fully deploy a Strategic Project Office.[45]

What does success look like? How will you know when you have arrived? Research studies allow us to paint a picture of the organization that has demonstrated competence in managing projects, and managing by projects:

- Top management understands project management basics.
- Effective training programs are in place.
- Clear project management systems and processes have been established.
- There is improved coordination of inter-group activities.
- There is an enhanced goal focus on the part of employees.
- Redundant or duplicate functions are eliminated.
- Project expertise is centralized.[46,47]

The Project-Centered Organization: A Fantasy?

"The model for the future is the [project-based] professional services firm … [O]rganize in project teams that change shape with regularity. It's a creativity-based world, a talent-based world. That logic is absolutely unstoppable."[48]

The project-centered enterprise, in which people are treated as though project performance really mattered to organizational performance, is not a theory. In fact, it is the logical outcome of the application of project management to business problems. In the industries where the practice of project management has long been accepted as the way to get work done, such enterprises already exist.

A recent study published in the *Project Management Journal* focused on the ways that these project-centered companies build the organizational capability (and of course, concurrently, individual capability) to perform projects and manage by projects. The study group consisted of successful Australian construction companies, but the authors went to great lengths to map their organizational strategies to those of IT. And, although conventional wisdom tells us that construction is so predictable that it has little to offer volatile IT projects in the way of management tips, survey research by the same authors showed that, especially in civil engineering projects, high levels of uncertainty are typical and managers in construction and IT see themselves as faced with equally turbulent environments.[49]

Here are some of their findings. Organizations with strong project management capability, and the related ability to leverage projects for competitive success, display the following organizational features:

■ *A different, systemic view of the role of executive management.* They "reframe the management task" so that the enterprise's objective is to improve the way the organization manages its project managers and its project management processes. Improved performance on individual projects follows as an outcome of the redesigned management structure and processes. This "systemic approach" contrasts with many organizations' habit of focusing on and intervening in individual projects on a case-by-case (and often, crisis-by-crisis) basis.

■ *A flat organizational structure.* The authors found business units in construction to have flat structures with no more than two levels separating project managers from executives, thereby ensuring ready access to powerful decision makers. They also found that functional departments are relatively small and therefore act as support units rather than empires that compete with projects. This structure clearly signals the importance of projects to the business. The result is that projects can be managed with the minimum of internal tensions and conflict. By having weak functional authority, the organization ensures that project directors are able to command organizational resources as and when they need them. By positioning project directors either as executives or as direct reports to that level, the organization secures strong identification with corporate interests and commensurate accountability.

■ *Project-centered role design.* Project managers are assigned sole responsibility for the conduct of the project, and at the same time, sufficient authority is delegated to them to deliver on that responsibility. Given the resources and authority to match their project responsibility, project managers are held accountable by their superiors for the extent to which they achieve targets. But, at the same time, a "project director role" is created and positioned as the immediate superior of a number of project managers. This role encompasses total responsibility and accountability for all phases of the company's involvement with a particular client's project, from business development through to post-implementation.

■ *Streamlined reporting processes.* The flat structure's short lines of authority combine well with tight and frequent reporting and control processes to ensure that the organization concentrates on project performance. Informal reporting keeps the project director informed about progress and difficulties, sometimes several times a day. This eradicates the long-lamented disconnect between project management and executive management.

■ *Methodology plus experience.* Methods, procedures, and standards structure the project management task and formalize some organizational knowledge; but are not expected to substitute for project managers' active skills, which often incorporate much tacit knowledge.

■ *Valued project managers.* Successful project-centered companies treat their project managers as an asset, retaining them in bad economic times, even when there are no projects to be managed. These companies are more tolerant of mistakes. With the expectation of continuity of employment and a sense that the company values the project manager, greater openness, innovation, and learning result in more accurate estimating and reporting, and in the preservation of organizational knowledge.

■ *HR management policies that are project-friendly.* Because of the learning curve for new hires, it is important to maintain a pool of skilled project managers such that, with continuing turnover of projects, there will be at least one appropriately skilled manager available as a new project commences. Companies compensate for the differential strengths and weaknesses of individual project managers by the selection of staff to fill other key team roles, such as contract administrator, program manager, planners, etc. (See

Chapter 4 and Appendix A for descriptions of primary and sup-porting project roles.) Training and development coordinators must therefore possess a deep knowledge of project management, not as something extra but as a central competency. Individuals' project management skills are developed through an extensive "appren-ticeship" combining formal training plus exposure to a range of roles, including close-hand observation of the practices of experi-enced project managers. Project managers are graduated through a sequence of projects of increasing complexity and difficulty with appropriate culling. Because much of this apprenticeship or men-tored learning takes place "just in time," it happens not under the purview of HR-based trainers, but within the community of project managers. Consistent with the development of a talented body of project managers, the valuing of project managers and the tolerance of understandable mistakes, the performance review practice also is more flexible, and project managers have significant input, compared with functional managers, in staff appraisal.

The synergy between these organizational characteristics creates "a self-reinforcing dynamic." For example, reporting processes work well because project managers, who are less fearful of being penalized for mistakes, report honestly, and because the project director's role and top management's performance focus mean that powerful managers act promptly on the basis of the reports they receive.

Figure 1.2 shows what can be done to enhance organizational and individual project management capabilities and to support the conduct of projects.

What do the authors recommend in order to institutionalize the devel-opment of individual capabilities and to create learning that extends beyond the individual project manager's skills and experience, and becomes organizational capabilities? "Create a focal point in the organi-zation ... a corporate project office," is the advice. "A corporate project office [is a] starting point for the company trying to transform itself into a project management–centered organization."[50,51]

This is a systemic solution to the problem of project performance and human capital development. The same result cannot be achieved by only addressing project performance issues case-by-case by ad hoc interven-tions. Companies become repeatedly successful at projects because they have developed both organizational and individual capabilities, which are then applied to every project as a part of normal organizational function-ing. The organization becomes stable and effective because its internal processes are logically consistent and mutually reinforcing, and because business goals, project actions, and human needs are balanced and inter-related in a way that supports success at all levels of the organization.

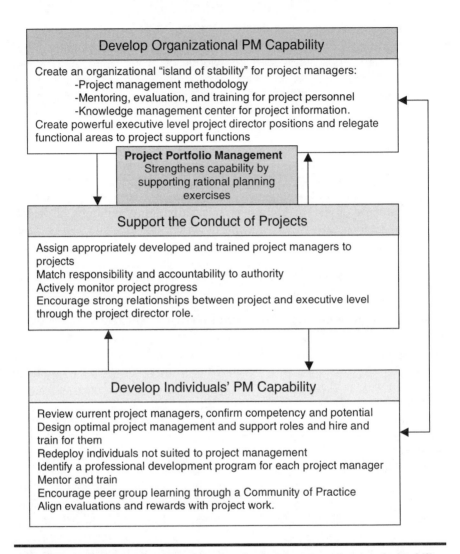

FIGURE 1.2 Building the project-centered company. Organizational capability in project management is built from the top down and from the bottom up. Supportive organizational structure *and* appropriately selected, trained, and developed individuals work together to produce project management excellence. (Adapted from Christopher Sauer et al., Where project managers are king, *Project Management Journal*, December 2001, with permission.)

"Project sponsors and managers need 'islands of stability' to guide teams and to ensure the integration of project deliverables into the organization," writes one researcher. "Without this stability, project results will not align with organization strategy and stakeholder expectations. Project participants and stakeholders will have difficulty comprehending the project's contribution to the organization's vision, resulting in unproductive activity and high levels of demotivation and frustration." If this description sounds familiar, one is not alone. Yet the elements of stability — a sustainable corporate strategy, a project management culture, capable and adequate human capital to deliver results, and a clear link between project activities and strategy[52] — is achievable. However, it will not be achievable by a fragmented organization in which projects are one problem, strategy another, and human resources something separate. The Strategic Project Office offers the hope of creating the island of stability in today's chaotic organizational life. However, all the organizational-improvement potential of the SPO discussed in this chapter depends on the knowledge and skills of project managers, team members, and other project personnel. Therefore, staffing the Strategic Project Office is the keystone to realizing the business potential of project management.

Notes

1. The Standish Group, *CHAOS Report,* 1999; see also www.standish-group.com and Johnson, James, Chaos: The dollar drain of IT project failures, *Application Development Trends,* January 1995.
2. Jeannette Cabanis-Brewin, Interview with Dr. Frank Toney, *Project Management Best Practices Report,* August 2002.
3. Robbins-Gioia, Inc., study on project failure, 1999.
4. M. Light and T. Berg, The project office: teams, processes and tools, *Gartner Strategic Analysis Report,* August 2000.
5. Andrew Osterland, *CFO,* April 2000.
6. Jim Johnson, Turning CHAOS into SUCCESS, *Software,* December 1999.
7. Light and Berg, ibid.
8. Preston Smith and Donald Reinertsen, *Developing Products in Half the Time,* Van Nostrand Reinhold, 1991.
9. Brian Dumaine, How managers can succeed through speed, *Fortune,* Feb. 13, 1989. Also Charles House and Raymond L. Price, The return map: tracking product teams, *Harvard Business Review,* Jan./Feb. 1991.
10. Johnson, ibid.
11. Value of Project Management Study, Center for Business Practices, 2001.
12. Lauren Gibbons Paul, Turning failure into success: maintain momentum, *Network World,* November 22, 1999.
13. Paul, ibid.
14. J. Roberts and J. Furlonger, Successful IS project management, *Gartner Group,* April 18, 2000.
15. C. Natale, IT project management: do not lose track of time, *Gartner Group,* May 9, 2000.
16. Bailey, Richard W, II, Six steps to project recovery, *PM Network,* May 2000.
17. Paul, ibid.

18. Bailey, ibid.
19. Natale, ibid.
20. Furlonger, ibid.
21. Paul Dinsmore, *Winning in business with enterprise project management,* AMACOM, 1998.
22. Jeannette Cabanis-Brewin, Weeding out the losers, *Best Practices Report,* September 2002.
23. Dennis Comninos and Anton Verwey, Business focused project management, *Management Services,* January 2002; see also Graham and Englund, *Creating an Environment for Successful Projects,* Jossey-Bass 1997; and J.M. Nicholas, *Managing Business & Engineering Projects: Concepts and Implementation,* Prentice Hall, 1990.
24. The Standish Group, 1998 *CHAOS Report,* see www.standishgroup.com.
25. J. Kent Crawford, Portfolio management: overview and best practices, in *Project Management for Business Professionals,* Joan Knutson, Ed., Wiley, New York, 2001.
26. James S. Pennypacker and Lowell D. Dye, Eds., *Project Portfolio Management: Selecting and Prioritizing Projects for Competitive Advantage,* CBP, 1999; see also Robert G. Cooper, Scott J. Edgett, and Elko J. Kleinschmidt, *Portfolio Management for New Products,* Perseus Books, Reading, MA, 1998. In addition, a collection of white papers and expert commentaries is available at www.pmsolutions.com/articles/portfolio_mgmt.htm.
27. *Project Portfolio Management: A Benchmark of Current Business Practices,* CBP Research, 2003, summary accessible at http://www.cbponline.com/Research/PPM percent20News.pdf. Other portfolio management resources: Scott Berinato, Do the math, *CIO,* October 1, 2001; F. Peter Boer, Real options: the IT investment risk-buster, *Optimize,* July 2002; Dianne N. Bridges, Portfolio management — one approach, *People On Projects Executive Briefing,* January 2003; Susan Cramm, Organizational physics, *CIO,* August 2002; Amir Hartman, What went wrong? *Portfolio Knowledge,* August 2002; John Howell, III, et al., Implementing portfolio management: integrating process, people, and tools, www.portfoliodecisions.com; Doug Lynn, META report: how to ensure IT projects boost profits, *Internet.com,* Aug. 16, 2001; Jan Malet et al., Running a tight ship, *Pharmaceutical Executive,* February 2002; Tracy Mayor, Red light, green light, *CIO,* Oct. 1, 2001; Melissa Solomon, Project portfolio management, *Computerworld,* March 18, 2002; Mike Strevel et al., Project portfolio management: case study implementation is a microprocessor design center, *Project Management Institute Proceedings,* PMI, 2000; Jim Tisch, Navigating the economic storm, *Portfolio Knowledge,* August 2002; Gary L. Tritle et al., Resolving uncertainty in R&D portfolios, *Research Technology Management,* November 2000.
28. Light and Berg, ibid.
29. Jeannette Cabanis-Brewin: Project Portfolio Management: Four-Part Series, *Primavera Magazine,* http://www.primavera.com/news/primavera_magazine.html#Archives. See also John Howell, III, et al., Implementing portfolio management: integrating process, people, and tools, www.portfoliodecisions.com.

30. Francis Webster, Setting the stage for a new profession, *PM Network*, April 1999.

31. C.W. Ibbs and Young-Hoon Kwak, Benchmarking project management organizations, *PM Network*, Feb. 1998, pp. 49–53.

32. A capability maturity model is an organizational assessment tool that helps companies identify process maturity — or lack thereof — by documenting how various processes are actually carried out against a standard of best practice behaviors for that process. While there are several versions of maturity model in circulation for project management, we naturally feel that the one developed by our company has many advantages for the user. This model is described in *Project Management Maturity Model*, by J. Kent Crawford, Marcel Dekker, 2001. One segment of the model, describing process maturity in human resource management for projects, is included in this book as Appendix B.

33. J. Kent Crawford, *Project Management Maturity Model*, Marcel Dekker, 2001.

34. Software Engineering Institute, Capability Maturity Model for Software Development, www.cmu.edu/sei.

35. Light and Berg, ibid.

36. Jeannette Cabanis-Brewin, The value of project management, *PM Best Practices Report*, Oct. 2000.

37. J. Kent Crawford, *The Strategic Project Office*, Marcel Dekker, 2001.

38. Glenn M. Parker, *Handbook of Best Practices for Teams*, Human Resource Development Press, March 1996.

39. Dinsmore, ibid.

40. Jeannette Cabanis, Making the world safe for democracy, *PM Network*, Dec. 1998.

41. Cabanis, Jeannette, ibid.

42. Cabanis, Jeannette, ibid.

43. Furlonger, ibid.

44. J. Kent Crawford, *The Strategic Project Office*, Marcel Dekker, 2001.

45. Dianne Bridges and Kent Crawford, "How to Startup and Rollout a Project Office," *Proceedings of the PMI Annual Seminars and Symposium*, PMI, 2000.

46. Ibbs and Kwak, ibid.

47. Dr. J. Davidson Frame, Understanding the New Project Management, Aug. 7, 1996 Presentation to Project World, Washington, D.C.

48. Tom Peters, quoted in "Passion Beats Planning ..." by Jeannette Cabanis, *PM Network*, Sept. 1998.

49. Christopher Sauer, Li Liu, and Kim Johnston, Where project managers are kings, *Project Management Journal*, December 2001. See also T.R. Block, and J.D. Frame, *The Corporate Project Office: A Key to Managing Projects Effectively*, Crisp Publications, Menlo Park, CA, 1998. Also A. Majchrzak, Management of technological and organizational change, in G. Salvendy (Ed.), *Handbook of Industrial Engineering* (2nd ed.), John Wiley & Sons, New York, 1991, pp. 767–797.

50. Interestingly, the authors also note that few of the project-centered enter-
    prises they interviewed had a corporate project office, but this is because
    the entire enterprise functioned as a Strategic Project Office.
51. Block and Frame, ibid.
52. Comninos and Verwey, ibid.

Chapter 2

People on Projects: A New Look at Project Roles and Responsibilities

"People do projects." While this may seem like an obvious comment, it has taken decades for organizations to fully appreciate the importance of the human element in project management. In 1995, in the first volume of the award-winning book series entitled *The Human Aspects of Project Management,* Vijay Verma noted that "human resource management is a vital component of project management … [yet] most projects have been managed as technical systems instead of behavioral systems."[1] He then went on to differentiate between project human resource management and the usual administrative human resource management that takes place in an "ongoing, operational context." His description of the split between managing people on projects and HR describes the situation in a typical matrix organization.

The matrix organization, as discussed in Chapter 1, was the result of project management taking place across rigid functional departments. Much has changed in business since this organizational structure was first described in the early 1970s.[2] Project management's development from a technical specialty to a crucial business competency has moved so quickly that the realities of project planning and execution have far outstripped our thinking about the organizations that perform the projects.

33

Thus, although significant amounts of research have shown that the so-called "matrix" organization is at best inefficient in accomplishing projects,[3] most companies still try to carry out the major projects that provide competitive edge without organizing fully around the project model. Functional department heads grudgingly give up staff hours to some temporary endeavor for which they are not rewarded or responsible, and a harried project manager (who might have heard that job description for the first time yesterday) tries to cobble fractions of people into a team without any authority over them or power to reward them. In the margin of the org chart, something called "project management" dangles, with dotted lines vaguely attaching it here and there. In these circumstances, it would be a miracle if projects did not face immense obstacles, and in all fairness, neither the project manager nor the team can be held responsible for many of the potential obstacles to success — things such as poor definition of the business case for a project, lack of alignment with strategic corporate objectives, inadequate funding, or refusal to cooperate cross-functionally among the departments. These types of obstacles can only be cleared away at the executive level of the organization, by an executive commitment to wholesale organizational change.

One aspect of this change lies in the way the organization manages the people who carry out its projects. In the matrix organization, projects are something extra, something out of the ordinary that are cobbled together from "real" functional departments. The people who comprise project teams in this organizational structure may temporarily wear a title such as "project manager" but they "belong" elsewhere: in marketing, research, engineering, or accounting. Under this type of structure, it can be argued that it makes sense for corporate HR to keep track of everyone, overseeing performance, rewards, and development. Nevertheless, the relationship between projects and HR has always been problematic. Traditional reward and review structures have not been a good match for project team efforts, and the stresses on the project caused by conflicting pressures from functional and project managers take a toll on everyone. As a company becomes more project oriented, so that it is managing the organization as a portfolio of projects, the traditional administrative role of HR fits the "managing by projects" paradigm less and less well.

Why Is This So Important?

After a couple of decades of looking for the silver bullet in tools and techniques, researchers have recently confirmed that "people do projects." The selection of the right project manager was found as the single most important factor in project success,[4] even overshadowing the implementation of methodologies, systems, and structures to assist project management.[5] If nothing we do is more important than nurturing high-performing project managers, then the present disconnect between the administration of HR and the staffing of projects, in our view, may be a key factor in project failure.

One clue to the effects of this disconnect is found in job descriptions for project and program managers, planners, analysts, and administrators. During a six-month period in 2003, we studied hundreds of job descriptions gleaned from Internet job postings in project management. Our central finding was that most of the job descriptions in the project management field are woefully inadequate. Many of the job descriptions conflate responsibilities ranging from portfolio management to project administration into a kind of "monster" job that no normal human being could possibly pull off. Others title a job that is primarily administrative "project manager" — a kind of cosmetic title.

As has often been pointed out in project management literature, one of the biggest traps a company can fall into is to lack a common language and vocabulary for dealing with projects. The drive within project-oriented companies to adopt standard methodologies has done a great deal to resolve this problem, giving team members from project to project and across the enterprise a shared language about tasks, steps, and methods. However, still lacking is a "methodology" for titling and describing the roles and responsibilities related to projects.

Why is this a problem? To begin with, it makes hiring the right people nearly impossible. When recruitment is done by people who have only a nodding familiarity with project work, they often fail to establish the line between project organization, project direction, project management, project administration, and the technical skills needed. Thus, project management job descriptions can include everything from executive roles to quasi-secretarial tasks. Here is an example: an actual job description from an advertisement for a "Senior Project Manager":

> The Senior PM is responsible for managing an application development team that provides business solutions to the Operations Division. This is a 6-month, right-to-hire position. Applications include image, document and workflow management, call center CRM applications, fulfillment processing and Internet based service delivery applications.
>
> Candidate will be responsible for the following:
> > Gather and analyze information (issues and requirements) and translate business requirements into structured functional specifications.

Analyze current applications and recommend changes to gain a competitive edge.

Identify business problems/opportunities and implement systems solutions.

Perform workflow analysis in functional areas, gathering information, understanding users' needs and translate them into business requirements.

Perform user acceptance testing and quality assurance, including executing, reviewing, and evaluating software development test plans.

In other words, they are looking for a business analyst, a software engineer, a team leader, a systems analyst, a testing coordinator — plus someone to make the coffee and take the blame when it all goes belly up — all wrapped up in the same human package (one who, incidentally, is only looking for temporary employment). It is not difficult to see how these kinds of role descriptions — which are far more common than realistic role descriptions, according to our survey — can set up both people and companies to fail.

At present, projects fail because organizations fail to support effective project managers. Project management researchers and practitioners have observed this seeming paradox, but few have examined what organizations can do to better support the challenging tasks that project managers and teams take on.[6-8] Most companies — despite the fact that nearly everything they do to create wealth falls under the descriptive heading of "projects" — have not learned much about how to hire, train, reward, manage, or mentor the people who keep the project wheels turning.

One of the barriers to better people management on projects is structural. Traditional HR was, and in many cases still is, characterized by lengthy, multistep administrative processes centered around compliance.[9] An organization *can* be designed around the flexibility and autonomy that characterizes that group of knowledge workers we call the project team. However, given the current structure of HR, it is difficult for this kind of change to originate there. With its historical roots within the accounting department — a relic of the era when people were merely "labor costs" — HR is often placed under a controller or CFO. Says Mitch Stem of Deloitte & Touche, when HR becomes an extension of accounting, HR programs and processes are implemented not so much for their strategic fit as for cost-effectiveness and ease of administration.[10] Bob Thomas of Accenture's Business Results Project says that HR professionals "have an enormous ability to generate data" but little idea of what to do with it.[11] The project office director of a major U.S. insurance company, interviewed for this book, characterized the inherent conflict between project

management and HR in her organization this way: "In a matrix organization, the pool of project resources all report to an HR manager, and also
report into the project managers. The rift here is between the project
manager and the business managers who are over the HR issues, because
project management isn't understood as well as it should be by those
people. They don't understand the impact of moving resources around
on schedules and delivery and so on. The project manager and HR
manager have almost conflicting goals: one is just trying to get the job
done, the other is trying to develop people." However, she pointed out,
even a lofty goal like career development can backfire if the HR staff
lacks an understanding of career progression in project management.[12]
(See Chapter 6 for more information on career development.)

Project-friendly human resource strategies have the potential to transform the inner workings of companies: to streamline resource management, make project rewards rational, provide training that addresses real
needs and issues, and gives people the job satisfaction that translates into
low turnover and higher productivity. Leading business thinkers Michael
Hammer and James Champy have stressed that, in a knowledge-based
economy, companies should be organized around processes (such as
project management) rather than functions.[13]

There are some signs that companies are taking steps in this direction.
Already, 12.2 percent of companies are moving traditional HR functions
to line managers and 62.8 percent are streamlining HR processes and
procedures, incorporating more self-service features into the data collection side of their work, and implementing enterprise-level HRIS systems.[14,15] These technologies — time and attendance reporting, resource
allocation and leveling, skills databases, decision-support tools — are
already familiar to project managers and are included in many enterprise
project management software packages. Meanwhile, advances in software
in the areas of knowledge management, project management, collaboration, and workforce planning allow us to begin putting systems in place
to collect, connect, and better manage the knowledge that individuals
create on projects. But no technical solution on the planet can create the
organizational climate that creates the "zest factors" leading to high performance described in our Introduction. Only organizational changes
favoring the project paradigm can do that.[16]

Our vision of the Strategic Project Office is as a full partner in HR
concerns: helping the organization to hire, train, measure, and reward
people in ways that make the project portfolio more productive and
profitable. In the chapters that follow, and in the appendices, we offer
practical ideas on the management of project personnel. But to create
change in organizational systems, we must "take it from the top" by first
examining the executive role in the organizational change project of
creating and sustaining a Strategic Project Office.

The Executive Role

One of the chief reasons for project failure, in all types of projects and across all industries, is actually built into most organization charts. We find it in the great divide between "the coal face" of project work and decision makers on the executive level. Study after study cites "lack of executive support (or involvement)" as a top reason that projects run into trouble.[17]

In the past, and in matrix organizations today, the project sponsor or project champion plays a critical role in the successful management of an individual project, smoothing out the inherent disconnects.

When initiating a major organizational change project — implementation of enterprise software, a project office, a knowledge management project, a merger, and the like — executive sponsorship is even more necessary. The level of authority required to drive this kind of change does not exist on the project team or even the departmental level. Only the company's executive staff has that authority and responsibility to architect and oversee the implementation of this magnitude of change. The executive leadership of the enterprise must commit the organization to this new direction and exhibit the resolve necessary to see these changes through to completion. Many sources in the literature on successful reengineering and implementation of new processes agree that executive commitment is the first and most crucial piece in any drive to improve or change organizations.

In a project management improvement initiative, the primary role of the executive staff is to provide the strong leadership, strategic vision, and program definitions necessary to implement the Strategic Project Office. A company can have a best-in-class project management process defined, but if the strategic vision that underpins that process is missing or ill-conceived, the process simply cannot make that company successful over the long term.

The executive staff must establish vision and direction for the project management initiative and allocate funding and resources to it. Such sponsorship from the members of the executive committee ensures a voice for programs and projects. Many organizations have strong support for project management at lower levels but very little acceptance or interest at the top. Such an organization is not managing effectively by projects, and is unlikely to derive the benefits that enterprise project management has to offer unless a cultural evolution takes place. It is not necessary for executives to become project managers, but it is necessary that they enthusiastically support, with words, actions, and funding, the aspirations of the project management community within their organizations.

Once the initiative is in place and the projects that fall under it are gearing up, the executive staff has minimal involvement in day-to-day project activities. However, although the executive team is not performing the day-to-day detailed work, it must be involved as an executive oversight team (or Steering Committee). Ideally, management must understand the strategic implications of the Strategic Project Office initiative and its impact on the company's bottom line in terms of more rapid new product development and the resulting increased return to shareholders.

Where Executives Fail

The dilemma that arises in most organizations is that the impetus toward improved project management begins at the middle management level. And because middle management tries to implement changes that are really beyond its scope of influence, the project management initiative usually receives inadequate funding. Middle management usually only receives enough support to cobble something together — *if* they do not get tied up with other things. Without executive management sponsoring/driving/overseeing this important organizational change project, a project management initiative does not deliver the promised value — not because the initiative itself was not a sound idea, but because the implementation is half-hearted. Without the backing of executive management, project office resources typically find themselves implementing the project office initiative as a part-time role, are periodically pulled from deployment efforts to manage current "hot" projects, and find themselves juggling multiple priorities — many times defocused to the point that the project office initiative loses its direction and momentum.

These are typical of the problems we see in companies that have tried and failed to implement better project management practice. Front-line or middle management might see the need for process improvement, but given their immediate pressures and responsibilities, it is almost impossible for them to rise above the tactical level to focus on the strategic level. Make no mistake: deploying and sustaining a corporate-level Project Office is a strategic program. So management has a critical role to play.

How To Succeed

What are the critical elements of successful management participation in a Strategic Project Office deployment? There are many, including the strategic decision making that supports the project, protecting the resources in the SPO so that they can focus on what they need to do; supporting the budget, supporting the plan, supporting the schedule, and providing conflict resolution when resistance to change arises within the departments most affected by the deployment. However, the keystone in the EPO deployment strategy is the Executive Sponsor. The Executive Sponsor paves the way for the EPO deployment by dealing with other executives as a peer when conflicts over resources arise. Without an Executive Sponsor as an initiative champion, the chances of successfully deploying a Strategic Project Office are very slim.

Identifying the Executive Sponsor

The project sponsor is the executive in charge of the area in which most of the business functions connected with the project reside. He or she initiates the project and is a member of the Oversight Committee. The sponsor makes business decisions at the various project phases, communicates the larger vision of the project throughout the organization, and, from the customer's (the executive leadership team, in this case) point of view, is ultimately responsible for the project's completion. Project sponsorship is most effective when accountability resides with one person, a person high enough in the organization that he or she has enterprisewide influence. There will of course be a project sponsor for every project undertaken by the company, but the sponsor chosen to spearhead the Project Office initiative will have a particularly important role in leading organizational and cultural change; thus, the sponsor of the Project Office initiative must be highly placed.

In our experience, in a mid-sized organization or within a business unit of a larger organization, the Executive Sponsor would typically be at the vice-president level. A simple rule of thumb for choosing a person with sufficient authority is simply this: does he or she have the authority to cancel the project management change initiative? Lack of an Executive Sponsor with sufficient authority is a major risk to the success of the initiative, and we recommend that work not proceed until one engages an effective project office sponsor. This step should take place early in the initiative to ensure that the project will move forward. Securing buy-in across the executive positions in an organization will significantly improve the probability of project office success, giving the project team the ability to resolve the kinds of issues, conflicts, and challenges that occur whenever one tries to deploy an organization-wide system of this magnitude.

Integration of multiple financial systems, coordination among the various organizations, compiling the resulting data, and generating appropriate tailored reporting only begins to reflect the complexity of the integration challenges surrounding the myriad of changes that an SPO deployment entails. Multiply this example by the issues raised by the additional issues faced by a developing Project Office — coordination of the project/program/organizational budgeting processes, procurement, inventory control, capital equipment funding and allocation, and suppliers — and we find there is a tremendous amount of coordination and systems integration required for a fully functioning Strategic Project Office. To expedite these integration issues, the Executive Sponsor must be a champion for the SPO, while serving as an effective organizational facilitator. Being seen as a proponent of this process change for the good of the organization as a whole allows the Sponsor to pave the way to work through some of the sticky issues of turf, information-sharing, and power.

It is tempting for executives to hand over these kinds of sticky issues to a project manager selected to lead the Project Office initiative. But the project manager, as a middle-management level manager, most likely will not have the influence, authority, or reputation to work through the toughest challenges of integration. Also, it is likely he or she will run into a political roadblock, or the department he or she is negotiating with has other issues that it views as more of a crisis and the SPO integration problem is put on the back burner until "later." If integration unveils some areas of duplication or inefficiencies between departments — as is likely to happen — the project manager as the bearer of bad news is likely to be subjected to that time-honored management technique of "shooting the messenger." The value of a higher-level executive sponsor is that he or she can help adjust priorities relevant to the priorities of the overall organization. He or she can cut through some of the political challenges that a mid-level Project Office "project manager" will have extreme difficulty in achieving.

The Bottom Line

Choose a sponsor for the SPO who can communicate the plan and keep the organization's priorities straight. He or she must be a strong advocate for the changes involved, extremely knowledgeable about the benefits of project management, and have the ear and confidence of the powers that be. The old saying goes, "You're never a prophet in your own land." If senior management does not fully understand and support the project management approach, it might be time to bring in an external consultant who has dealt with a number of companies in your market segment to explain and execute the advantages of project management and the results achieved by others who have successfully implemented a Project Office.[18,19]

More Management Participation: The Project Office Steering Committee

As the liaison between senior corporate management and the SPO project team, the Executive Sponsor should be the chair of the Project Office Steering Committee. This committee is normally composed of the director of the SPO; the Project Sponsor; the heads of key functional organizations (members of business units affected by the project or projects being dealt with at any one time); and a senior corporate official, such as the CEO or COO. It should consist of three to seven individuals in total. This committee is formed to change the corporate project culture and is active on a continuing basis to select, prioritize, and evaluate the entire corporate portfolio of projects. In addition, it acts specifically on very large projects having overall corporate impact, such as the SPO initiative. When major issues or problems with the project must be escalated, the Project Office Steering Committee provides a forum for issue/problem resolution. This committee initiates the project in a management oversight role, and also continues to hold end-of-phase reviews throughout the duration of the deployment project, monitoring progress against the objectives to determine whether or not the SPO is meeting the objectives that were established at initiation. The Project Office Steering Committee may also discover the need to include technical and internal client representatives — senior staff from other business units that might be affected by the SPO deployment. If there are external customers who are critically affected, one may want to include them on this committee as well. This group is, in effect, the board of directors for the SPO and other mega-projects.

As a "board of directors," the Project Office Steering Committee has input into the strategic direction and will play a part in the review of the SPO charter. In some cases, members of the committee will need to sign off on key elements of the deployment plan (such as the project charter) because the charter defines the scope of the proposed SPO and its specific roles and responsibilities with respect to functional departments and business units. While the SPO Project Office Director will write the initial draft of the charter for the Project Office Steering Committee meeting, he or she will ask committee members to sign the charter to verify that its provisions have been agreed to. If a conflict arises in the future, the members of the committee will revisit originally agreed-upon terms of scope, priorities, and strategy prior to initiating change. The Project Office Steering Committee will also continue to revisit the goals and objectives of the SPO, as well as the critical deliverables, and continue to work within the organization to achieve executive buy-in to all those areas.

The Project Office Steering Committee is also involved in the commitment of all the various resources that the SPO deployment will require, from budget and personnel, to space, equipment, and time.

In the early stages of an SPO deployment, the Project Office Steering Committee will be required to meet more frequently, perhaps as often as monthly. As the project begins to deploy, the committee will meet less often. As part of project planning, the Project Office Steering Committee may wish to identify key end-of-phase points when it will come together to review progress to date, determine whether the objectives of that phase have been achieved, whether the schedule has been maintained, whether proper cost controls have been put into place, etc. Another way executive management can make sure that Project Office Steering Committee representatives fully appreciate the importance of the project is to ensure that committee members devote sufficient time to committee proceedings; that they in fact attend meetings and provide meaningful input, and provide feedback to senior executives on progress and problems. It may be necessary to conduct a session of executive-level training in project management before the SPO deployment project is launched to ensure that the Project Office Steering Committee fully understands its role, responsibilities, commitments, and value.

Functional managers seldom have a sufficient grasp of the enterprise advantages of project management to fully appreciate "what all the fuss is about." The members of the Project Office Steering Committee must understand enough about the project management process and its value to be strong advocates; and they must also have a high-level understanding of the phases and processes of the discipline in order to provide leadership and guidance during project reviews.

Periodic progress reviews are a normal part of the "controlling" processes of project management. On the SPO deployment project, as on any other organizational project, executive participation will be necessary in these project reviews. These reviews will be scheduled into the implementation plan. One reason executive involvement is important in these reviews is that the Project Office Steering Committee must have the authority to both launch and cancel the project if necessary. Otherwise, the Committee will not have sufficient authority to make other critical decisions necessary for the successful outcome of the project. Project control is all about identifying problems, risks, or issues early in the deployment initiative, and then addressing them as a project moves through its life cycle of planning, deployment, and transition to ongoing operations.

Keep in mind, however, that the Project Office Steering Committee must be aware of the highlights of the program only: a very high-level roll-up of all the project activity. The SPO project manager should also provide the committee with an agenda and a menu of decisions that must be made during the Project Office Steering Committee meetings. Some of the typical issues this committee will be asked to address include major changes in the direction of the Strategic Project Office deployment project or other significant change control items, budgetary impacts, resource conflicts, need for involvement from other organizations, or lack of support from a critical "power center" in the organization. A simple word from the CEO or COO to a recalcitrant player is sometimes all that is needed to get the Project Office deployment back on track. All the issues the project team itself is not able to resolve should be elevated to the Project Office Steering Committee so that the committee can use its influence or decision-making ability to redirect, correct, provide funding or resources, reprioritize, or take other action. And, as always, it is necessary to document committee decisions and incorporate them into an updated plan or issues log.

Finally, one of the most important areas in which the Project Office Steering Committee plays a role is in the realm of culture change. As discussed in Chapter 1, managing by projects is an entirely new way of doing business in many organizations and anyone attempting to align projects and strategy will impact not only those individuals doing project management, but also functional teams and managers, and systems from HR to payroll to facilities to procurement to finance. Changes of this magnitude cannot take place without management support and advocacy, and this will be a primary role for the Project Office Steering Committee. It has been said that much of implementing project management is "missionary work," and the executives involved must be the primary "missionaries" of this new business doctrine. Table 2.1 shows a set of Steering Committee guidelines adapted from the practices of the Australian government.[20] Table 2.2 offers suggestions for basic project management training for Steering Committee executives.

The Expanding Role of the Stakeholder

Because key stakeholders form the backbone of a Steering Committee, it is worth noting that, recently, several authors and experts have suggested a broader view of and role for stakeholders.

What the Gurus Say

Project management is unique among business approaches in the attention it lavishes on stakeholders; and according to some business thinkers, this feature of the discipline makes it a kind of model for how business will be carried out in the future. Ann Svendsen details recent research showing that when companies treat their employees well, create jobs in the local economy, develop innovative products and services, take care of the environment, and contribute to the community, they are often more

TABLE 2.1   What the Steering Committee Does

A Steering Committee's role is to:

Take on responsibility for the project's feasibility, business plan, and achievement of outcomes.

Ensure the project's scope aligns with the agreed requirements of the Business Owners and key stakeholder groups.

Provide those directly involved in the project with guidance on project business issues.

Ensure effort and expenditure are appropriate to stakeholder expectations.

Ensure that strategies to address potential threats to the project's success have been identified, costed, and approved, and that the threats are regularly reassessed.

Address any issue that has major implications for the project.

Keep the project scope under control as emergent issues force changes to be considered.

Reconcile differences in opinion and approach, and resolve disputes arising from them.

Report on project progress to those responsible at a high level.

Depending on the nature of the project, take on responsibility for progressing any corporate or strategic issues associated with the project.

What role do individual members perform?

Individual Steering Committee members are not directly responsible for managing Project Office activities, but provide support and guidance for those who do. Thus, individually, Steering Committee members should:

Understand the strategic implications and outcomes of initiatives being pursued through project outputs; appreciate the significance of the project for some or all major stakeholders and perhaps represent their interests.

Be genuinely interested in the initiative and the outcomes being pursued in the project.

Be an advocate for the project's outcomes by being committed to and actively involved in pursuing the project's outcomes.

Have a broad understanding of project management issues and the approach being adopted.

In practice, this means they:

Ensure the Project Office's outputs meet the requirements of the key stakeholders.

Help balance conflicting priorities and resources.

Provide guidance to the project team and users of the project's outputs.

Consider ideas and issues raised.

Foster positive communication outside the Committee regarding the progress and outcomes.

TABLE 2.1 (continued)   What the Steering Committee Does

As members are selected based on their individual knowledge and skills that they bring to the Committee, there can be some confusion and conflict in the accountability of members. The first responsibility of members is the achievement of Project Office success and second to their business area. Similarly, members who have expertise in a particular area should avoid taking a narrow view of their responsibility.

What happens before each meeting?

At least five working days before each scheduled meeting, you should receive:

An agenda

Minutes of the last meeting, including an action list

A progress report on the status of the project since the last meeting prepared by the project manager

Other documents to consider at the meeting (if any)

What happens during each meeting?

The Executive Sponsor usually chairs the meetings. The chair will conduct the meeting according to the agenda, ensuring that all members are encouraged to provide input throughout the meeting and that any decisions or recommendations are adequately resolved and confirmed by the members. A basic agenda would include:

Confirmation of minutes from previous meeting

Reviewing the status of action items from previous meeting

Report on the status of key projects by the Strategic Project Office Director or CPO

Discussion on other documents to be considered (if any)

Confirmation of date, time, and venue for next meeting

Within a week of the meeting, a copy of the minutes of the meeting should be circulated to all members.

Source: Adapted from the Tasmanian Governmental Project Management Guidelines, accessed at http://www.projectmanagement.tas.gov.au/res_kits/pm_scresourcekit.htm.

profitable.[21] Attention to the relationships between and among all the people, both within and external to a business organization's activities, not only minimizes conflict today, but also builds a fund of goodwill that can mitigate the potential for future problems. In a crowded global marketplace, with scarce talent and hair-trigger litigation, such relationship-based thinking becomes less and less of a luxury.

Svendsen's insights are confirmed by Steven F. Walker and Jeffrey W. Marr. In their book, companies are urged to build commitment and loyalty by developing ethical core values and practices for dealing with their

TABLE 2.2   Project Office Steering Committee Training

Barriers to Executive Education	How to Overcome the Barriers
Executives are too busy to take time for training.	Deliver information in bite-size components (e.g., two hours maximum length for any one session).
Executives will never use project management; that is for their direct reports.	The goal is not to create experts, but to increase their awareness of the potential of project management: to enlighten them as to how it can help them achieve their personal and professional objectives.
	Do not focus on tools and techniques; instead, give them the information needed to interpret the various types of reports generated by project management professionals.
	Teach enough project management so that they can ask the right questions to get the right picture from the project data.
	They should understand the realities of managing projects, so as to avoid unrealistic expectations. They should be able to connect the improvement in the management of projects with the company's business strategy.
Executive education must be delivered differently than the traditional classroom approach.	Senior executives must be engaged in a dialogue of exchange rather than the classroom paradigm of "I teach, you learn."
	An executive session requires a much smaller audience, preferably 12 to 15 at most.
	Use an action-oriented format: analyze where the organization rates on the project management maturity scale, identify steps needed to move toward maturation, and assign action items to the members of the executive staff. This sends a message to all attendees that they are expected to be active participants in the process.

Source: Adapted from Jimmie West, Even executives sing the blues, *The Project Management Best Practices Report,* June 2000.

"immediate family" of employees and customers.[22] But they do not stop there: citing research on the positive business returns on ethical community relations, they explore stakeholder relationships with community leaders, the media, and government. Using a stakeholder relationship model as the basis for developing corporate strategy, they argue, has significant long-term benefits.

So, corporate strategists and thought leaders are using stakeholder relationship management ideas from project management as a model for reinventing business. This should be a sobering thought because, in project management, stakeholder relationships are an area that often receives scanty attention.

What the Statistics Say

The project failure statistics generated by the Standish Group's CHAOS Reports are dismal. By analyzing what failed projects have in common, the CHAOS Reports have, after nearly a decade of data gathering, been able to pinpoint key success factors and failure red flags for projects. What are some of those red flags? "Lack of user involvement," "unrealistic expectations," and "lack of executive support" are the top three, all of which result from poor attention to stakeholders early in the concept and planning processes. In fact, British engineer and author John McManus identifies stakeholder mismanagement as "the critical risk in project management." He goes on to say that stakeholder theory represents "a challenge to conventional economic analysis, an approach that does not adequately consider the distribution of costs and benefits among different stakeholders: the winners and losers." According to McManus, projects both public and private will continue to have high failure rates unless better ways are found to incorporate various interests in planning, and to anticipate and deal with stakeholder opposition and conflict. In fact, he notes, only "the adoption of a stakeholder approach to project management and management in general will contribute to the long-term survival and success of a project organization." When stakeholder relationships are mutually supportive, they encourage trust and stimulate collaborative efforts that engender "relational wealth" — those organizational assets arising from familiarity and teamwork. By contrast, conflict and suspicion set into motion formal bargaining, limit efforts and rewards to stipulated terms, and set up reactive, information-hoarding "need-to-know" dynamics in the area of knowledge sharing. All this wastes time and money. When assessing the importance of stakeholders to the success of a project — especially a strategic project, such as a project management change initiative — he suggests the use of "checklist" questions to structure thoughts and obtaining answers to which policy or strategy might be developed. For example, which problems, affecting which stakeholders, does the project seek to address or alleviate? For which stakeholders does the project place a priority on meeting their needs, interests, and expectations? Which stakeholder interests converge most closely with policy and project objectives?[23]

Other Executive Roles: Portfolio Management, the CPO, and the SPO Director

If the SPO is to play the central role in guiding project management in the organization, staffing is complex. The Project Office Director position within the organization should be equivalent to that of a high-level functional manager — even a vice president, in some cases. The SPO Director at this level is supported by large numbers of professional associates and administrative personnel. Typical project office sizes range from five to twenty; in very large organizations, there may be hundreds of project managers linked directly or indirectly to the project office.[24]

As companies or divisions take on multiple projects, the process for deciding which projects to execute, and when, and what resources to assign to each project, becomes critical to whether or not the company meets its business objectives. At this level of maturity, a portfolio manager becomes a key role in facilitating project prioritization, resource allocation, and project approval decision making. In larger organizations with many projects underway, the job responsibilities might be split between two different positions: (1) a "portfolio manager" who maintains the most strategic view of business objectives and how various projects fit within those objectives, and is most responsible for the overall prioritization criteria and process and making decisions (or recommendations to executive management); and (2) a "resource manager" who works most closely with functional managers and project managers to understand the resource needs of each project (skills, expertise, timing, and numbers from various functions) and coordinate resolution of resource conflicts.[25]

See Appendix A for possible divisions of responsibility and roles at this organizational level. Depending on the size of the company, executive roles will vary in number and complexity. Figure 2.1 shows a fully mature corporate-level Strategic Project Office's roles and fit within the enterprise. Keep in mind that these roles, as we explain in the introduction to Appendix A, can be easily scaled down to describe roles and responsibilities for a divisional SPO. Whether the SPO is corporate or divisional, however, choosing its director will be a critical success factor.

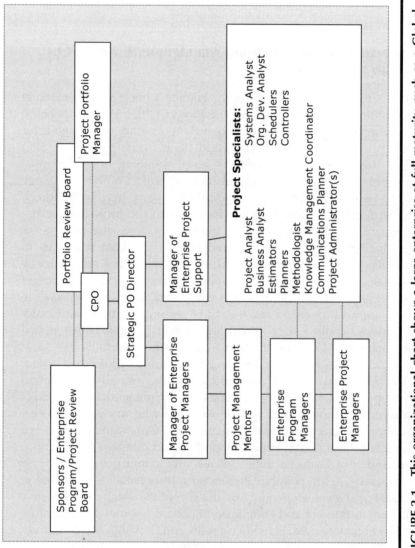

FIGURE 2.1 This organizational chart shows a large enterprise at full maturity, such as a Global 2000 firm, or federal or state government with a Strategic Project Office. Obviously, this structure must be tailored for many companies. For organizations that will never reach this level, the role descriptions must be combined and "scaled down" to fit the organizational circumstances.

The Strategic Project Office Director

If one's organization is prepared to make the SPO the central driving force behind the management of projects, one will want to consider establishing a director of project management who will sit at the director or vice-president level with other senior executives in the organization. This position, which we will call the SPO Director, provides project oversight in virtually all areas of the organization, managing corporate-level projects and overseeing corporate-wide resource distribution and allocation on all projects. Any project that crosses divisional boundaries, as well as some large projects performed within a department, would be under the auspices of this enterprise SPO Director.

But the SPO Director position is more complex than simply a glorified project manager. He or she will have to fill several critical roles. The SPO Director must ensure that the project management process runs well while also seeking to continuously improve it. As the expert on project management, the SPO Director also serves as an ad hoc consultant and advisor to project leaders and teams. The existence of an SPO Director guarantees a focus on the consistent use of the project management process throughout the organization.

Michael Hammer wrote of the "two flavors" of manager: (1) one a process manager who oversees a process end to end, with skills of performance management and work redesign, and (2) one an employee coach who supports and nurtures employees.[26] A good SPO Director must be both the overseer and "owner" of project management methodology and a leading mentor to up-and-coming project talent within the organization.

The SPO Director must possess enough stature and respect throughout the organization to champion projects from start to finish — and to recommend canceling projects whose objectives either cannot be met or are no longer valid. He or she must have the demonstrable backing of senior management, especially critical early in the transition to the SPO structure. However, instituting an SPO Director alone is not enough to bring the organization into a mode of "managing by projects." It is also necessary to alter the role of functional managers from resource owners to project resource suppliers — an equally significant change that organizations must make to fully realize the value of effective, cross-organizational project teams.

An SPO Director can wear many hats, depending on the size and scope of the SPO. Here are a few of the general areas of responsibility that he or she will take on:

■ The SPO Director is a "relationship manager" working to smooth the interfaces with the business units and develop project requirements through consensus with customers. Serving as a liaison to executive and functional management, the SPO Director communicates the mission, vision, scope, and benefits of the SPO, and interfaces with all aspects of the business to increase a level of awareness of the services provided by the SPO and the benefits of using those services.[27]

■ A Human Resources Manager develops the skills of the SPO staff and project managers throughout the organization, prioritizes the application of Project Office resources, and contributes to definition of training requirements on corporate project management training, and project management methods and processes. He or she might also act as a professional development coordinator — or oversee such a position — to ensure that job descriptions are created, maintained, and refined for the project management career path. Criteria are defined for interviewing, rating, and hiring for project management skills, as well as for identifying people in the organization who are currently acting as project managers and those who are interested in developing their skills in an effort to become project managers. Depending on the size of the Project Office, the SPO Director might also work with each individual to identify strengths and weaknesses in the project management discipline and assist them in identifying opportunities for developing the appropriate skills and knowledge, work with the internal training organization to identify project management training courses, and work with management to identity individuals or assignment opportunities to develop skills and experience.[28]

■ A Program Manager, providing corporate project oversight, checkpoints, and controls, reviewing and analyzing the process of project management throughout the organization, defining and conducting project audits, and managing the Project Office budgets. The SPO Director must ensure organizational compliance with tax laws, governmental guidance such as the Sarbanes–Oxley Act, and accounting or financial standards. Regular and accurate reporting must be provided at all levels of the organization with information appropriate to the needs of the recipient.

■ A Mentor and Evangelist for PM: as "owner" of the project office methodologies, the Director might also be in charge of the following areas, either by taking personal responsibility for these items or by employing a methodology expert to fulfill the functions: authoring, maintaining, and adapting the project management methods and processes; evaluating and selecting project management tools; developing knowledge management standards and processes for archiving and disseminating project documents, lessons learned, and other intellectual capital derived from project activities; developing tools for measuring the level of usage and effectiveness of project management methods used by the organization; and soliciting and incorporating feedback from project managers for the continuous improvement of the methods and processes.

In short, the SPO Director is an integrator of processes, a manager of staff, a coordinator of project resources (including project managers), the coordinator of standards and methods as well as developer and maintainer of tools expertise, a mentor, training coordinator, and point of interface between projects, programs, and the executive staff. A tall order — and one that must be filled with the same care that companies take in placing a CIO, a CFO, or a CEO. We believe it is time to institutionalize a role called the "Chief Project Officer" (CPO) on a peer level with other executives in the organization; and in mid-sized companies, the CPO and the director of the corporate SPO might be one and the same.

The alternative — spreading out the project-management-related responsibilities among existing executives in the organization — is cumbersome. This arrangement has been tried before, under the title of "matrix organization" and, as we discussed in Chapter 1, the jury is in: it is too slow and bureaucratic a system to satisfy today's rigorous time-to-market needs.

Notes

1. Vijay Verma, *Organizing Projects for Success*, PMI, 1995, pp. 19–20.
2. J.R. Galbraith, Matrix organizational designs, *Business Horizons*, February 1971.
3. R.J. Karen, White, Functional to matrix: avoiding the pitfalls, *Best Practices Executive Briefing*, August 2002. This issue also contains an excerpt from Frank Toney, *The Superior Project Organization*, CBP, 2001, and other research on the matrix organization.
4. Frank Toney, *The Superior Project Manager,* CBP, 2000.
5. *Performance Measurement for Project Management*, American Productivity and Quality Council, 2003.
6. J.D. Frame, *The New Project Management: Corporate Reengineering and Other Business Realities,* Jossey Bass, San Francisco, 1994.
7. R.M. Kanter, The role of the technical leader, in R. Katz (Ed.), *The Human Side of Managing Technological Innovation*, Oxford University Press, Oxford, 1997. See also J.K. Pinto and O.P. Kharbanda, *Successful Project Managers: Leading Your Team to Success,* Van Nostrand Reinhold, 1995.
8. James J. Jiang, Gary Klein, and Houn-Gee Chen, The relative influence of IS project implementation policies and project leadership on eventual outcomes, *Project Management Journal*, September 2001.

9. Breaking HR's vicious cycle, *Canadian HR Reporter,* December 3, 2001, www.hrreporter.com, article #1448.

10. Ibid.

11. Ibid.

12. Personal interview, August 2003.

13. Michael Hammer and James Champy, *Reengineering the Corporation,* HarperCollins, 1993.

14. Human Resource Department Management Report, March 2002.

15. Andrew Lee-Mortimer, Clocking on to extra value, *Works Management,* February 2001.

16. Arie de Geus, *The Living Company,* HBS Press, 1997. See also "An Organic Approach to Management" at http://www.cbi.cgey.com/journal/issue4/features/organic/author.html.

17. The Standish Group, *CHAOS Report,* 1999; see also www.standishgroup.com and James Johnson, Chaos: The dollar drain of IT project failures, *Application Development Trends,* January 1995. Additional reading on project failure: *Best Practices Executive Briefing,* August 2000.

18. J. Kent Crawford, *The Strategic Project Office,* Marcel Dekker, 2001.

19. Project Connections role templates, accessed at www.projectconnections.com.

20. Tasmanian Government Project Management Guidelines, accessed at http://www.projectmanagement.tas.gov.au/res_kits/pm_scresourcekit.htm.

21. Ann Svendsen, *The Stakeholder Strategy: Profiting from Collaborative Business Relationships,* Berrett-Kohler, 1998.

22. Steven F. Walker and Jeffrey W. Marr, *Stakeholder Power: A Winning Plan for Building Stakeholder Commitment and Driving Corporate Growth,* Perseus, 2002.

23. John McManus, The influence of stakeholder values on project management, *Management Services,* June 2002.

24. M. Light and T. Berg, Gartner Strategic Analysis Report: The Project Office: Teams, Processes and Tools, August 1, 2000.

25. Project Connections, ibid.

26. Michael Hammer and James Champy, ibid.

27. M. Light and T. Berg, ibid.

28. Carolyn M. Hennings, Proposing a program office for a service organization, *Proceedings of the 30th Annual Project Management Institute Seminars & Symposium,* PMI, 1999.

MANAGING PEOPLE AS THOUGH PROJECTS REALLY MATTER: BEST PRACTICES FOR CAPITALIZING ON PROJECT PERSONNEL

II

Chapter 3

The Right Stuff: Competency-Based Employment

Chapter 2 focused on the importance of executive involvement in building organizational project management capability. But even an informed, involved executive is not going to deliver great project results without the right project managers leading solid project teams.

It is not just that projects are the value-creation engine of today's economy, as discussed in the Introduction and Chapter 1; and it is not simply that a good project manager has been cited as the number one factor in project success.[1] There is another point that should be stressed about the importance of identifying high-performance project managers. From within their ranks will come the next generation of project executives: Project Office Directors, Portfolio Managers, CIOs ... perhaps even CEOs. Experienced project managers with the aptitude for business bring a valuable project-focused intelligence to corporate leadership. But these leaders must be developed, from team members into project managers, from managers into leaders. "At the heart of organizational project management capability is the company's ability to empower and support project managers," says Oxford University's Christopher Sauer. "Individuals do not innovate and advance organizational learning just because to do so improves organizational capability; they do so because human resource policies and the organization's values encourage them to feel they have a personal stake in helping the organization perform better in the long term."[2]

Sauer, in his study of successful project-based organizations, points out that organizational capability is built from the ground up — by making it possible for the people who do projects to do their best. A first step in this building process is defining what "best" means.

Focusing on building project manager competencies to the "best" level means first identifying what needs improvement. To do this requires a comprehensive competency assessment program. The results of this type of individual assessment help organizations begin to harness the power of their project personnel's skills and abilities. It also allows the organization to focus training where it is most needed. Matching project manager and team competencies with the types of projects they are prepared to handle will result in more effective project execution, and thus better organizational performance. Competency-based project human resource management is a bold approach to the professionalization of the role of project manager — not only in terms of providing them with the means to acquire the needed skills and competencies, but also making it possible for experienced project managers to bring their knowledge up through the ranks to senior-level positions in the organization.

Caution: This is not a small change. To optimize the benefits of project management, organizations need to completely change their approach to hiring and training project personnel. They also need to more aggressively develop the knowledge, skills, and competencies of their project management staff. To accomplish this, the organization must focus on both developing the individual and on linking organizational roles to individual skills. Once a company begins viewing role description, recruitment, rewards, and professional development through the lens of competence, many time-honored structures and patterns existing in our human resource management will change. Behaviors in the workplace are the building blocks of competence but they are also an expression of organizational culture. It is no exaggeration to say that designing organizational human resource processes around competence on projects is a paradigm shift. If you are ready for this shake-up, read on.

What Is Competence?

Even the dictionary writers must go to great lengths to adequately describe the quality of "competence." In this word, the concepts of ability, skill, knowledge, and qualification are combined. For our purposes, perhaps the legalistic definition suits best: "the quality or condition of being qualified to perform an act." Although, unlike Australia, the United States does not at present have laws defining who can call themselves "project managers"; the unforgiving marketplace does punish companies for failing to first define project management competencies, and then to hire, measure, reward, and promote within a competency-based system. Project failure rates describe just how much punishment companies endure due to ineffective methods for choosing and retaining good project personnel.

Competence is not a management fad; it is nothing new. David Frame points out that it is a major topic in Plato's *Republic* and in the Old Testament, and that competence (or its opposite) continues to be pondered in modern culture … by Dilbert, for example. Frame writes that the concept of competence in the workplace derives from philosopher William James' philosophy of pragmatism, which can be briefly stated as "it's results that count."[3] In a competency-based environment, one determines the result one needs and works backward from that goal to pinpoint the skills and behaviors that individual players must possess to arrive at it.

That sounds simple; but because people are complex and organizational life is often chaotic, it never is simple. There is more to encouraging productive behaviors than making sure everyone has a certain educational background or certification. Competence in the work setting is the result of an interplay between several factors: knowledge, skills, experience, personal qualities or traits, team dynamics, and organizational culture. Certain aspects are inborn or come naturally, a function of talent, aptitude, preference for processing information, or learning style. Others are a matter of education, practice, and socialization. The factors that contribute to the team and organizational environment are just as crucial as individual competencies, but are often overlooked. (See the Competency Pyramid, Figure 3.1.)

Dimensions of Individual Competence

Various writers on the theme of competence in business have broken down competence into its components in different ways. However, the following four dimensions seem to be universally acknowledged.

Knowledge

The first recorded musings on the nature of knowledge belong to the ancient Greeks. The ideas of Plato and Aristotle have long formed the basis for our concepts of what knowledge is and how it can be accumulated. For our purposes, knowledge can be defined — as the dictionary defines it — as the "familiarity, awareness, or understanding gained through experience or study; the sum or range of what has been perceived, discovered, or learned." For project managers, the "body of knowledge" contains more than simply specific knowledge about how to plan and

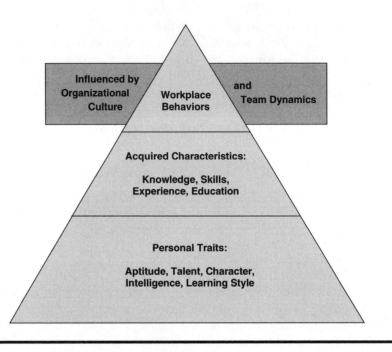

FIGURE 3.1 The Competency Pyramid.

control projects. There is also knowledge in their chosen discipline (e.g., engineering, marketing, information systems, etc.); knowledge of other disciplines that come into play in the industry in which they work, such as regulatory law or technology advancements; and knowledge of the business side (finance, personnel, strategic planning). Knowledge in all these areas can be built up through reading, classroom training, research on the Internet, and the kind of informal knowledge transfer that takes place constantly in the workplace and in professional associations.

Skills

Webster's dictionary describes a skill as "proficiency, ability, or dexterity" — learned behaviors with practical application that require practice to perfect. For a project manager, such skills can fall into any of three areas: their area of subject matter expertise (engineering, marketing, information systems); project management skills related to planning and controlling; or human skills (influencing, negotiating, communicating, facilitating, mentoring, coaching). The technical skills become less and less important as the project manager's responsibility for the managerial skills grows; this is one reason why excellent technologists have often failed as project managers. As roles become more abstract — one of the hallmarks of knowledge work — the difficulty of defining the competencies necessary becomes complex. Skill at typing is easy to quantify; skill in strategic thinking, innovation, or teambuilding much more difficult.

Personal Characteristics

On the intangible, but extremely important, side of the ledger are things like energy and drive, enthusiasm, professional integrity, morale, determination, and commitment. In recent years, a number of project management writers have focused on these traits as being perhaps the most important for project managers, outweighing technical knowledge and skills.

Experience

When knowledge can be applied to practice, and skills polished, experience is gained. The great thing is that it does not stop there. Experience also increases knowledge and skill. As Webster's dictionary describes it, "Active participation in events or activities leading to accumulation of knowledge or skill." Joan Knutson describes project managers' experience as "getting their hands dirty in their areas of expertise, in their industry and in project management; [accumulating] layer(s) of scar tissue which show that they have been there and done that."[4]

Modeling Competence

The quality of competence can be more specifically described in terms of *competencies*. Competencies are statements about the characteristics, in each of the areas listed above, that result in effective or superior performance at work.

Defining competencies for critical jobs helps a company identify criteria that can be used to assess employees for recruitment, in performance appraisal, and in making professional development choices. From the individual's point of view, competency-based management means that work makes sense: the job you apply for is the one you actually end up doing; and your performance in it is judged on some logical criteria. In truly competence-driving organizations, pay and other rewards are also linked to competency, as are training opportunities and other forms of professional development.

While some competencies are universal to business or to project management, a subset must be unique to each organization. A generic model is a useful starting place for competency-based management, but each company must adapt competencies to fit its competitive market, management style, and culture.[5]

Competency-based management brings focus and order to the complex web of tasks, responsibilities, goals, skills, knowledge, and abilities in today's knowledge-based roles by clarifying the critical few competencies that differentiate high performance. Because these critical competencies tend to be more enduring than the immediate priorities, this step can help companies avoid the dangers of short-term thinking in the management of people.

The first step toward competency-based management is to understand the patterns that are repeated by the most effective employees in their knowledge, skills, and behaviors — in other words, competencies that enable them to be high performers. By highlighting these competencies, companies provide managers and employees with guidance on how to increase workplace effectiveness, and also give individuals some control over their own development and performance. This "architecture" of effectiveness for a given position is a *competency model*. Companies such as the Royal Bank of Scotland, Consignia, Amazon, and Goldman Sachs use competency frameworks of this type.[6]

A *competency model* comprises a list of differentiating competencies for a role or job family,[7] the definition of each competency, and the descriptors or behavioral indicators describing how the competency is displayed by high performers. Options include developing models for entire families of jobs (all project management personnel) or whole departments, such as all information technology employees.

There are two types of competency models. *Descriptive competency models* define the knowledge, skills, and behaviors known to differentiate high performance from average performance in the current environment or recent past. Descriptive models can have high validity because they are built from actual data about the difference between average and star performers. *Prescriptive models* lean toward describing competencies that will be important in the future. They are helpful in dynamic environments or to help drive a major change in culture or capabilities. Competency models provide a catalog of the leadership traits desired by the organization in its managers. These traits, in turn, become the key attributes to be developed.

The business needs addressed by competency models include:

- *Clarifying work expectations:* defining the skills required and the behaviors that lead to success. This serves the company's interest by getting the work done, and serves the individual's interest by making work make sense, by taking the arbitrariness out of hiring, rewards, appraisal, etc.

- *Hiring the best people:* for more on the costs of bad hiring practices, see Chapter 5.
- *Maximizing productivity:* workers are more effective when they know what behaviors are valued by the organization. A competency model communicates organizational values to the individual. At the recruitment stage, this allows candidates to make an informed choice about the organization.[8]

The first competency models were designed in the 1970s by the leading authority in organizational psychology, David C. McClelland. He tried two approaches: (1) asking a panel of experts from management to identify the tasks, skills, and qualities needed; and (2) interviewing top performers about their best practices. Most of what was identified from the top down turned out to be irrelevant. McClelland's research proved that people who do the jobs are the best source of information about what those jobs consist of and what is required for them. And, even this early on, McClelland identified social sensitivity as a competence — something we are only now fully realizing in project management and other technical occupations.[9]

There are many advantages in using competency models to manage knowledge workers. First, they are often constructed around tangible dimensions — behaviors, outcomes, or activities. These can be measured. Second, they send a clear message to an organization about the specific attributes that are considered valuable. Third, they provide a framework or checklist for both individual managers and their organizations to benchmark themselves; in other words, to see which competencies are strong or weak within the individual and within the management ranks of the organization.[10] So, while the work processes might be intellectual in nature, and the work product somewhat intangible, effectiveness can still be gauged in an objective manner. Anyone who has ever been through a performance review that seemed to have little to do with their performance and a lot to do with organizational politics will appreciate the potential for competency-based management to bring fairness into the review process. Performance review processes that incorporate competency models usually enable multiple inputs (such as 360-degree feedback with subordinate, peer, and manager), which improves assessment or review quality.[11]

While implementing competency-based management tools can be expensive in the short term, the costs are outweighed by the financial benefits. Craig Russell examined the value of competency-based selection in 98 candidates for executive roles in a Fortune 50 company. Monitoring their performance over three years, he calculated that general managers selected using a competency-based process each generated an additional $3 million in annual profit as compared with recruits who were selected using a previous process that was not based on competencies.[12]

Developing a Competency Model

James Warner, Ph.D., director of strategic performance modeling practice at Personnel Decisions International, in an interview in *Workforce Week* reminds us that a competency model is a "worker-focused" view, not a detailed task analysis. To maintain a worker-focused view, ask the question: What characteristics are most likely to lead to successful performance? Therefore, the first step is to make sure that one understands the most important results, or outcomes, from the job. This step links performance to organizational goals. Once one identifies general strengths needed to perform in the organization, one must examine what separates an excellent performer in this job, job family, or organizational level (such as senior executive, project manager, or team member) from someone who is not successful. Warner cites studies showing that using a comprehensive, competency-based system results in the selection of higher-performing individuals and lowers the overall costs that can result from bad hires.[13]

When a company sets out to develop its own competency models, the process is usually to gather information through interviews or focus groups, with managers and employees who understand what it takes to be successful. Information from executives who have a strategic view of the organization and who know what kind of performance will be required to achieve success as that strategy unfolds in the future will be important even when adapting a standard competency model. The analysis of these interviews typically provides a prioritized list of competencies that should be the focus of the recruitment and selection process. Sometimes, cognitive or intellectual capability is most important. At other times, especially when individuals work independently, personality attributes that enable them to develop partnerships, yet work without guidance, are most important.

Interview the Job — To derive descriptions of competence from them, job descriptions should be both accurate and complete (Appendix A provides a thorough discussion of job descriptions in project management). A well-written job description weeds out those not suited for the position, helps the candidate evaluate the job opportunity, helps determine the appropriate compensation, enables the company to assess how long it will take to find the right candidate, and assists the manager in evaluating employee performance once the person is on the job. Naturally, this will require thoughtful analysis of the position being described. Develop a list of the required tasks and personal traits (problem-solving skills, communication skills, the ability to motivate people). If the resulting list is not both realistic and manageable, analyze your expectations and the roles of related jobs to see if the "job family" can be adjusted to make success achievable. Many companies collect long wish lists of personality traits, qualifications, and potential tasks and projects such that they are unlikely to find real human beings who can measure up. This sets up both the company and the candidate for failure. The time invested in job analysis results in significant time savings throughout the selection process. If you fail to complete this essential step, expect delays, increased turnover, and potential problems when trying to defend your selection process from grievances or legal actions.[14]

Another benefit of clear job descriptions is that they minimize the influence of racial and sex stereotypes in the interview process. Interviewers with little information about the job may be more likely to make stereotypical judgments about the suitability of candidates than are interviewers with detailed information about the job.

One way to test the validity of a model before implementing it in the organization is to evaluate the most successful employees to determine if they have more strength in these competencies than those who are not as successful. One of the advantages of adapting a standard competency model, such as exist for project managers, is that, to a certain extent, such validation has already taken place.

When choosing or developing a competency model as the basis for selecting and developing individuals, the predictive validity of the model is only one consideration. Here are five additional criteria that should be considered. A competency model (and its associated assessment procedures) should be:

1. *Practical.* Ease of use is important, especially where there are many positions or multiple roles to be filled.
2. *Scalable.* Results from competency assessments should be applicable across levels and job roles. A test of project management knowledge can be useful for project support team members, project team leaders, project managers, and even program managers, for example.
3. *Cost-effective.* The ROI of investing in better recruitment, selection, and development methods will vary from company to company, but should be calculable. (See information on the costs of turnover in Chapter 5 for inputs to ROI calculations.)
4. *Acceptable.* The employees or candidates being assessed should find the questions reasonable; and the managers responsible for administering the assessment or doing selection or reviews should find it helpful rather than an administrative burden. Candidates should be able to see a link between the contents of an assessment and the requirements of the job for which they are applying.

Assessments should not leave people wondering, "Why are they asking me this?" Research also suggests that qualified candidates prefer well-structured assessments to more informal hiring practices. Assessments that are perceived to be intrusive, inappropriate, or inconsistently used can damage a company's reputation among both candidates and newly hired employees. They should also be appropriate in length: long enough to yield actionable information, but not overwhelming.

5. *Legal.* Because there is always a legal dimension to hiring and promotion practices, ensure that the model or assessment process does not infringe on candidates' human rights or discriminate unfairly against minority groups. In general, a staffing assessment will be considered legal if it is job related, predicts job performance, and is consistently administered. However, the complexity of legal compliance makes it important to consult an expert before designing and using any staffing assessment.[15]

Models for Project Management

Within the past decade, research attention has focused on identifying competencies for project managers. The seminal work in this field was done by the Australian Institute of Project Management (AIPM), whose National Competency Standard for Project Management was adopted by the Australian Government as part of that country's national qualification system. In England, the Association of Project Management (APM) has created competency standards for project controls specialists and project managers. The publication of U.S.-based PMI®'s competency standard in 2002,[16] after five years of developmental work, established a new framework for thinking about the components of competence in a project management context. This standard, along with other work by educational institutions and private-sector companies, is framed on the concept that, when it comes to managing projects, many of the competencies required are specific to the discipline but not to the organizational context. That is, a project manager who has cut his or her teeth on projects in the telecom industry might do very well on other types of projects that require either creating or introducing new technology. The existence of project manager competency models streamlines the adoption of competency-based management for project-oriented companies. Although all these assessment frameworks are quite different, they do have certain themes in common (see Table 3.1.)

From our point of view, a project manager competency assessment should determine who has the best mix of traits and skills to be a superior project manager, or the potential to become one. By examining the

TABLE 3.1 Project Management Competence: A Comparison of Competency Models

	Australian National Competency Standards	*Boston University Competency Model (BUCEC)*	*PM College Competency Model*	*PMI Competency Development Framework*
Component 1 (PMBOK-based)	Project management-specific competencies	Technical skills	Knowledge assessment	Project Manager knowledge
Component 2	Common business competencies	Personal skills	Behaviors in the workplace (multi-rater tool)	Project Manager performance
Component 3	N/A. Many personal competencies (communication, initiative, leadership) are covered within Component 2	Business/leadership skills	Project Manager potential profile	Project Manager personal competence
Unique Features	Embedded within government-accredited qualifications that are part of the Australian Qualifications Framework	Focused more on business acumen, leadership traits, and other aspects of the "art" of project management; includes competencies in "big-picture" areas like *organizational savvy and strategic thinking*	Predictive element (Component 3) based on extensive research by Caliper, an assessment firm with a database of more than two million individuals assessed for business competencies	"Units of competency" (tasks and behaviors) sorted into "competency clusters" according to PM Process areas as defined in the *PMBOK® Guide*

knowledge, potential, and behaviors of project managers (or project manager candidates), the organization can achieve the following results:

- Project managers are appropriately recruited.
- Project manager training is more effective.
- Projects are managed at a higher level of quality.
- Projects are delivered on time and within budget.
- Project failure rates decline and time to market increases.
- Profitability improves.

Implementing a Competency-Based System

The first step in competency-based management is not simply testing people against a competency model, however. The implementation of competency standards is a process-improvement project with the usual steps:

1. *Understand the current state.* What is the hiring process? The selection process? What are the organization's strengths and weaknesses? What are the organization's priorities? What is the review process? How seriously do manager and employees take it? Is hiring the best people really a serious goal? (When an organization hires people who are less than the best, there are reasons, even if they are not articulated — benefits it receives from hiring mediocre performers, such as the unwillingness to challenge existing employees, resistance to monetary expense, a commitment to the status quo. Change agents will need to identify and address these "hidden" values.)

2. *Model the desired state.* Who do you want, and why? What is the vision for human resource development? What should be the relationship between reviews and compensation and career planning?

3. *Establish the objective.* What difference will it make to the organization to change its project management selection and training practices?

4. *Build a case for the need.* Identify the project human resource problems (turnover, poor quality, project failures). Describe the consequences of those problems, describe the solution, and identify the benefits of the solution, including the personal benefits to individuals (think of these as "selling points" for cultural change): financial gain, career advancement, prestige, simplification, accomplishment, growth and learning, social satisfaction, community commitment, job security.[17]

5. *Implement the competency model.* Once the groundwork for this change project has been laid, one can begin assessing individuals, either as part of the new-hire selection process or across the organization, in order to bring professional development and reward practices in line with the organization's definitions of competence.

A few important reminders about conducting competency assessments:

1. *Communicate the results.* What is the objective of the program? Let people know how assessment results will be used to modify future training and professional development.
2. *Make it easy for employees to complete the assessment.* Evaluations make people anxious. Provide adequate notice, and allow enough time to complete the assessments. These steps decrease anxiety and help one obtain a truer reading of knowledge and skills.
3. *Do not keep secrets.* Once the assessments have been completed, communicate the aggregated results. One can increase support for the process by closing the loop with employees and providing details on the next steps.
4. *Protect confidentiality.* To ensure that the data is used appropriately, protect confidentiality by conducting assessments in privacy, without management present. Online assessment instruments have an advantage in this area. Make it difficult for people to guess about individual responses by reporting aggregated data for groups of ten or more.[18]

Assessing Competence

Staffing assessments are nothing new, and tools for assessment are widely available in the HR marketplace. These range from simple prescreening questions asking about salary expectations and work eligibility to complex "talent measures" that assess underlying motives, traits, and soft skills. Research has shown that well-designed assessment tools predict job success with much greater accuracy than traditional employee-selection practices such as résumé reviews and unstructured interviews. In addition, because staffing-assessment tools can often be administered via computer, they can also increase the efficiency of the hiring process. For example, Sherwin–Williams estimates that its use of automated assessment tools reduced the number of employment interviews conducted each year by more than 5000. This increased accuracy and efficiency can have a big impact on organizational performance and costs.

So the question is not whether conducting assessments of competence is a good idea; the question is what tools to use for the assessment. HR experts recommend that, to be effective, staffing-assessment tools should meet three key conditions:

1. They must be chosen on the basis of a clear definition of performance for the job in question.
2. They must effectively measure the key candidate characteristics that influence job performance.
3. They must be deployed in a standardized, consistent fashion that ensures that all candidates are assessed in the same way.

Common types of staffing-assessment tools (the first three are pre-employment; the second three can be used for hiring or for "tuning up" the existing workforce):

1. *Qualifications screens.* These questionnaires screen out candidates who do not meet minimum requirements, such as relevant experience or educational degrees.
2. *Structured interviews.* A systematic process for evaluating candidates on the basis of their responses to predefined questions built around key job competencies. Structured interviews can be conducted face-to-face, by phone, or over the Web.
3. *Job simulations.* These evaluate how people respond to work-related situations. Job simulations can be "paper-and-pencil" exercises (such as analyzing and responding to cases), role-playing, or computer simulations. In addition to assessing competence, simulations can provide candidates with a realistic preview of job roles. Labor intensive to create, simulations may require extensive training to administer (especially the role-playing option).
4. *Knowledge and skills tests.* These assess knowledge and skills in specific technical knowledge areas such as computer programming or business applications such as project management.
5. *Talent measures.* These measure personal characteristics that have been associated with success for the role in question. Problem-solving ability, work ethic, leadership characteristics, and interpersonal style are a few areas that are frequently tested for in business. These measures predict two kinds of performance: (1) what a person *can* do (abilities) and (2) what a person *will* do (behaviors). When appropriately matched to the job, these kinds of measures are the best predictors of superior job performance. They are also the most difficult to develop because they require looking below the surface.

6. *Values/culture inventories.* These help determine how well an applicant will fit into a particular work environment. While not indicative of the individual's abilities, they may indicate how those abilities will function within the specific organizational context. This is a useful measure for predicting retention.

The best competency assessment programs use multiple assessment tools.[19]

What Project Manager Competency Assessment Looks Like

Once competencies are defined, it is time to conduct an assessment of the identified project management populations. A communication plan about the assessment should precede administration of the tests in order to inform the candidates about what will be expected of them and the reason behind the assessment. It is human nature to view something like this as a way to justify an organizational realignment. The assessment process should clearly focus on building strengths, not eliminating staff; mitigating fear of assessments through open communication is critical.

As much care should be given to the appointment of a project manager for a mission-critical project as is given during the hiring process for a key position in corporate leadership, according to Boston University's project management program leaders.[20] Yet most organizations have no process for choosing project managers, and little idea what skills and personality traits are needed by project managers to help them succeed. Poor project manager competency accounts for 60 percent of project failures, according to IT research firm Gartner, Inc. Lost profits due to late, over budget, and failed projects have encouraged more business decision makers to look at project manager competency assessment programs. These in-depth evaluations help executives make better, more informative decisions about project manager recruitment and training initiatives.

The best way to demonstrate how to assess project management competency is to look at an existing model in detail. The model co-developed by PM College and Caliper International, a leading human resources assessment firm, The Project Manager Competency Assessment Program (PMCAP) provides us with a ready example.[21]

The PMCAP gives organizational leaders a holistic view of an individual's current project management knowledge and skills, along with his or her potential to effectively fill a project manager role. Armed with this diagnostic information, companies can determine which individual project managers have the highest potential to grow and excel. The assessment results also help organizations target training only where deficiencies are recognized, thus eliminating unnecessary training programs and ensuring more productive results from training investment.

Like other effective competency assessment systems, the PMCAP has three components: (1) a multilevel knowledge test, (2) a personality and cognitive assessment, and (3) a multirater survey reviewing the current workplace performance of project managers. These three instruments address three aspects of competence: (1) knowledge of project management concepts, terminology, and theories; (2) behavior and performance in the workplace; and (3) personal traits indicative of the individual's project manager potential. (Sample questions from all three instruments are included in the Appendices.)

Knowledge

The *knowledge assessment tool* measures the level of an individual's project management knowledge. It tests the candidate's working knowledge of the language, concepts, and practices of the profession with questions based on the Project Management Institute's *PMBOK® Guide*, the ISO-approved industry standard. The advantage of using this standard is that the *PMBOK Guide* has created a uniform language of project management that can be used across all industries. Knowledge assessment should address both the five process areas (initiating, planning, executing, controlling, and closing) of the *PMBOK Guide* as well as the nine knowledge areas (integration, scope, time, cost, quality, human resources, communications, risk, and procurement management).[22] Figure 3.2 is an example of results from a completed knowledge assessment test. On an individual basis, the candidates can see how they scored on each knowledge area, how they compared to the highest score, their percentile ranking, and how many areas they passed. For the organization, an aggregate table provides insight into the areas of strengthened areas that need improvement for their entire population. This information is used to begin developing a targeted education and training program designed to meet those needs.

Behavioral Assessment

A second area of assessment is of behaviors exhibited in the workplace. This approach requires the use of a multirater tool (sometimes called a 360-degree tool), which allows the acquisition of feedback on the project managers' behavior from a variety of sources — typically peers, subordinates, supervisors, or clients — but always someone who has first-hand

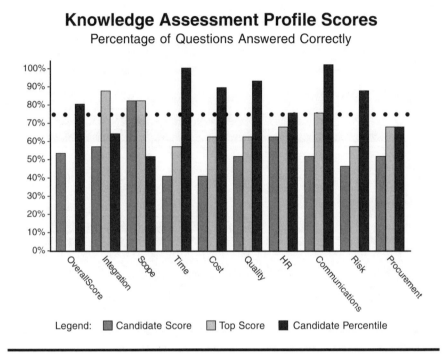

Knowledge Assessment Profile Scores
Percentage of Questions Answered Correctly

Legend: ▨ Candidate Score ☐ Top Score ■ Candidate Percentile

FIGURE 3.2 Example of a completed Knowledge Assessment report. Dotted line represents a passing score.

knowledge of the candidate's behavior in the workplace. This type of assessment should focus on the desired behaviors that effective project managers exhibit in the execution of their jobs. For example, it might examine the creation of a stakeholder communication plan, the development and distribution of a team charter, or the execution of a risk management plan. Individuals also rate themselves on their competency in several key performance indicators. The independent assessors then rate the individuals on those same criteria. Ratings are compared. A multi-rater assessment provides a holistic view of the individual's project manager behaviors and serves as a gauge for determining which behaviors are present or absent, how well the behaviors are displayed, and which behaviors demonstrate areas for potential growth.

There is a dual focus to this assessment: confirmation of behaviors and analysis of competency. The analysis of this assessment looks for significant gaps between the candidate and rater. These gaps are created either by the candidates rating themselves higher than the rater or the candidates rating themselves lower than the rater. When there is little or no gap found, the important thing to review is the level of agreement.

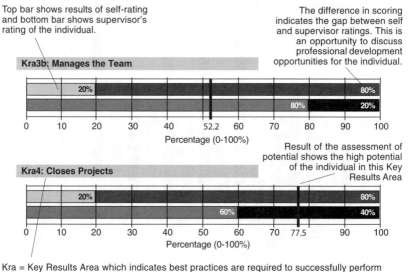

Kra = Key Results Area which indicates best practices are required to successfully perform a project

FIGURE 3.3   Example Behavioral Assessment report. Top bar shows results of self-rating and bottom bar shows supervisor's rating of the individual. The vertical bar indicates assessed level of potential.

Both the candidate and rater could agree on the level of performance but, in reality, that level may be less than the desired level. In that case, the organization has an opportunity for developmental actions if required. Figure 3.3 is an example of a behavioral assessment report.

Potential to perform the project manager role is evaluated through a series of questions that test the ability to think and solve problems in specific situations. The role of project manager carries with it a number of critical factors that, when used together, can identify the potential of the project management candidate to be successful in managing projects. In addition, these factors can indicate whether the candidate would be best used in small, noncomplex projects or large, highly sophisticated and complex projects. Factors to consider include the abilities to handle stress, be flexible, negotiate, deal with corporate politics, and manage personal time; organization skills; and conflict management. The candidate's score is compared with high performers (project managers who show the highest level of competency). The instrument for measuring potential in the PMCAP is the Caliper Profile, an assessment battery developed by Caliper that provides competency-based reporting to the project management industry.

Extensive research and interviews have been conducted to ensure that the project manager competencies being measured are fully validated. Caliper has performed two million of these profiles across multiple industries and multiple professions.[23] The results of this assessment indicate an individual's potential to survive and thrive in the role of a project manager.

The information generated by the three assessment instruments is analyzed to identify the top three to five areas for growth opportunities. Together, the knowledge, potential, and behavior assessment profiles determine the individual's:

- Suitability for the project manager job, or if he or she should be redirected toward another career path
- Potential to become a superior project manager
- Skill area strengths and weaknesses
- Need for training and what types of training programs will be most effective

The assessment of this information is done through gap analysis. The knowledge gaps are determined by examining the differences between the demonstrated level of knowledge and the level of knowledge required. The behavioral gaps are identified by examining the differences between the self-rating of the project manager candidate and the rater's score. The gaps in both knowledge and behavior, based on the size of the gap, are targeted as developmental opportunities. The results of this integrated assessment are used to create professional development plans for project manager candidates.

While an individual assessment is being conducted, the organization should be determining what roles they will need to ensure an improved level of project performance. Possible roles include team leaders, multiple levels of project managers, program managers, project portfolio managers, project executives, project office directors, and chief project officers. With each of these roles, the organization will need to create effective job (role) descriptions that define performance or competency expectations, experiential requirements, and prerequisites of whatever technical skills are required. Suggested project management roles are described in Appendix A; a fuller discussion of competencies for project managers and project planners can be found in Chapter 4.[24,25]

With these role descriptions in place, the organization can conduct a gap analysis between their desired state and the existing state. This analysis is accomplished by aggregating the individual results of the knowledge assessment with the multirater assessments. Once this gap analysis is completed, the next step is to examine the results of the assessments of potential to identify the project managers who display the most potential to succeed in the project manager role. The key to examining this data is to identify the project managers who will be successful in either the small, noncomplex projects or the larger, complex projects.

Benefits to Organizations and Individuals

The PMCAP is designed to improve the effectiveness of project management training and development programs. A gap analysis is performed to analyze the project manager's current capabilities and skill areas requiring improvement. Therefore, training and development initiatives can be tailored to individuals' needs, saving countless dollars on unnecessary training.

The PMCAP also increases the quality of project management recruitment and job placement decisions by identifying immediately which candidates are or have the potential to become effective project managers. Thus, the "right" people are placed in the "right" jobs.

Because of the impact of excellent project managers on project outcomes, the more qualified the staff is to manage projects, the better the organization will be able to execute, manage, and complete projects. This leads to fewer project failures, increased organizational efficiency, faster project and product delivery times, reduced costs, and higher profitability.

From the individual's point of view, the PMCAP provides career guidance. Individuals are able to view their assessment results to determine their best career path. If the results indicate that they are or have the potential to be effective project managers, they can learn which knowledge and skill areas to improve upon.

Of course, a series of tests does not in and of itself guarantee all these results. Ancillary activities to assessment might include individual feedback review and coaching, remediation plans for identified skill gaps, performance/profile correlation and industry benchmarking, and curriculum development for courses in project management and leadership.

Developing Competence

> If you do not change some rooted human behavior on projects, you cannot improve anything because humans lie at the heart of any organization and its systems.
>
> **—Gerald I. Kendall, PMP and Steven C. Rollins, PMP in *Advanced Project Portfolio Management and the PMO***

The nature of work today is that individuals are often expected to take responsibility for their own professional growth. However, no one exists or works in an independent vacuum. There are clear and very necessary roles for organizations to play in creating an environment that fosters successful project managers. And, it is in the organization's interest to do so.

This collective information from assessments should be used to structure both a developmental program and an organizational project management career path. A developmental program is ideally a coordinated track that combines educational, training, and professional experiences for each role in the project management area.

The developmental program should be aligned with a career path that clearly demonstrates how an individual can progress from a team leader to a project executive within the organization. It can also be used to assist in recruiting candidates to the organization. (For more on career paths, see Chapter 6.)

The ultimate goal in using this approach is the creation of sustainable performance in managing projects. This can be accomplished by creating a well-trained, effectively positioned workforce that is capable of maximizing their potential in the various roles required in project management.

The real value of these assessments is learned by aggregating the results of all three assessment areas (knowledge, behavior, and potential) and using the output reports to develop a comprehensive view of their project manager population. A possible output could be that the candidate has adequate knowledge, poor execution behaviors, and solid potential. Using the combined information, the organization can determine where the gap really exists. It may be a matter of education, adding a mentoring relationship, or providing more directed experiences to improve performance. Another possible scenario is that the candidate has high knowledge, poor performance, and low potential. Analysis of this situation may determine that the candidate may be best suited to a specific role in the technical area rather than as a project manager. Using these assessments together allows organizations to more effectively develop and deliver targeted professional development interventions for their project management population.

Of course, competency-based management still comes down to someone making decisions about who gets what pay, and for what reasons. Best practices include group reviews where managers review competency assessment decisions and then obtain approval of the manager's recommendations by the level above. The method for determining those differences is most often where the individual employee falls on a scale relative to the competency model.[26] If competencies are the "wheels" for managing knowledge work, pay remains the engine. In most organizations it is not enough just to reveal the most critical competencies or to provide training and development in competencies. Employees will continue to pay attention to whatever gets reinforced by pay even if it merely reflects the individual biases of their managers. Company after company has come to the same conclusion about managing with competencies: nobody really cares until they are linked to pay. In the past, some project-oriented companies have linked rewards to Project Management Professional (PMP®) certification, yet it is possible for a PMP to acquire the technical knowledge needed for project management but still lack many of the business and interpersonal skills needed to lead projects successfully.[27] (More discussion of rewards is found in Chapter 7.)

Competence-Building Activities

One way to approximate the real-world application of professional skills is to create cases that highlight complex situations that demand skillful performance. Reading and studying such cases, the learner sees how to exercise judgment in applying any particular guideline. As an organizational learning activity, project personnel can practice their problem-solving skills, either online or at lunch-hour learning sessions, by reviewing cases based on an actual organizational story or event. Executives responsible for developing project managers can create a hierarchy of cases, where the simplest cases focus on one polarity and the more difficult focus on the simultaneous interplay of several polarities.

Competence building takes on the flavor of mentoring and coaching if project managers' supervisors or trainers can identify, through peer nomination, managers who are regarded as the "best." Just as artificial-intelligence researchers interview seasoned professionals to create an expert system, the best project managers can be interviewed to elicit how they have solved difficult problems in the past. A task force of project managers, for example, can ask the "best" to respond, by talking out loud in response to a particular case study. Alternatively, the best project managers can be asked to recount stories of when they confronted and solved especially challenging problems.[28,29]

The best project managers, if they are willing to do so, can mentor and coach individuals whose assessment has shown they are in need of improvement in specific skills. Having the results of the assessment to start from focuses mentoring activities and makes them more productive.

Assessing and improving individual competence in the ways described in this chapter is an important step in improving organizational project management capability. But just as individuals do not work in a vacuum, organizations are not blank slates. Let us consider the organizational culture dimension of competence, which, as seen in Table 3.1, impacts individual behavior and performance.

Applying Systems Thinking to Competence

It is worth noting that competency-model experts Lucia and Lelpsinger[30] start their book on the topic by listing three things that support organizational success:

1. Competent leadership
2. Competent employees
3. A corporate culture that fosters and optimizes competence

Often in our discussion of competence, we focus narrowly on the personal traits and abilities of individuals. But this is only one level of the three that must be analyzed when seeking, as Christopher Sauer said at the beginning of this chapter, to build organizational project management capability: How capable are individuals? How well do the teams they work in function? And how supportive is the organization? Capable individuals still cannot work miracles within dysfunctional teams and organizations. That is why culture change, not merely individual competence assessments, are required.

"Organizational pathology," says David Frame, is behavior rooted in an organizational culture that works against the best interest of the organization and its members. Organizations that punish the bearers of bad news are an example. Organizations that insist on applying outworn solutions to new problems similarly stifle personal competence in their members. The result? A "a profoundly unhappy workforce."[31]

To develop the organization's project management capability, says Sauer, it is desirable both to institutionalize the development of individual capabilities and to create learning, which extends beyond the individual project manager's skills and experience. He recommends the project office, as "a focal point in the organization" where an environment conducive to the development and practice of project management capabilities can flourish.[32] Yet even the best-run project office cannot sustain brilliant project managers unless it is nested within a corporate culture whose values are the values of project management: teamwork, flexibility, merit-based rewards, and realistic planning.

Kerzner has identified actions that the organization can take to set the tone for the support of projects and project teams as well as the overall project management system. The project-centered organization:

- Shows a willingness to coordinate efforts
- Demonstrates a willingness to maintain structural flexibility
- Shows a willingness to adapt to change
- Performs effective strategic planning

- Communicates promptly and accurately
- Exhibits enthusiasm
- Recognizes that projects contribute to the capabilities of the whole company

When a project is being performed for a client organization, the client can exert a great deal of influence on the behavioral aspects of a project by minimizing team meetings, rapidly responding to requests for information, and simply allowing the contractor to conduct business without interference. The positive actions of client organizations include:

- Showing a willingness to coordinate efforts
- Maintaining rapport
- Establishing reasonable and specific goals and criteria for success
- Establishing procedures for making changes
- Communicating promptly and accurately
- Committing client resources as needed
- Minimizing red tape
- Providing sufficient authority to the client's representative, especially in decision making

Kerzner adds that when executive sponsors take the following actions, project success is more likely:

- Selecting a project manager at an early point in the project who has a proven track record in behavioral skills and technical skills
- Developing clear and workable guidelines for the project manager
- Delegating sufficient authority to the project manager so that he or she can make decisions in conjunction with the project team members
- Demonstrating enthusiasm for and a commitment to the project and the project team
- Developing and maintaining short and informal lines of communication
- Avoiding excessive pressure on the project manager to win contracts
- Avoiding arbitrarily slashing or ballooning the project team's cost estimates
- Developing close, not meddlesome, working relationships with the project manager and other key stakeholders

"Behavioral success" — as indicated by such project environmental attributes as openness and honesty among the stakeholders, an atmosphere that encourages healthy, but not cutthroat, competition, adequate funding, informal lines of communication and a flat organizational structure, prompt decisions and close working relationships — is how Kerzner describes the outcome when organizations are competent at supporting competence.[33]

Assuming that an organizational context exists in which project managers and teams can "be all that they can be," let us now turn our attention to the tasks and responsibilities faced by key project personnel.

Notes

1. Frank Toney, *The Superior Project Manager*, Center for Business Practices, 2002.
2. Christopher Sauer, Li Liu, and Kim Johnston, Where project managers are kings, *Project Management Journal*, December 2001.
3. Antoinette D. Lucia and Richard Lelpsinger, *The Art and Science of Competency Models*, Jossey-Bass, 1999.
4. Joan Knutson, Project manager competencies, *People on Projects*, May 2003.
5. Rob Yeung and Simon Brittain, Beyond the interview, *Financial Times (London)*, Nov. 12, 2001.
6. Howard Risher, *Aligning Pay and Results*, Amacom, 1999.
7. See the discussion of project management job families in Chapter 4.
8. Antoinette D. Lucia and Richard Lelpsinger, *The Art and Science of Competency Models*, Jossey-Bass, 1999.
9. Antoinette D. Lucia and Richard Lelpsinger, *The Art and Science of Competency Models*, Jossey-Bass, 1999.
10. Louis Carter et al., *Best Practices in Organization Development and Change*, Jossey-Bass, 2001.
11. Howard Risher, *Aligning Pay and Results*, Amacom, 1999.
12. C.J. Russell, A longitudinal study of top-level executive performance, *Journal of Applied Psychology*, 2001, 6, 510–517.
13. James Warner, interview in *Workforce Week*, March 2002.
14. Performance-based Selection, www.hrstrategy.com.
15. Rob Yeung and Simon Brittain, Beyond the interview, *Financial Times (London)*, Nov. 12, 2001.
16. *Project Manager Competency Development Framework*, PMI, 2002.
17. Michael Zwell, *Creating a Culture of Competence*, Wiley, 2000.
18. Jeffrey M. Anderson, Ph.D., interview in *Workforce Week*, May 6, 2003.
19. Charles Handler and Steven Hunt, Using Assessment Tools for Better Hiring, *Workforce Magazine*, July 2003.
20. BUCEC Introduces Project Management Competency Model, *Business Wire*, Jan. 8, 2003; Freeman and Gould, The Art of Project Management: A Competency Model for Project Managers, White paper, accessed at www.BUTrain.com.
21. PM College can be accessed at www.pmcollege.com; Caliper at www.caliperonline.com.

22. The adoption of any new knowledge areas will be reflected in updates to the testing instruments.

23. Personal interview, Dr. Jimmie West, February 2003.

24. Jimmie West and Deborah Bigelow, Competency assessment programs, *Chief Learning Officer*, May 2003.

25. Building Project Manager Competency, White paper, PM College, June 2004. Accessible at http://www.pmsolutions.com/articles/pm_skills.htm.

26. Howard Risher, *Aligning Pay and Results*, Amacom, 1999.

27. Freeman and Gould, ibid.

28. Larry Hirschhorn, Manage polarities before they manage you, *Research Technology Management,* Sept./Oct. 2001.

29. Barry Johnson, *Polarity Management: Identifying and Managing Unsolvable Problems,* HRD Press, Inc., 1992.

30. Antoinette D. Lucia and Richard Lelpsinger, *The Art and Science of Competency Models*, Jossey-Bass, 1999.

31. J. Davidson Frame, *Building Project Management Competence,* Jossey-Bass, 1999.

32. L.P. Willcocks, D.E. Feeny, and G. Islei (Eds.), *Managing IT as A Strategic Resource,* McGraw-Hill, 1999; and Christopher Sauer et al., ibid.

33. Harold Kerzner, *In Search of Excellence in Project Management*, John Wiley & Sons, 1998.

Chapter 4

Why Project Managers Fail ... and How to Help Them Succeed

Project Manager and Team Member Competencies

> Organizations manage projects with ... project managers who are project managers in name only — project managers who spend most of their time "running with scissors.[1]

One of the main reasons for troubled or unsuccessful projects is the lack of qualified, committed project management professionals. In many organizations, employees have very little incentive to assume the position of project manager, largely due to a disconnect surrounding what the role entails. Organizations have historically recognized the technical capabilities of individuals and assumed these skills could be translated into project management expertise. Because of this, professionals who have worked for years to earn the title of senior engineer, technical specialist, or technical consultant are unwilling to exchange their current jobs for the role of project manager. The role is added to their regular job description, instead of being viewed as a legitimate function to be valued by the organization, and that requires a special set of skills. Therefore, many organizations still have not connected the value of the project manager to the success of the organization.

A second, related reason is that poor role definition — for all the roles in a project, but especially for the project manager — places even qualified personnel into situations where they are doomed to failure by requiring them to do too much and be expert in everything: the phenomenon that we referred to in Chapter 2 as "the monster job."

Research reveals that while more organizations recognize the need to improve their project management initiatives, they have a difficult task in creating a corporate culture that supports the mechanisms needed to effectively deploy a project management process.

The performance of project managers varies from project to project; and within any given organization today, there is a wide range of experience in project managers. At one end of the spectrum are project managers who are new to the practice or who fall into the category of the "accidental project manager." New project managers are those individuals who are just beginning to practice the art of managing projects. Accidental project managers are appointed to the role because they were seen as having the time to take on a project along with their other work. Both of these types of project managers struggle to be effective because they lack familiarity with the basic project management concepts. They lose focus on the project's big picture, and instead get drawn into the minutiae, slowing down progress and damaging team health.

At the other end of the spectrum are the experienced project managers. These individuals have either learned to manage projects by the "seat of their pants," through an ad hoc training program, or through some other means. The challenge to the organization is to get consistent performance from these project managers.

Because there are varying degrees of capability, competence, and confidence among project managers, organizations are experiencing an inconsistency in the quality of how projects are managed. This inconsistency can be traced to a number of factors. One obvious factor is that many organizations are recruiting project managers from other organizations. These project managers have been exposed to a variety of approaches and apply them to their current effort. Because each manager's approach is different, it is difficult for organizations to create and maintain a consistent approach to project implementation.

Another factor is the failure by organizations to manage project knowledge. The lack of systematic knowledge transfer and collection from project to project means that each project "reinvents the wheel." New project managers are not given time to review previous organizational projects to see the lessons learned, to review possible templates for project planning, or to identify possible areas of reuse in a new project. As a result, the costs of projects escalate, the time to complete them increases, and customer satisfaction is negatively affected.

In terms of resources, most organizations lack a pool of individuals who are trained in the art of managing projects. Instead, they adopt a "just-in-time" mentality when· it comes to developing the skills of the project managers.

As a result, organizations lack an effective approach to identifying and delivering the right training to the right people. Even if employees are given classroom training, they are not given appropriate job assignments to practice those skills. Then they are expected to utilize their training without the benefit of a mentor to guide them once their training is completed.

Clearly it is time for organizations to become more systematic in the way they deal with the human resource challenges posed by the project environment. As a result of our research and experience within Project Management Solutions, Inc., we have developed a framework for the division of labor on projects that we think works both for the people and for the project outcomes. Let us start by examining the historical role of the project manager.

What Does a Project Manager Do?

The project manager's challenge has always been to combine two distinct areas of competence:

1. *The art of project management:* effective communications, trust, values, integrity, honesty, sociability, leadership, staff development, flexibility, decision making, perspective, sound business judgment, negotiations, customer relations, problem solving, managing change, managing expectations, training, mentoring, consulting
2. *The science of project management:* plans, work breakdown structure (WBS), Gantt charts, standards, CPM/precedence diagrams, controls variance analysis, metrics, methods, earned value, s-curves, risk management, status reporting, resource estimating and leveling

Because of the nature of the enterprises that were early adopters of project management (military, utilities, construction industry), the profession "grew up" in an environment with a strong cost accounting view and developed a focus on project planning and controls — an emphasis on the science. This is the kind of project management that we think of as being "traditional" or "classic" project management. However, the reality is that it probably simply represents an early evolutionary stage in the life of the discipline. More recently, project management is being used in nearly all industries and across all functions within those industries.

Since then, the industry has seen the emergence of countless trends. Organizations have flattened out, matrixed organizations have taken root, new information technology has allowed people to communicate more effectively and reduce cycle times across all business processes. As a result, management began pushing more projects onto an increasingly complex organization and the project manager suddenly became the "Jack-of-All-Trades" — forced to be everything to everyone. The role of project manager is now very demanding and requires an ever-expanding arsenal of skills, especially "soft" or interpersonal skills.

"New project management" is characterized by a more holistic view of the project that goes beyond planning and controls to encompass business issues, procurement strategy, human resource issues, organizational strategic portfolios, and marketing. The new project management places its focus on leadership and communication rather than a narrow set of technical tools, and advocates the use of the project office to change corporate culture in a more project-oriented direction.

As a result, the role of the project manager has expanded in both directions, becoming both more business and leadership oriented on one hand while growing in technical complexity on the other. The result has been that the title "project manager" today often falls to an individual who is not only poorly prepared for the role, but carries a "kitchen-sink" job description that ranges from strategic and business responsibilities to paperwork to writing code — the "monster job" we discussed earlier. However, there is hope. The now-widespread use of the project office means that companies are developing specialized project roles and career paths, defining specific competencies for these roles, and providing "a fork in the road" that allows individuals who are gifted strongly either on the art side of the ledger — as program and project managers and mentors — to flourish, while allowing those whose skill lies in the science of project management to specialize in roles that provide efficiency in planning and controlling projects. While, on the surface, an enterprise project office might seem to add more bureaucracy, in fact it can simplify project management by making it possible to break out, cluster, and create specialties from the many project management tasks that have up until now often been lumped together into one near-heroic role.

The present challenge lies in defining these two separate paths. Because the project leader has been found to be one of the most (if not the single most) critical factors in project success, much published research exists on the roles and skills of project managers. Current industry research has found that a deficient project management workforce is one of the leading culprits of failed projects, which can cost companies millions of dollars annually. In fact, Gartner, Inc., reports that poor project manager competency accounts for 60 percent of project failures.[2] Much effort has therefore been devoted to understand what project managers can and should do to enhance the chances of project success and have found that leadership, communication, and networking skills top the list. Despite the importance of leadership characteristics for project managers, researchers and practitioners observed that project managers in many organizations are seen by senior management as implementers.[3] (More work remains to be done in defining and researching the role of the "implementer," but in the section that follows we will share the analysis of the role that has been done within our own organization.)

Organizations can avoid this problem by determining beforehand who has the best mix of traits and skills to be a superior project manager, or the potential to become one; and by creating career paths for both technical project managers and leadership-oriented project managers so that senior management can fully appreciate the breadth of the roles necessary to the effective management of projects. Technical project managers tend to focus more on process, while business project managers are more concerned with business results. Ideally, a balance between the two is required, as determined by the project type, organization culture, and systems.[4] Confusion of roles and responsibilities would be averted if these two very different roles were not both referred to as "project managers," and this is an important step in developing project-friendly human resource policies.

And there are other roles that can be broken out of the "monster" job description, further streamlining the leadership work of the project manager. Many tasks that have long been part of the project management landscape feature elements of administrative work, for example.[5] In addition, project managers must be "grown" in the organization through a series of roles that develop the individual in positions of increasing responsibility. (See Chapter 6 for career pathing information.)

Next, it is important to review your existing project managers in terms of their appropriateness for these roles, confirm your ablest individuals as well as those who have potential. Review the remaining project managers against established inventories of skill sets or competencies to identify areas for development, then prepare and implement a development plan for individuals. To quote Oxford University's Christopher Sauer, "It is crucial to demonstrate that the company is willing to invest in enhancing individuals' competencies. Redeploy unsuitable people in positions where their strengths can be used."[6] We should note that what may be "unsuitable" in a project manager is often exactly suitable to the role of project planner or controller.

What Makes a Good Project Manager?

> He is the best sailor who can steer within fewest points of the
> wind, and exact a motive power out of the greatest obstacles.[7]

Nature or nurture? Education or experience? Soft skills or nuts and bolts?

The debate about project manager skills and competencies is well into its third decade. The good thing about a topic that stirs plenty of debate is that there is plenty of research data generated. In a pinch, one can look at lists compiled by a dozen or so organizations, academics, and consultancies to check out where their views on "the good project manager" converge. When resources as diverse as software companies, professional associations, and academic researchers agree on something, one can probably take it to the bank.

What project manager skills, competencies, and characteristics are in this zone of convergence? A modicum of technical or industry knowledge seems to be taken for granted; that is what gets a project manager candidate in the door. After that, the role appears to succeed or fail based on what are variously termed "Organization and People Competencies" (Assoc. for Project Management, U.K.), "Personal Competencies" (PMI®), or "High Performance Work Practices" (*Academy of Management Journal*, 1995). PMI's list of project manager roles (from *A Framework for Project Management*, PMI, 1999) reads like a soft-skills wish list: decision maker, coach, communication channel, encourager, facilitator, behavior model .... This last item was explored in research by Dr. Frank Toney of the University of Phoenix, who states that "honesty" trumps education, experience, and even intelligence as a desirable quality in project managers.[8]

What are the "generally accepted" project manager competencies? According to research conducted by PM College in conjunction with Caliper, 70 percent of the competencies of a project manager overlap with the competencies of a typical mid-level functional manager in Global 2000 organizations. These competencies can be summarized as follows.

Leadership

Usually characterized by a sense of ownership and mission, a long-term perspective, assertiveness, and a managerial orientation. While management focuses on systems and structures, short-range goals, and supervision of *when* and *how* work gets done, leadership focuses on people and relationships, takes a long-range view, and seeks to communicate *why* the work is worth doing. Leaders focus on developing people, creatively challenging the system, and inspiring others to act. Project managers are often expected to combine the two sets of skills. Areas of competency related to leadership include:

Communication

Written and oral communication, including listening skills, and using all available communication tools, is a critical component of leadership. Many teams are made up of poor communicators who rely on less-than-adequate verbal skills. By understanding the unspoken message — often relayed through nonverbal and visual cues — a project manager can gain more insight into his or her team and develop ways for the members to work together more effectively. Understanding communication differences, and not letting them become a barrier to project success, is key to clearly delegating responsibilities and instructions to the project team. Project managers also must serve as the liaison between the project team and executive team. Skilled project managers know when to speak, when to listen, and how to resolve issues and conflicts in a calm, professional manner.

Negotiation

A related skill, negotiation is a daily feature of the project manager's life. Among the issues that must be negotiated with clients, executives, contractors, functional managers, and team members are scope, changes, contracts, assignments, resources, personnel issues, and conflict resolution.

Problem-Solving Skills

These include proactive information gathering or strategic inquiry. This goes hand in hand with the "bias for action": project managers actively seek information that might impact the project instead of waiting for it to surface, and apply that information in creative ways). Project managers must be able to both focus on the details of a problem and see it in the context of the larger organizational or business issues — otherwise known as systemic thinking.

Self-Mastery

Best-practice project managers are able to consider their actions in a variety of situations and critically evaluate their performance. This introspective ability enables the great project managers to adjust for mistakes, adapt to differences in team personalities, and remold their approaches to maximize team output.

Influencing Ability

This is the ability to influence others' decisions and opinions through reason and persuasion, the strategic and political awareness and the relationship development skills that are the basis for influence, and the ability to get things done in an organizational context.[9]

In reviewing other sources of information on competence in leaders and managers, we find additional or related areas that apply to the role of a project manager.

Efficiency

The best project managers work efficiently to complete only what is necessary to deliver projects on time, within budget, and without sacrificing quality. They take the fewest possible steps to get things done. They follow the simplest possible methodologies, standards, procedures, and templates. Along with efficiency come good prioritization and organization skills. Efficient project managers know what to do, when to do it, and in which order to complete tasks. They are the ultimate "task jugglers," able to shift direction when the situation requires. Many effective project managers rely on collaboration tools to facilitate communications, increase understanding, and finish projects on time. The ability to have two teams on opposite sides of the world look at the same document at the same time while comparing notes can significantly speed the project management process … and ultimately speed a product's time to market.

Technological Savvy

Knowledge of technology is an important qualification for any good project manager. In today's multifaceted, global business environment, virtual or Web-based collaboration tools are necessary to bring together project teams that are geographically disbursed and in different time zones. Effective project managers are able to develop a high-performing project team from resources that are not co-located. They are proficient in project management support tools — not only traditional project scheduling tools, but also e-mail and calendar tools, and virtual meeting tools. And of course, they must have a working familiarity with the technology important to the industry within which they work.

Project Skills

Successful project managers know that communication, trust, and reliability are key elements to forming a winning project team. However, even with the right personal and professional attributes, the project manager must be knowledgeable in the language and concepts of project management to be successful. The superior project manager displays a high degree of expertise in applying structured project management methodologies and procedures. He or she understands how the methodology of project selection, planning, implementation, and termination are applied to different projects in a variety of cultural environments. He or she knows how to apply character, leadership, and management skills to optimize team performance. Finally, the superior project manager knows how to align project goals with corporate strategy.

Personal Attributes

Effective project managers also display certain personal traits that contribute to success. Some that have been identified in the literature include enthusiasm for the project and for project management, tolerance for ambiguity, the ability to manage change, and a talent for building relationships with others, from the project team to customers and vendors. Here are a few of the most crucial:

Honesty — Project managers are role models for the entire project team. They must conduct themselves honestly and ethically if they are to instill a sense of confidence, pride, loyalty, and trust throughout their project team. An honest and trustworthy project organization leads to greater efficiency, fewer risks, decreased costs, and improved profitability.

Ambition — Ongoing behavioral studies establish that ambition is an important factor in business goal achievement. Project managers must be careful that their ambition does not make them ruthless or selfish. They must use their determination to accomplish goals for the organization, as a whole, rather than for their own personal gain. It is critical that the project manager understands that he or she is part of the team, not above it, and is responsible for its successes and its failures. A successful project manager leaves his or her own ambition at the door, and concentrates on what is good for the organization. However, achievement orientation, as defined in the ground-breaking work on motivation by David McClelland, comprises a focus on excellence, results orientation, innovation and initiative, a bias toward action, and is very desirable in project managers.[10]

Intelligence — Overall, this enables better job performance and occupational success. Nonetheless, while a project manager must be intelligent, he or she does not have to be a genius. The project manager should possess strong analytical skills, good judgment, and strategic thinking capabilities. These qualities are more important to project management achievement than natural intelligence. The respected project manager will acknowledge the limits of his or her knowledge and will know who in the organization possesses the needed knowledge.

Confidence — Leaders who are confident in their decisions are most likely to succeed. The most confident project managers believe that they have full control of their actions and decisions, versus the belief that outcomes are due to luck, fate, or chance. Superior project managers are confident in their decisions, proactive rather than reactive, and assume ownership for their actions and any consequences. All of these qualities stem from self-confidence.

One can see how all these play out in the following list of actions that project managers can take to ensure the successful completion of projects, according to Harold Kerzner:[11]

- Insisting on the right to select the key project team
- Negotiating for key team members with proven track records in their fields
- Developing commitment and a sense of mission from the outset
- Seeking sufficient authority from the sponsor
- Coordinating and maintaining a good relationship with the client, parent company, and team
- Seeking to enhance the public's opinion of the project
- Having key team members assist in decision making and problem solving
- Developing realistic budgets, schedules, and performance estimates and goals
- Maintaining backup strategies (contingency plans) in anticipation of potential problems
- Providing a team structure that is appropriate and yet flexible and flat
- Going beyond formal authority to maximize their influence over people and key decisions
- Employing a workable set of project planning and control tools
- Avoiding over-reliance on any one type of control tool

- Stressing the importance of meeting cost, schedule, and performance goals
- Giving priority to achieving the mission or function of the project
- Keeping changes under control
- Seeking ways to assure job security for effective project team members

Emerging Competencies

Having said all that, the definition of the "good project manager" is a moving target. As economic and cultural factors change, the project manager role alters in response. And, the elements of the role have different importance to different people in the organization. To an employer, a "good" project manager is one who brings the project in on time and does not waste any money. To a project team member, it might be more important that the daily environment of the project is not one that careens from crisis to crisis, accompanied by raised voices and slammed doors.

And, as project managers expand into new industries, additional areas of competency will emerge. Recently, field research in biotechnology suggests that good project managers are skilled in "polarity management," which Barry Johnson defines as those organizational dilemmas that we must manage rather than resolve once and for all. For example, the skilled manager of a team is aware that she must constantly tack back and forth between focusing on the team's performance as a whole and on each individual team member's performance. Were she to focus on one to the exclusion of the other, one would surmise that she was not as effective as she could be. Table 4.1 describes the six "polarities" that project managers must manage.[12,13] These polarities provide a look at how the project manager's role is evolving away from technical, tool-based project management (especially in knowledge-based organizations such as R&D), and toward a broader "art" of leadership. However, that does not mean that the science can be left behind. Equally important are the competencies that many companies are successfully sorting into a new "starring role": the *project planner*.

The Emergence of the Project Planner Role

The development of the *project planner* position has been an evolutionary process. Initially, many organizations created a position called "coordinator." The coordinator was responsible for handling administrative tasks,

TABLE 4.1 Project Managers and "Polarities"

On one hand	And on the other ...
Take account of the big picture of the project.	Pay attention to the details.
Help team members advance a project; be an advocate for the project.	Help team members shut down a project, or rationally anticipate and plan for possible failure.
Play a supporting role to enable the team leader to lead. Inspire team leaders to be effective in negotiating for the resources and commitments needed from team members and functional groups.	Provide project leadership in the areas that are not adequately addressed by team leaders, or which are beyond his or her scope or skill level.
Be responsible for the outcomes of a particular project and advocate strongly for it.	Be responsible for the outcomes of the company's portfolio of projects. The project manager must be able to situate the project in the context of the portfolio of all the projects under development. At any given moment, the firm, facing scarce resources, must create an up-to-the-minute assessment of which projects should be accelerated and which should not. The project manager must be aware of what is going on in other projects in order to be effective on his or her own project.
Negotiate resources for the team from the functional groups. Timely assistance from functional areas can significantly accelerate or retard the project schedule.	Protect the functional groups from excessive demands on their time, attention, and resources. If each project in the organization insisted that its effort was most important, allocation of resources would be based on which project had the most political influence, rather than on a rational basis. Thus, at times, the project manager must protect the functional groups from the inappropriate or excessive demands of his or her own team.

gathering status information, entering data into a timekeeping and scheduling system, and helping to produce status charts.

Over time, additional responsibilities — such as tracking issue and risk logs, analyzing schedules, and facilitating planning sessions — were added

TABLE 4.1 (continued)   Project Managers and "Polarities"

On one hand	And on the other ...
Focus on the demands of the project itself. A project suffers when its leader and members are not single-minded. The project manager must help the team leader focus everyone's efforts on the goals that will advance the project.	Focus on the context for the project. Projects do not operate in stable settings. Surprises come in the form of technical glitches, competitors' actions, and from other sources. The project manager must help the team leader step back from the immediacy of the project's tasks and rethink the strategic assumptions that led to the project in the first place.

to the coordinator role. More recently, their responsibilities increased to include handling resource constraints and allocations, schedule and critical-path analysis, financial reporting of earned value, and other documentation sufficient to comply with the Sarbanes–Oxley Act.

Today, the role of project coordinator has evolved into that of project planner. The new project planner supports the project manager by taking over critical, detail-oriented, time-intensive tasks, such as the ones discussed above. As a result, the project manager is free to focus on more strategic project goals and objectives.

Earlier in this chapter, we discussed the core tasks of the leader. It is worthwhile noting that the core tasks of the manager have been identified as:

- Planning the work
- Organizing the work
- Implementing the plan
- Controlling the results

These tasks align with the role of planner. Together, the project manager and planner (controller) resolve the leader (manager) dilemma by supplying both aspects of these roles in collaboration.

Job Responsibilities of the Project Planner

The project planner is a key member of the project team and works directly with the project manager to help define the project's vision, goals, and objectives; analyze progress reported against the work schedules; and recommend and take action to improve progress. For a visual representation of how the two work in tandem, see Table 4.2.

**TABLE 4.2   Duties of the Project Manager and the
Project Planner by Knowledge Area**

PMBOK® Guide Knowledge Areas	Project Manager Duties	Project Planner Duties
Scope Management	Work with project owners to ensure all scope (features/functionality) is explicitly defined and documented. Accountable for maintaining integrity of scope, or authorizing scope changes.	Document scope baseline. Track scope changes. Gather data and analyze impact of change. Make recommendation(s) to project manager.
Quality Management	Charged with making sure project fulfills business needs. Overall responsibility for the quality of any products delivered by the project. Accountable for overall health of the project.	Collect project documentation for quality reviews. Prepare project status reporting on a set-interval basis — i.e., project dashboard giving high-level view of project health. Document project requirements.
Time Management	Obtain approval on schedule and any revisions. Proactively improve timeline through parallel tasking or finding smarter ways to carry out work.	Develop and maintain schedule. Collect status updates for tasks. Analyze variations, slipping tasks, impact of task changes, critical path, overall ability of project to deliver on time. Perform earned value analysis. Perform burn rate projections. Recommend improvements.

TABLE 4.2 (continued)   Duties of the Project Manager and the Project Planner by Knowledge Area

PMBOK® Guide Knowledge Areas	Project Manager Duties	Project Planner Duties
Cost Management	Work with owner/sponsor to obtain initial budget. Proactively obtain further funding if needed. Charged with ultimately delivering project within set budget.	Track all expenditures. Analyze spending trends and project final costs; report any deviation from baseline. Recommend method to keep project under budget.
Risk Management	Canvas team to identify all issues and risks; liaise with other business partners or project managers who have completed similar projects. Develop mitigation ideas and work to have strategies in place should they be needed.	Facilitate team session to identify risks. Document/track issues, risks. Oversee risk analysis and impact. Provide project manager with status report of open issues, risks, mitigation. Escalate, as necessary, extraordinary risk impacts and /or issues.
Procurement Management	Ultimately responsible for procurement of all products, resources, and materials necessary to successfully complete project. Maintain open communication with suppliers/procurement to ensure quality products/services from suppliers.	Build sub-schedule to determine procurement dates. Collect updates from suppliers and analyze impacts to project schedule.

TABLE 4.2 (continued)   Duties of the Project Manager and the Project Planner by Knowledge Area

PMBOK® Guide Knowledge Areas	Project Manager Duties	Project Planner Duties
Communications Management	Communicate with entire organization, from the project team to the C-level. Negotiate conflict resolution when needed, between team members or business partners. Honestly represent project status to project sponsor and other stakeholders.	Communicate with team to coordinate execution of tasks and provide status of project activities and milestones. Facilitate planning sessions including development of Project Charter, Project Plan, WBS, Network Diagram, and Schedule. Facilitate risk sessions. Facilitate lessons learned sessions.
Integration Management	Charged with making sure that project plan and processes are followed throughout project; negotiating with sponsor or key stakeholders should modifications to the plan become necessary.	Work with project team to develop project plan, including facilitating processes for handling risks, issues, scope, quality, and general project communication.
Human Resource Management	Resolve conflict within project team. Boost morale and reward project victories — i.e., hitting milestone dates. Negotiate with project sponsor to obtain scarce resources or materials. Garner team buy-in and support of the project.	As part of schedule development, determine that project has all needed resources. Ensure resource allocations are current — i.e., that resource has adequate project hours to cover tasks and has availability to work on project. Educate project team on status reporting techniques and manage the process.

To achieve required consistent documentation and reporting, many organizations are positioning the project manager and project planner as part of a centralized project support organization, usually referred to as the Project Management Office (PMO) or the Strategic Project Office. Typically, the SPO reports to a high-level business executive who is responsible for driving the business in his or her domain, whether a CIO, VP of Operations, or head of New Product Development. It is their desire to implement consistent processes across all their projects.

Specifically, the project planner is responsible for carrying out the following six responsibilities:

1. *Advise the team on proper processes.* The project planner educates and advises the team on project management policies and standards, methodologies, and processes across all phases of the project: initiating, planning, controlling, executing, and closing. This includes describing the processes' purpose, utilizing scheduling and costing tools, determining who is responsible for deliverables, and detailing approval procedures.

2. *Facilitate or oversee project planning sessions.* Organizing and facilitating team planning sessions also falls within the realm of the project planner's role. These sessions may deal with a variety of topics such as planning, developing the WBS, developing the network diagram, integrating the WBS and network diagram into the project schedule, estimating resource hours and task durations, controlling issue or risk management, capturing lessons learned, and project reporting.

3. *Develop the project schedule.* Using project office standards, the project planner works with other key members of the team to develop the project schedule, including resource leveling and critical path analysis. Once baselined, the schedule is used to measure work progress, manage resource assignments, track milestones, and monitor and report on project performance metrics.

4. *Control progress to ensure success.* The project planner proactively manages the schedule to ensure that the project is delivered on time. As part of this responsibility, the project planner must regularly collect task statuses; update the schedule; analyze any variation or forecasted variation to the plan, emphasizing items such as critical path, slipped tasks, and upcoming tasks; calculate, analyze, and present metrics such as earned value; manage resource assignments, including submitting resource requests, monitoring current allocations, and forecasting future needs; and meet with the project manager to discuss project status.

5. *Track and analyze costs.* The project planner must work with available accounting and project management software tools to track actual (or blended) costs, actual time charged against the project, equipment usage, procured resources, etc. He or she must also analyze cost run rates and variations to extrapolate or forecast total costs, as well as report findings to the project manager, project office, and any financial oversight committee.

6. *Manage issue, risk, and change control.* The project planner ensures that issues, risks, and change requests are identified, analyzed, and estimated so they can be escalated to the appropriate levels of management for disposition, and documented or tracked in the project's collaboration database. The project planner monitors issue, risk, and change request resolution dates; contacts team members listed as responsible parties for status and documentation; offers assistance to responsible parties to facilitate progress or resolution meetings; and provides the project manager with the status of open issues, risks, and changes.

What Makes a Good Project Planner?

To efficiently handle the responsibilities outlined above, the successful project controller or project planner must possess technical expertise in project management software and related spreadsheet or database (financial, resource) tools, as well as business process expertise in cost budgeting and estimating, risk analysis, critical path diagramming and analysis, resource forecasting, and change control. In contrast to the project manager candidate, the ideal project planner has the following personal and professional characteristics:

- Logical thinker and problem solver
- Organized and detail-focused
- Numbers-oriented
- The ability to interpret complicated and interconnected data
- Communication skills, especially as they apply to project information
- Project management software expertise
- Application software expertise (accounting, procurement, etc.)

Table 4.3 describes the various areas of competence we have identified for top planners.

It is important to note that the project planner may be supporting several projects simultaneously (based on project size and work experience). Therefore, he or she must also be flexible in dealing with multiple

TABLE 4.3   What We Look for in a Project Planner

Schedule Management	WBS development, critical path analysis, float analysis, schedule analysis, baseline, procedures and processes, general logic, frequency of updates and how obtained, change control, tools (software), scope management.
Resource Management	Method for managing, resource-loaded schedules, baseline, utilization analysis, scope management, frequency of updates and how obtained, change control, tools (software).
Cost Management	Baseline, procedures and processes, types of analysis — break-even, roi, trend, estimating, frequency of updates and how obtained, change control, tools (software).
Reporting Management	Determine effective reporting needs, determine level of management to receive reports; baseline, financial reports, earned value (bcws/bcwp/acwp) analysis, types of reports — schedule, resource, cost, trend analysis.
Facilitation Requirements	Effective meeting leadership, effective management of difficult stakeholders and team members, knowledge of requirements for the project charter and project plan, capability to obtain necessary input for project charter and project plan, capability to obtain updates and status.
Communication Skills	Conflict management, proven oral communication skills, proven written communication skills — reports, e-mails, team written communications, effective communications in difficult situations.
Experience	Type of industry (government, construction, utility, etc.), type of experience and number of years, job responsibilities, decision making roles, level of reporting, industry tools (software).
Education	College degrees and field of study, specialized classes, certificates, specialized certifications, project management professional (pmp), certified cost engineer.

project managers, while maintaining the required level of standards demanded by the organization.

Just as with project managers of varying experience and skill, one will find a hierarchy in the project planning and controls arena. A serious project controls person will have a breadth of experience that encompasses many of what we have termed "specialty areas," such as change (configuration) control, risk management (from the perspective of quantifying risks with the tools), issues management, action item tracking, multiproject reporting, executive reporting, scheduling integration, organizational resource management, multiproject resource analysis, forecasting, and leveling, multiproject what-if analysis, management of the organizational (enterprise) resource library, schedule estimating, cost estimating, etc. And, just as with project managers, the organization will benefit from establishing a career path from the specialist team member level to a sophisticated divisional project controls position.

Results: Increasing Project Efficiency and Success

There is no denying that the role of project planner has the power to positively impact project performance and project success rates. In fact, organizations that have already installed project planners, such as State Farm Insurance Companies, have seen immediate improvements. Jeanne Childers, Director of State Farm's Systems Project Office, states, "We've been using the project planner role for the past six years, and with solid results. What our project managers are finding most helpful is that they can delegate time-consuming yet critical tasks like updating and analyzing schedules. This enables the project manager to focus more time on higher-level issues and leadership responsibilities. By utilizing the planner role we've been able to expand the capacity of our project managers to handle more projects concurrently."

Childers concluded, "We're finding that our project planners at State Farm are an excellent asset during the project planning phase. Many of our planners have become very skilled at organizing and leading project planning meetings. In addition, we're in the process of expanding the role of our planners to take on other project management responsibilities — under the direction of a project manager — for segments of our larger efforts."[14]

Another insurance executive characterized the roles relationships in this way: "We like to think of the project manager as the CEO of the project, and the project planner as the CFO. Like the CEO and CFO, both the project manager and project planner carry out crucial duties, and both need to possess significant, albeit different, skill sets and experiences in order to bring the projects in on time, within budget, and at agreed quality levels."[15]

In building the business case for planner, some of the benefits of developing this as a separate position and career path include:

■ It allows project managers to take on additional projects.
■ It reduces risk in schedule slippage.
■ It allows for more consistent and accurate status reporting.

- It increases morale in both project managers and planners or controllers.
- Project documentation improves.

Other Roles and Their Areas of Competence

Project support team members on projects make it all happen by executing the tasks necessary to move a project through all its phases to successful closure and delivery. Typically, the number of team members is highest during project planning, stabilizes as the project progresses, and decreases as the project approaches delivery and closure. Full-time dedication to the team is also more prevalent during the planning and execution stages.

Human behavior is also a consideration in assigning staff to project support teams. Team members should not be assigned to a project solely on the basis of technical knowledge. It must be recognized that some people simply cannot work effectively in a team environment.

The team member position is where the actual day-to-day work of project planning, estimating, statusing, and analysis is done. This is where the organization accounts for plans and actual charges against time and dollars as the programmers write code, the installers install equipment, subcontractors provide their deliverables, etc. Within this level, more definitive project management roles — depending on the organization — can include:

- Project controllers
- Project analysts
- Schedulers
- Planners
- Business analysts
- Knowledge management coordinator: sometimes formerly known as the "librarian," this role has grown to include the maintenance of project records, standards, methods, and lessons learned that must be stored in a project database or repository. In a large organization, the maintenance of such a repository can develop into a full-time job. Once envisioned as a clerical task, the SPO librarian is now evolving into a sophisticated knowledge-management function and will become a fruitful source of benefits and value to the entire organization for historical data, successful practices, and effective templates, with knowledge that was previously lost with changes in and transitions of personnel.
- Estimators

- Systems analysts
- Communications planners
- Project administrators: back-office tasks, report generation, software support, calendars, etc.
- Methodologists: best practice or process experts, they provide training, project oversight, quality assurance, and methodology development.
- Resource manager: in organizations with significant project activity, the responsibility for resource management may become a full-time job. One major insurance company titles this role "The Project Manager Role Steward." Individual project managers, rather than having to "beg, borrow, and steal" resources wherever they can find them, turn to the resource manager (RM) for assistance. The RM prioritizes resource requests, manages the "fit" of resource skills to project requirements, manage and balance scarce technical resources, forecast and aid in planning for acquisition of resource shortfalls, and secure assignment of key resources to projects according to the project's relative rank on the organization's prioritized project list.
- Organizational development analysts: Another project human-resource management role that has been identified in some organizations, the ODA "floats" among projects, identifying the human issues that often derail projects before they become a problem and working to resolve them. ODAs are a liaison between projects and the HR department. Is corporate HR a partner or the enemy? The relationship between IT organizations and the HR function has not always been harmonious: IT often views HR as slow, unresponsive, and out of touch with the realities of the IT labor market, while HR perceives IT as the group of people that upsets the organization's compensation schedules. Establishing a boundary-spanning role such as the ODA can help alleviate some tensions with corporate HR, while making sure the project personnel's needs are addressed.[16]

These roles are fully described in Appendix A.

Competency development has matured for project managers but there is still a lot of work to do for all the other job descriptions. Chapter 6 describes the "job families" into which we have sorted and clustered project roles and responsibilities in an effort to identify roles that can be combined, or that can serve as stepping stones in a development program. However, it remains for organizations that have "best practice people" in all these roles to identify what the top performers' behaviors might be. In the meantime, we close this discussion of competence by reminding readers that, like any systematic analysis of human behavior, competency identification does not explain everything about human performance on projects. Sometimes, the most unlikely people do the most amazing things. In the words of the philosopher, "These are days when no one should rely unduly on his 'competence.' Strength lies in improvisation. All the decisive blows are struck left-handed."[17]

Next let us turn our attention to the hiring and selection practices for today's knowledge workers and project team members.

Notes

1. Dennis Smith, in "Questioning Enterprise Project Management," *People on Projects*, May 2004.
2. Gartner Group, Research Note, June 2002.
3. Frame, J.D., *The New Project Management: Corporate Reengineering and Other Business Realities,* Jossey-Bass, 1994.
4. Dennis Comninos and Anton Verwey, Business focused project management, *Management Services,* January 2002; see also R. Graham and R. Englund, *Creating an Environment for Successful Projects*, Jossey-Bass 1997; and J. Nicholas, *Managing Business & Engineering Projects — Concepts and Implementation,* Prentice Hall, 1990.
5. Tom Mochal, Is project management all administration?, *TechRepublic.com*, posted Nov. 29, 2002. Accessed May 2004.
6. Christopher Sauer, Li Liu, and Kim Johnston, Where project managers are kings, *Project Management Journal*, December 2001.
7. Henry David Thoreau (1817–1862), U.S. philosopher, author, naturalist in *A Week on the Concord and Merrimack Rivers,* "Friday," 1849.
8. Frank Toney, *The Superior Project Manager,* Center for Business Practices, 2001.
9. Jimmie West, Building Project Manager Competency, white paper, accessed at http://www.pmsolutions.com/articles/pm_competency.htm, January 15, 2005.
10. David McClelland, *The Achieving Society,* Van Nostrand Reinhold, 1961.
11. Harold Kerzner, *In Search of Excellence in Project Management*, John Wiley & Sons, 1998.
12. Larry Hirschhorn, Manage polarities before they manage you, *Research Technology Management,* September 2001/October 2001.
13. Barry Johnson, *Polarity Management: Identifying and Managing Unsolvable Problems,* HRD Press, Amherst, 1992; and Gary Klein, *Sources of Power,* MIT Press, Cambridge, MA, 1999.
14. Robert Wourms, Attention Project Managers: Project Relief Is within Sight, unpublished article, May 2004. Also, "A New Way to look at PM Roles: Where do you fit in?," presentation, April 28, 2004, PMI–Great Lakes Chapter Symposium.

15. Robert Wourms, ibid.
16. Ritu Agarwal and Thomas W. Ferratt, Enduring practices for managing IT professionals: assessing existing business practices to determine staff recruitment and retention capabilities, *Communications of the ACM,* September 1, 2002.
17. Walter Benjamin (1892–1940), German critic, philosopher, in *One-Way Street and Other Writings,* 1978.

Chapter 5

The Turnover Solution

Recruitment and Retention Practices for the Project-Based Company

Chapter 4 discussed the use of competency-based management to help identify and develop project talent. As noted, understanding the project management competencies that are important to an organization takes some of the guesswork out of recruiting and hiring. Hiring mistakes are costly — to the individual as well as to the company.

On the company's side of the ledger, the full cost of turnover is difficult to calculate and is rarely seen on a profit and loss statement. Nevertheless, most experts agree that bad hiring decisions affect the bottom line. The estimated cost of a hiring mistake ranges from 1.5 times to 5 times the departing person's salary; add another $8,000 to $12,000 per new employee for advertising, recruiting, and training expenses. Assessing tangible and intangible (or soft) costs can be an eye-opener for most managers. Because time is money, personnel costs — the number of hours multiplied by wages — mount up when one considers staff's time to interview, check references, review, and place employment ads. Hard costs also include advertising, employment agency fees, professional assessment, relocation expenses, start-up costs (business cards and incidentals), training, salaries and benefits, staff changes, termination, and outplacement fees. Meanwhile, the intangible costs, those that cannot be weighed accurately, are business losses resulting from customer relations problems, ebbing employee morale, lost productivity due to lack of contribution during training, and the decline in a department's overall productivity while other employees get used to a new co-worker, compensate for his lack of productivity, answer his questions, correct his mistakes, and integrate him into the group. With clients or customers, there are missed opportunities and lower quality results while waiting for the new employee to get up to speed (see Table 5.1).[1,2]

TABLE 5.1   Turnover Costs Calculation Worksheet

This is a worksheet for use in calculating turnover costs. It includes direct costs, such as the cost of background checks, as well as indirect costs, such as lost productivity. The chart below can be used to show the "green money" or actual costs of turnover, and the "blue money" or softer costs of turnover.

Blue Money and Green Money Turnover Cost Calculations

Notice Period

Green Money (actual) Costs:

1. Last paycheck, accrued vacation, separation pay	$_____
2. Increased unemployment tax	$_____
3. Continued benefits	$_____

Blue Money Costs:
(appropriate salary/hour × time spent on each activity):

1. Administrative costs for processing the separation: process benefits; contact unemployment office, payroll, IS departments; schedule exit interview; etc.	$_____
2. Lower productivity: employee, peers, supervisor, subordinates	$_____
3. Exit interview, transition meetings	$_____

Vacancy Period

Green Money (actual) Costs:

1. Advertising and recruiter fees	$_____
2. Interview expenses (meals, mileage, or other)	$_____
3. Printing costs for company marketing materials	$_____
4. Assessments	$_____
5. Criminal checks, reference checks, credit checks, etc.	$_____
6. Medical exams and drug tests	$_____
7. Temporary/contract employee costs	$_____
8. Overtime costs	$_____
9. Relocation expenses and salary	$_____

TABLE 5.1 (continued)   Turnover Costs Calculation Worksheet

Blue Money Costs
(appropriate salary/hour × time spent on each activity):

1. Lost productivity: peers, supervisor, subordinates $_____
2. Advertising creation and placement $_____
3. Recruiter selection $_____
4. Administrative costs: ordering forms and copies of
   annual reports, scheduling and scoring assessments,
   coordinating with hiring manager and others, etc. $_____
5. Résumé screening $_____
6. Interviews: first, second, third $_____

Hiring/Orientation Period

Green Money (actual) Costs:

1. Orientation materials
   (handbook, video, handouts, etc.) $_____
2. Formal training programs (materials, course fees) $_____
3. Informal one-on-one training (materials, if any) $_____

Blue Money Costs
(appropriate salary/hour × time spent on each activity):

1. Orientation participants' salaries $_____
2. Lost productivity: peers, supervisor, subordinates $_____
3. Administrative costs: orientation setup, ordering
   materials, etc. $_____
4. Informal training and one-on-ones $_____

Hidden Costs

1. Missed deadlines and shipments $_____
2. Loss of organization knowledge $_____
3. Lower morale due to overwork $_____
4. Learning curve $_____
5. Client issues due to turnover $_____
6. Loss of client relationships $_____
7. Disrupted department operations $_____
8. Chain reaction turnover $_____

Total Replacement Cost $_____

Source: Adapted from the work of Nancy S. Alrichs
(copyright 2003, all rights reserved). Accessed June 2004 from
www.edo.ca/member/NAO/ The_Cost_of_Turnover_Worksheet.doc.

These describe the issues for a team-member position, so it is easy to see that replacing a management-level position creates even greater impacts. Analytical tools for measuring human capital developed by Mercer Human Resource Consulting have helped FleetBoston Financial reduce its turnover rate by about 40 percent among salaried employees and are estimated to have saved the bank $50 million.[3] Yet in a recent survey, executives said they spend an average of only 16 minutes to determine whether a candidate might be a good match for a position.[4]

Sixteen minutes? Why is it there is never enough time to do the project of staffing right the first time — but always time (and resources) to do it over? Instead, why not set up a process specifically geared to bring the right project personnel into your organization, and plan to keep them? This chapter provides a review of the literature and some guidelines on recruitment and retention for knowledge workers. These guidelines will move an organization toward the goal of becoming an "employer of choice" — an organization that outperforms its competition in the attraction, development, and retention of people with business-required talent. According to Deloitte & Touche and the *Wall Street Journal,* employers of choice enjoy a direct positive impact on the shareholders' (owners') value.

At this writing, some of the focus on retaining top performers, especially in the IT field, has lessened. Economic factors and the offshoring market have caused a rise in the unemployment rate. However, many experts feel that this is a temporary phenomenon, and that the next five to ten years will see a continued "people shortage." As noted recently in *CIO Magazine,* "While headlines are filled with stories of massive layoffs and abrupt bankruptcies, CIOs still struggle to find and retain skilled employees." Intellectual capital will always be necessary to effectively exploit new opportunities and to maintain old sources of capability; resulting in recurrent IT staff shortages. Companies that have not bothered to put any effort into retaining their employees will find out that they are "a way-station" for talent until the economy improves.[5]

Also, as the "baby boomers" begin leaving the workplace and transitioning into retirement in the next ten years, many years of capabilities such as expertise, attitude, and practical knowledge will be lost unless companies have a plan in place to capture their knowledge, and new employees to put that knowledge to work.[6]

Another angle on the talent shortage issue was explored recently when SHL surveyed corporations in the United States and discovered that employers lost $105 billion annually by failing to recognize the talents of current workers and potential job candidates. Many firms place workers in the wrong positions, and experts suggest that this has caused the "illusion" of a talent shortage.[7] In any case, companies can only benefit from developing a systematic process for the recruitment and retention of high-value employees.

What Workers Want

Studies of highly talented employees reveal certain values that cause individuals to join or stay at their place of employment. These quality employees seek organizations with a strong sense of direction, an emphasis on training and development with clear opportunities for advancement, an organizational culture and environment that place a premium on innovation and creativity, competitive reward strategies linked to performance, innovative benefit plans that are designed to meet individual needs, and an open and fair culture that values diversity and respect for individual differences. According to studies by Towers Perrin and the National Association of Colleges and Employers (NACE), the desires of top performers (that is, those individuals who have the potential to be the best-performing, most successful employees in an organization) today include challenging work, change on the job, opportunities for growth with the employer, performance-based pay, and the autonomy to complete work assignments. These same studies identified what top performers do *not* want in their jobs: rules, regulations, policy manuals, and long meetings topped the list. Top performers want work to be fun in the sense that highly skilled employees find enjoyment in being able to utilize their skills and expertise. Top performers have very high expectations for themselves and for the people with whom and for whom they work. Employers who seek top performers must be prepared to meet the needs of this group.[8]

One more clue that the talent shortage is real: major IT service firms such as IBM and EDS spend about half of their marketing budgets to support recruiting. Apparently they have less trouble finding projects than people to perform them. That is why results from a study of IT personnel practices in 32 organizations in the United States concluded that companies should shift their focus from myopic HR remedies (such as one-time inducements or bonuses) to more holistic or systemic solutions such as better management of workloads, rewards, and training and development.[9]

Recruitment

Most companies practice a "firefighter approach" to staffing: each unexpected job opening becomes a fire to put out as quickly as possible. Here is a better idea: create a system for evaluating all candidates fairly and practice it consistently. Hiring the right people means taking time up front to analyze the position being filled (job description); determining the type of person who will best fit the position (competency identification); and then conducting structured interviews and performing due diligence: assessments (competency evaluation). The investment in performing these steps can be significant but is not likely to be more expensive than the turnover costs already described.[10]

Recruitment efforts, which have traditionally focused on enticing individuals to accept available jobs, now have to first find interested individuals to entice. The demographics of today's workforce have evolved to a point that traditional recruitment and retention strategies have lost much of their effectiveness. Approximately 30 percent of American workers are in nonstandard work arrangements (part-time jobs, temporary jobs, on-call jobs, independent contractors, contract employees) and many of these employees desire this type of work arrangement. Some of them are the "project nomads" written about several years ago in the *Wall Street Journal*.[11]

Clearly, the shift in the way many of us view our work (as *life*, not as "just a job") calls for a corresponding shift in the way companies treat people, from the very first contact. We can no longer afford the kind of cheap, offhand bureaucratic procedures that have become standard in hiring. In developing a pool of candidates, the following suggestions will be helpful.

Cast a wide net — Friends, colleagues, consultants, professional associates, board members, ex-employees, search firms, trade groups, and Internet job sites all help to proactively locate talent. Stay on the lookout all year, whether or not you have an open position. Search newsgroups on the Internet for people with the skills you need. Develop partnerships such as relationships with academic institutions.

Use an employee referral program — Employees will not refer people unless they want to work with them. One firm reported that as many as 60 percent of its new hires came from internal referrals. In the year 2000, 71 percent of all managers surveyed by Meta Group ranked internal referrals as one of their top-three IT recruiting methods.[12]

Recruit from within — Promoting from within boosts morale because it tells other employees that they too can be promoted. Internal hires also do not need the extra orientation and training to become familiar with corporate culture.[13]

Exercise courtesy — When recruiting, make everyone feel respected. The person you do not hire today may be the person you need in six months. Basic manners are seldom followed in dealing with prospective hires: that is, acknowledge receipt of their résumés, return their phone calls, and communicate about decisions and processes.[14]

Do not passively run ads and sort résumés — Top talent probably will not be looking in the want ads. Particularly with project management and technical personnel, to reform the hiring process, instead of reading HR journals and going to HR conferences, recruiters should read industry trade magazines and go to industry conferences. Technical people often write the kind of résumés that recruiters reject because they include clusters of acronyms and jargon. But when recruiters choose well-written, but less substantive résumés, unqualified candidates can get on the short list.

Pare the bureaucratic processes — Talented people do not have much patience for bureaucratic processes; so instead of loading up candidates with a pile of paper forms, engage personally.

Bring the managers into the picture — In many companies, HR will not let the hiring managers get involved until recruiters have selected a short list of candidates, even though the hiring manager is the person with industry contacts. This is why we recommend that the project office have a dedicated position for recruiting and nurturing project talent. Too often, HR staff members in charge of hiring project managers have never spent time "in the trenches."[15]

Keep process metrics — Researchers at Watson Wyatt list recruiting excellence as one of five human resource practices that affect the bottom line, yet few organizations formally evaluate their recruitment efforts. Only 44 percent of organizations surveyed formally evaluate any recruitment outcomes.[16]

A survey conducted by International Data Corp. (IDC) and *Computerworld* of more than 70 IT recruiters found that one of the keys to good hiring is keeping accurate statistics and metrics on the hiring process itself. Some of the metrics suggested include:

- *How long it takes to hire a person.* Having a clear understanding of the hiring timeline helps managers approach hiring in a systematic manner.
- *How many applicants one needs in the pipeline to generate a hire.* The IDC/*Computerworld* survey found that the average company chose 26 qualified résumés to yield three interviews before hiring someone.
- *Where the best hires have come from.* The survey found that the most efficient channel for hiring (in terms of offers accepted per résumés gathered) was employee referral.[17]

Interviewing Strategies

Approximately half of companies of 100 employees or less do not have established policies and procedures describing criteria for new hires.[18] These criteria must be established long before the interview takes place; but assuming that they are in place, the first contact with a new member of a company or team begins with the interview.

Interviews have some weaknesses as a method of selecting employees. Their validity and reliability is relatively low as a way of predicting future performance. And stereotyping by interviewers, in addition to the generally subjective nature of the process, may allow biases to creep into the selection process, especially if the interview process is not standardized. (This is why most HR management experts now recommend performing validated testing of candidates to add an element of objectivity to the hiring process. See Chapter 3.)

The *unstructured interview* is a free-for-all conversation that typically begins with a request such as, "So, tell me about yourself." Such interviews are susceptible to "contrast effect," in which applicants are compared to the person who was interviewed just before them, or "first impression effect," where a snap decision is made. Unstructured interviews showcase "impression managers," who skillfully direct the conversation to irrelevant topics such as sports or travel. While such conversations might be enjoyable, less than 20 percent of the workforce hired by this method are top performers.[19]

However, companies that take interviewing seriously can sidestep some of these pitfalls. *Structured and competency interviews* ask interview questions relevant to the job and, working from a competency-based role description, each interviewee receives the same set of questions and is scored using suggested responses. A five-point performance-based rating scale is used to evaluate the completeness and correctness of applicant responses. The following are some guidelines for performing structured interviews.

Develop a range of targeted, core questions that you ask all applicants. In addition to inquiries designed to assess general project management and industry knowledge, gauge an individual's interpersonal skills and "fit" with your firm's corporate culture (see Table 5.2). Hypothetical job-related scenarios also can reveal a lot about the applicant's enthusiasm, attitude, and ethics.[20]

Read résumés in teams. A team of three to five people offers about the right mix of multiple perspectives. Approximately 60 percent of applicants should never be granted an interview in the first place, some experts say. Because interviewing too many unqualified applicants can interrupt productivity, carefully read résumés and match candidates to job descriptions. Watch out for big changes. Is the candidate moving from a

TABLE 5.2   Searching Questions

When I call your references, what will they say?
What accomplishments are you particularly proud of?
What motivates you? How do you motivate people?
Why are you in the job market?
What are the best, and worst, aspects of your current position?
How do you resolve disputes?
Have you ever gone out on a limb on a project? Tell me what happened.
What is the biggest mistake you have made in your career?
Describe your current organization chart and how you fit into it.
Describe your participation in team efforts. What worked, what didn't?
Have you ever been terminated from a job? Why?
Tell me about a project experience in which you had to use good communication skills.
How many levels of management have you interacted with? How many different departments?
Have you ever made an unpopular management decision? What happened?
If you could have made improvements in your previous position, what would they have been?
What is the most interesting or challenging project you have been involved with in your career?
Tell me about a situation at work in which you had to suddenly reschedule your time and reprioritize projects.

Source: Adapted from Great Expectations: How to Hire Top Performers, *California CPA*, July 2001, by Max Messmer.

small organization to a large one? Is the person moving from an entrepreneurial culture to a very structured one? While this should not disqualify anyone, it should spark some questions.[21]

Prepare for the interview by allowing plenty of time — one or two hours — when interviewing technical and managerial positions. Limit distractions such as phone calls.

Put the candidate at ease. Come out from behind your desk, encourage the use of first names, and share something personal with the candidate to break the ice.

When doing a structured interview, armed with a list of suggested responses available for each question, do not "lead" the candidate by using the suggested responses as a checklist. If you ask applicants if they have experience with any of a list of skills, they almost always say, "Yes, I can do that," but this can be misleading.

Starting questions with "Why," "What," or "How" generates more expansive responses. In addition, ask the candidate to respond to a few hypothetical questions relating to your organization or the project. Ask all your questions at once. If you hand the candidate a set of printed questions, it forces you to listen, and it allows the candidates to see the road map. As the candidate answers the questions, the interviewer can occasionally ask for more information or examples.

Take notes. Research has shown that the first person interviewed often has the least chance of getting the job because hiring managers might not recall their thoughts about him or her. Develop a rating system to simplify comparisons of each applicant's skills and abilities. Note when further amplification is needed. Ask why the candidate left (or wants to leave) a previous employer. Note accomplishments, or the absence thereof.

Try to evaluate personal qualities such as insight. When has he or she has faced adversity? Does he or she display honesty and humility? Ask the interviewee to describe his or her weaknesses and steps taken to overcome them. Ask about peak experiences. What does the candidate brag about? What would he or she do during a hypothetical 12-month sabbatical? Identify productive traits. When has the candidate flown in the face of convention? Look for curiosity and creativity.

Tell candidates that you will check references. Ask, "What will we hear from your detractors?" If this type of question is followed by a long silence, be patient.

Listen carefully. Ask prospective candidates what projects they are particularly proud of, or look at their résumés to see what projects they have listed. As the interview draws to a close, a candidate will usually say something very important in the last five minutes. Do not rush this phase.

Put problems on the table. All candidates have them; and if you have not discovered them, then you have not paid attention.

When closing the interview, consider giving an assignment. This allows you to see the caliber of work and eliminates candidates who are not motivated enough to follow through.

Save time for the candidate's questions. The quality of the questions will tell you a lot about the candidate. If candidates appear uncertain about accepting a job offer, do not jump to the conclusion that money is the problem. As discussed later in this chapter, money is rarely a knowledge worker's prime concern. Ask, "Are there aspects of this job that concern you?" Make sure candidates know that you appreciate their interest and let them know when to expect to hear from you.

After the interview, review your notes in a timely manner. Make a balance sheet (plusses and minuses). List questions to be addressed during reference calls or as part of a second interview. Then check references. To get more than "name, rank, and serial number," ask finalists to encourage their references to provide you with feedback. Do not automatically rule out an applicant because of one negative reference. Try to verify any criticisms with other contacts.[22] One simple and legal method of getting better-quality information is to call a reference when you are likely to reach voicemail. Say, "John (or Jane) Doe is a candidate for (the position) in our company. Your name has been given as a reference. Please call me back if the candidate was outstanding."

Finally, hire for attitude. One can teach specific skills to someone who has a thirst for knowledge and sound judgment. However, one cannot teach a positive outlook or the aptitude for interpersonal skills.[23]

Yet, hiring a top performer is only the start of the journey. It is a myth that high performers are more reliable, longer-term employees. An employee can be extremely capable; but if that person is bored or unhappy with co-workers, he or she will soon be out the door.[24] Table 5.3 displays the personal characteristics of a high performer.

TABLE 5.3   Hire an ACTOR

When screening for leadership positions such as project managers, you want ACTORs — people who are:

Adaptable. Leaders must be adaptable to change. A leader's job is to allow change to occur and, in some cases, be the catalyst. The last thing a leader wants is to be the keeper of the tradition that creates the roadblock to progress.

Considerate. Leaders can no longer think in terms of "the end justifies the means." Leaders must consider the personal effect of their actions on followers if they are to build the commitment that is required for long-term success. Leaders do not use their position to gain special perks. What is good enough for followers should be good enough for leaders. Leaders should also look to celebrate the successes of their followers as often as possible. They recognize, reward, and praise them frequently.

Trustworthy. Chances are good that if they view the leadership as being trustworthy, the organization will also be considered a trusting place to work. Creating a foundation of trust encourages commitment among the followers that will generate incredible loyalty toward the leader and the organization.

Optimistic. Leaders must provide a positive vision of the future. They model the way.

Resourceful. Leaders should provide the required training to ensure that their followers are prepared for their jobs and responsibilities. They encourage collective intelligence and working with others. They break down walls within an organization. Being resourceful can be almost anything in the context of getting things done. Leaders view any failure as a learning event.

Source: Adapted from Your best leader — an ACTOR, *Workforce Magazine*, October 2002, by Ed Rose.

Retention

All too often, recruitment is only viewed as getting someone in the door. This approach can be costly, as our statistics on turnover at the beginning of the chapter showed. Luckily, there is a wealth of recent research focusing on motivation, commitment, and retention in the R&D and high-tech sectors having applicability to project management.

Jac Fitz-enz of the Saratoga Institute has noted that the most important human capital issue is the relationship between a company and each of its employees. Employees today want open, two-way communication with their employers, clearly articulated expectations with continual feedback, and significant opportunities for growth and development throughout their careers.[25]

A global study by *Fortune* magazine and the Hay Group revealed that knowledge transfer success is determined by the culture of the organization. The world's most successful organizations do not just claim that their people are their best asset, they act on it. These organizations view career development as an investment, not an expense; they promote internally, they reward top performers, and they make sure that their employees are satisfied with their work. In short, they inspire a culture that recognizes the importance of people.[26]

The AON Consulting Workforce Commitment Index compares workforce commitment levels across high-technology firms to national figures, and compares the reasons why workers join employers versus why they stay with those employers. Their studies identify sources of "psychic income," concluding that, although engineering benefits and rewards programs to address work/life needs is expensive, it has paid huge dividends for employers that have made the commitment. Several sources of "psychic" income include stock options, understanding how performance is evaluated, internal pay equity, effective supervisors and managers, and satisfactory communications about the benefits programs.[27]

A recent survey by Robert Half International looked at the most important line of questioning by job candidates in interviews. The results indicated a shift from interest in compensation and benefits to concerns about corporate culture. Some of the areas most important to knowledge workers (a category that includes all the project management positions described in Appendix A) are the length of the workday and frequency of weekend work, flexible hours or telecommuting, the style of management (participatory or authoritarian), educational opportunities, and mentoring programs.[28]

As these responses indicate, management involvement makes a difference. Kepner-Tregoe interviewed ten "retention leaders" — companies with successful track records in holding on to talent — to find out what works. The result was a list of "key drivers of retention success" that included:

- Balance a culture of caring with a tradition of excellence.
- Resolve conflict with a "stair-stepping process" that allows employees to bypass their immediate supervisor.
- Take stock of the turnover rate, then take action.
- Focus on the star performers.
- View people management as a strategic business issue.
- Pursue improvement relentlessly.[29]

Probably the best place to start paying attention to retention is to find out why people leave their jobs in your organization. Some of the top reasons across all industries include lack of job satisfaction, lack of challenge and interest in the work, dissatisfaction with their leadership or with the organization's image and overall position, and incompatibility with the work group.[30] Professional employees have additional reasons to add, such as lack of talent development, apparent lack of trust by supervisors, lack of genuine involvement, perceived lack of objectivity and fairness in the organization, higher management's disregard of or disinterest in human relations, and disproportionately low compensation.

Most important, according to the Society for Human Resource Management (SHRM), is to remember that retention comes from building emotional bonds between the workers and the employer. These emotional bonds are strengthened when managers pay attention to issues that are important to their employees.

Orientation

Day one is a good time to start building those emotional bonds. For an employee to get off on the right foot and feel comfortable in his or her job, a thorough orientation must be conducted. New employees who feel lost, ignored, or inadequately prepared tend to bail out quickly. And employees who were hard to find in the first place have many available alternatives and they will leave if they feel uncomfortable.[31]

The orientation should be done as though the new employees will be staying for 20 years. Frequently, because of short staffing, new employees are hustled onto the project unprepared. Ideally, an experienced staff person should be their mentor, but only if they want to do so. Employees who are forced to orient new employees but do not want this responsibility will do a poor job. Nothing makes new employees feel more welcome than to have a mentor take an interest in them.

Make sure there is congruence between the orientation and the actual work setting. A new employee should not come in expecting the greatest job in the world, only to find the actual job far different than the one described. If the orientation's aim is only to get the employee working as quickly as possible, then this recruitment effort will be a failure. It is rare for employees who have not been properly oriented to develop a sense of loyalty toward the organization.[32]

Part of orientation should be to introduce new staff to the corporate mission statement and strategies and help them internalize the meaning behind the words. Set up times when mixed groups of new and old employees meet and review the mission and strategies, and offer the opportunity to ask questions or provide feedback. By bringing together the new and old employees to discuss the main goals and values of the organization, you will ensure that everyone understands them and also build a sense of camaraderie. Such dialogue leads to a refreshed enthusiasm for fulfilling the organization's mission.[33]

Many companies skimp on retention activities because they are afraid that, once you start to develop good project managers, those managers will sell their new skills to a new employer at a higher price. Obviously this does happen, but it can be addressed through attention to the terms of the employee "contract." Companies that wish to retain project managers must pay the market price to do so — including costs of retention programs. If they wish to ensure that employees stay until the end of a project, they can write suitable incentives into project managers' contracts. The true challenge is to recognize the economic value of project managers and to change contracts of employment accordingly.[34]

To discover what those contracts should include, we can look at three areas crucial to retention — rewards, benefits, and organizational culture — starting with the least important and working up to the most important.

Rewards

Financial compensation alone, the factor that is easiest for employers to adjust, may have the least effect unless the problem is severe. People will tolerate a slight perception of being underpaid more than they will a bad job — even a bad job in a great company.

Probably the biggest surprise in human resources research over the past decade or so has been the consistency with which compensation comes in last as an important consideration in how people feel about their jobs. Technical workers especially are less likely than those in other fields to be lured away by more money. Competitive compensation may be of importance initially, but it comes in third behind career growth and training and development where retention is concerned.[35]

Money is the most common extrinsic reward but it does not make people passionate about their jobs. Intrinsic rewards, however, can generate the kind of passion required to make them achieve high levels of performance. Although knowledge workers can be motivated with extrinsic rewards, the evidence suggests that intrinsic rewards are more effective motivators. These include technical challenge, opportunity to pursue research interests, flexible career paths, the challenge of project work, and the sense of entrepreneurship.

But reward systems also need to motivate performance with extrinsic rewards. Because high performers can make substantial financial contributions to the company, reward systems must be flexible enough to reward them commensurately with their contributions. Many companies are replacing the traditional narrow salary ranges with broad salary bands. They also reward cross-functional and team performance, create pay-for-skills plans, and provide bonuses based on company profitability.

Fairness is also important to high performers, so internal pay equity should be carefully managed. Rewards to technical staff should be attached to performance targets rather than activity cycles, and these targets should include team performance.[36]

Unfortunately, organizations have not figured out how to effectively reward teams and team members. Project managers would love it if there were a correlation between the performance of project teams and the rewards those teams receive, but such correlations do not usually exist. A study of 87 project teams showed that the current method of rewarding teams and team members is primarily a qualitative assessment of how well the team is meeting the traditional cost, schedule, and performance goals. And in the absence of adequate project performance metrics — a problem in many companies — this means that rewards are based on the "gut feel" of a manager about how the project is progressing. This is a self-reinforcing cycle because when project managers responsible for teams are not being rewarded for their team-building efforts, there is a decrease in their motivation to make team building and teamwork a priority.[37]

The most radical — yet most obvious — change is to base all performance appraisals and review systems on the team, and make the team accountable for team results. For true teamwork to occur, people need common purposes, measurable goals, and a common fate. Thus, moving toward a project-oriented organization means creating a team-oriented appraisal and reward system. Because the team is in the best position to control the task, the team should be the primary focus of any performance measurement. Functional expertise is very much a prerequisite to team participation but it is appraising performance based on the team's results that encourages people to wear two hats.

Glenn M. Parker of human resource consulting and research giant Watson Wyatt recommends reward structures that foster collaboration, in which individuals are acknowledged, but primarily for being strong team players — those who "help the crowd stand out, rather than standing out from the crowd."[38]

Benefits

Benefits have typically been viewed as a necessary evil, but it is time that companies make friends with them because, even more than direct compensation, benefits express how a company cares for its employees. The credibility of the organization is, in part, measured by how well benefits promises are delivered. Some benefits are more powerful than others in saying that "the company cares about you." Topping SHRM's list of effective retention practices are health benefits, competitive vacation and time-off programs, retirement plans, flexible work schedules, and training and development.

To address the issue of retention, employers are offering what have been traditionally viewed as management perks to rank-and-file employees. These perks focus on quality-of-life issues faced by today's workforce: flexible work schedules, educational reimbursement, elder care benefits, and a host of employee conveniences such as on-premise laundry and dry cleaning services or fitness centers. While these popular benefits are typically of little cost to the employer, they provide employees with options that can simplify the pressures faced by today's working families and are thus deeply appreciated.[39]

How can companies determine what to offer? Too often, benefits packages are based on what the competition is doing, leading to a "me-too" approach that does not necessarily reflect the needs of the employees.

Few organizations actively survey their population to determine whether the programs address employees' needs. Less than one third of high-tech companies reported conducting a benefits-related attitude survey in the past two years. This is unfortunate because retention practices work best when tailored to the needs of each type of worker. Companies should develop flexible packages of benefits that fit the employee demographics (age, gender, marital status, and number of dependents, etc.). When deciding among benefits of equal cost, employers that look at the value of the benefit in action can maximize the payback. If, for example, a high percentage of the workforce includes working mothers of school-age children, a comprehensive child-care assistance program may be more valued than tuition reimbursement. Because no single perk will retain professional employees, develop a total package that appeals to a wide variety of people. Then communicate it effectively to everyone. Eliminate benefits that are no longer used or valued.[40,41]

Culture

A recent survey by Robert Half International looked at the most important line of questioning by job candidates in interviews. The results showed "that corporate culture rivaled benefits in terms of importance."[42] Table 5.4 shows some of the most important retention factors, by job function.

"Culture" or "environment" is the most complex aspect of recruitment and retention. Everyone wants to work in an interesting and innovative environment but no one has defined exactly what that means. Organizational culture has been widely studied by anthropologists and other organizational researchers, and is generally defined as a set of values and ideas shared by members of a social unit. These shared values are acquired through socialization and social learning processes as individuals experience membership in an organization. Recent research into the needs and preferences of knowledge workers gives us some more specific ideas for the project-oriented organization.

TABLE 5.4   Top Retention Drivers by Job Function

Retention Items	Information Services (%)	Manufacturing/ Operations (%)	HR/ Consulting (%)
Exciting work/challenge	63.4	47.7	46.7
Career growth, learning	37.9	39.7	48.6
Good workplace relationships	40.4	42.4	42.4
Fair play	29.0	37.6	25.7
Supportive management	25.4	25.4	26.8
Feeling recognized/ valued/respected	24.0	22.1	23.4
Benefits	14.7	26.3	21.1
Meaningful work	19.7	14.0	18.6
Great environment/culture	11.0	14.6	16.7

Cultures conducive to retention emphasize employees' self-concept and professional identity, recognize competing demands on their attention, emphasize communication to give a sense of inclusion, and provide recognition. Technical people and project managers today want to do more than show up; they want to make a contribution to the company's bottom line. Companies that erase barriers to success — technical, funding, and bureaucratic barriers — set them free to enjoy their work and take home the "psychic income" so important to knowledge workers.[43]

Work culture begins at the top with HR policies that can support one of two strategies. An organization following *a long-term investment strategy* views people as worth developing and retaining due to their specific knowledge and competencies. Organizations implementing the long-term investment strategy experience the least turnover. An organization following a *short-term producer strategy,* on the other hand, views people as providing highly valuable contributions to the organization in the short term and see them as driven by financial goals. Compared to other strategies, the short-term producer strategy puts relatively greater emphasis on compensation and recruitment, and creates the greatest turnover.[44]

When thinking about what makes knowledge workers happy and productive, Abraham Maslow's "hierarchy of needs" is a useful model (see Figure 5.1). Maslow's hierarchy of needs established a new way of looking at the order in which human beings seek fulfillment. Basically, Maslow said that when basic needs — compensation and safety — are satisfied, people become freer to form relationships and create intellectual assets. AON Consulting's Performance Pyramid hypothesizes a hierarchy of organizational practices that impact workforce commitment and retention, modeled on Maslow's ideas. The Workforce Commitment Index (WCI) rose progressively when expectations were met at each level. When safety or security issues were below expectations, the WCI was 80. When employees indicated that all levels were met, including work/life harmony, the WCI was 114.27.[45]

Security means not only physical safety, but also psychological well-being. A company that is experiencing constant change, including downsizing and economic stress, sees higher stress levels among the workforce. As uncertainty saps commitment, less and less gets done. Higher-order activities such as innovation come to a halt. The antidotes, in many instances, are communication and involvement of employees in change. Encouraging employees to participate in professional organizations can help insulate them from the sense of vertigo brought on by organizational change, as it gives them a venue for identifying with peers outside the workplace.

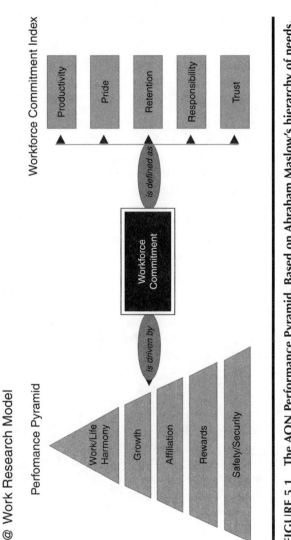

FIGURE 5.1 **The AON Performance Pyramid. Based on Abraham Maslow's hierarchy of needs, this model asserts that there are five levels of needs that drive workforce commitment: Safety/Security, Rewards, Affiliation, Growth, and Work/Life Harmony. (Accessed October 2004 at http://www.aon.com/hc_consulting/loyalty_institute/at_work/research/default.jsp.)**

Elements of Culture

Based on the studies cited above, we have determined that there are at least seven aspects of corporate culture, apart from compensation and benefits, that can make a real difference to project management personnel: equity and fairness, work/life balance, a collegial environment, professional growth, effective management, recognition, and a performance-based culture.

Equity and Fairness

Three key items — compensation, assigned work, and recognition — are important factors in determining perceptions of inequity. Workers who believe that they are fairly paid in relation to others in their organization exhibit higher levels of commitment. Yet more than one quarter (27 percent) of high-tech employees feel that internal pay is inequitable. In the same study of IT employees, they also perceived contractors as getting the best assignments, such as projects involving new technology, while full-time employees got the grunt work, such as legacy system maintenance. They noted that some managers gave out recognition awards more frequently than others, and some managers did not give any awards at all.[46,47]

Yet equity drives commitment to a greater degree than the amount of compensation or the package of benefits. The workplace is not only a source of income, but it also meets important affiliation needs. When employees feel that "we're all in it together," the sense of work effort equity contributes to employee commitment.

Work/Life Balance

Recognizing that employees' personal and family life is important and promoting benefits that address work/life balance is essential. These days, most working families suffer from "time starvation." Meanwhile, at work, burnout plagues nearly half of workers at one time or another. A Department of Labor study found that 84 percent of respondents would trade future income for free time, while nearly half would forego a 10 percent raise for more free time.

This is why flexibility in work hours has an indirect impact on the bottom line. Rather than increasing overhead by boosting payroll, flexing time enhances both employee commitment and performance. Although implementing alternative work schedules and other family-friendly approaches requires a commitment by the employer to reevaluate its processes and culture, flextime, in one form or another, has taken hold in about half of companies surveyed by SHRM. Other strategies are compressed workweeks (27 percent), telecommuting (26 percent), and job sharing (22 percent).

The U.S. Department of Labor estimates that between 13 million and 19 million full- or part-time employees telework. Executives recognize that the real savings, however, may be beyond productivity improvements. According to several studies, telecommuting employees save their employers up to $10,000 per year in reduced absenteeism and retention costs. For large employers, telework programs can reduce overhead by cutting office space needs. For example, IBM saw savings of $1 billion from 1992 to 1997, just from lowered real estate costs.

At IBM, about one third of the workforce works outside the office; and at Sun Microsystems, thousands of employees work from home or other remote locations. IBM reports that productivity has increased by 10 percent since it began allowing workers to telecommute, and Sun Microsystems says it has reduced its real estate spending by about 30 percent since it began allowing telework.[48] But the emotional bonding benefits may be even more valuable to stressed, pressed-for-time employees.

Collegial Environment

Watson Wyatt's Human Capital Index, a model for determining which HR practices lead to better financial performance, lists "a collegial environment" as a top contributor to bottom-line success. In the knowledge era, this makes perfect sense because the capability of an organization resides in the minds and energies of individuals within the organization, and on the collective minds and energies of well-functioning groups.[49]

When one considers that knowledge is converted from tacit knowledge into explicit knowledge through the socialization process,[50] it is not surprising that organizations with a healthy atmosphere of teamwork and camaraderie also lead the pack financially. Not only in R&D and high-tech, but also in a study of motivation and retention at a U.S. Department of Energy (DOE) site, good working relationships (teamwork) proved a key motivator.[51]

Effective teams enable organizations to achieve the high levels of performance that are essential to survival and prosperity in today's extremely competitive and rapidly changing environment. The long-term benefits of successful teams include higher performance, increased morale, and a strong commitment to the mission of the organization that can withstand almost any kind of adversity. However, a study by a Boston-based management consulting firm that researched teams in Fortune 1000 companies found that only 13 percent of the 179 teams researched received high rankings for effectiveness.

Professional Growth

Many companies fail to nurture a relationship with employees through career development. Without a focus on career development, however, employers ensure that some employees will fall behind the skill curve to the point of obsolescence. Knowledge workers are less likely to put up with an environment where they are not learning and keeping up with the latest developments in their field.[52]

A commitment to helping employees grow professionally must be balanced with an organizational openness to change because not only what employees need to know, but how they learn it is changing rapidly today. Online learning, company "universities," educational reimbursement, and tuition assistance are expected, not optional. For knowledge workers, boredom is as dangerous as dull skills.

Thus, in a retention culture, training is a top priority. Ironically, less than 14 percent of organizations have established targets for a formal training program.

Effective, Participatory Management

Traditional technical managers operated as "captains'" through command and control systems; they provided direction, plans, procedures, and rules, and enforced them. Today we are shifting from the captain role to the catalyst role; they assign broad objectives and create a work climate that helps project teams define and control their work.

Once hired, knowledge workers are often poorly managed. The traits of poor talent managers include withholding praise, withholding critical information, showing a lack of caring for others, motivating by fear, slamming doors and hitting tables, micromanaging, and giving only negative feedback.

The more managers act as catalysts, the less they are required to act as captains, because a stimulating work environment negates the need to direct the work.[53]

Therefore, managers must be trained in management and human relations skills. Management should reinforce that the values and actions they desire be displayed in the workplace. This includes placing people into supervisory and management positions that display the desired performance characteristics. Finally, management credibility needs attention. Management credibility is impacted by inadequate communications, perceived or actual inconsistencies, and a perception of a lack of interest in employees' needs.[54]

One recent study asked workers to rank, on a five-point scale, how closely their managers' words and actions were aligned to managers'

TABLE 5.5   Talent Magnet … or Deterrent?

Here is a checklist for managers to answer to determine how they are doing at managing knowledge workers for retention: I inquire about how to make work more satisfying for my employees. I realize that I am mainly responsible for retaining the talent on my team. I know my employees' career ambitions. I take steps to ensure that my employees are continually challenged by their work. I respect the work/life balance issues that my employees face.

Source: Beverley Kaye, Career Systems International,
http://www.careersystemsintl.com/engagement-retention%20articles.htm.

behavioral integrity by evaluating statements such as "My manager delivers on promises" and "My manager practices what he or she preaches." The key finding: integrity pays. No other single aspect of manager behavior had as large an impact on profits.[55] A self-assessment for managers is presented in Table 5.5.

Recognition

Employee recognition plays an important role in lowering the turnover rate among technical employees. Most often, this recognition takes the form of monetary compensation but there are alternative ways to reward good performance. Many are a symbolic gesture of thanks. Beyond financial compensation, recognition practices, some of which can be low-cost and highly effective, such as birthday cards and welcome baskets, lunch or dinner out, and getaway weekends are important.[56]

Performance-Based Culture

A results-oriented culture appeals to knowledge workers' need for professional achievement. Yet more than 27 percent of high-tech workers do not understand how their performance is evaluated. This is often the result of flawed or weak performance evaluation systems. When reviews are not fair, accurate, and timely, they fail to reward star performers, fail to provide encouragement and guidance to borderline workers, and fail to give proper feedback to those whose work is substandard. Although HR can do its part to make sure the performance appraisal process is reasonable and that managers are adequately trained, the buck stops with line managers who are responsible for the reviews.[57] For more information on building a performance-based culture, see Chapter 7.

Graceful Exits

No retention plan is perfect, of course, and there will always be those who leave your employ — voluntarily or otherwise. When you think you need to terminate a high-value knowledge worker, avoid missteps by following these "firing best practices":

Take the time to think through the situation. If you are clear about what the problem is, then it should also be clear would be happening if the problem disappeared. If analysis finds there are external constraints, such as insufficient training or resources, affecting the person's performance, can you remove the constraints?

The problem employee could be in the wrong job. A frank discussion with problem employees may be the first step toward correcting a problem. Do it as soon as you notice the problem behavior. They may be working off the wrong set of priorities, and telling them what one expects may be enough to do the trick.

Do not make a final decision prior to talking with other managers; always discuss a decision with an immediate supervisor or the human resource department manager. If you cannot explain your decision to an objective third party, then maybe it is the wrong decision.

Delay firing someone until you feel calm — never when you are angry. If you feel that you have done your best to help the person succeed, but feel troubled about the decision, it is best to wait. Talk with HR; figure out why you are not comfortable with the decision. However, do not delay too long.

Collecting Data on the Way out

In the case of a voluntary resignation, an exit interview, if conducted appropriately, can provide some information about why a person is resigning. Many employees are not truthful in the exit interview, fearing a poor recommendation. This does not help the company find out why employees are quitting. For an exit interview to be effective, it must be conducted by someone who has been trained in interviewing and who is outside the employee's department. And confidentiality must be guaranteed. Some companies have a third party call and interview people six months after they leave, which gives more accurate information than the exit interviews.

Exit interviews also provide useful clues to the needs and feelings of other staff members. Obtaining staff feedback is critical, and exit intervention can be a powerful tool not only for redesigning the workplace, but also for retaining departing staff. IBM discovered it could save a number of people headed for the door by just talking with them and finding out what they were unhappy about. They found that more than 50 percent of people who were leaving could have been retained if anyone had bothered talking to them about their issues. What a waste!

Notes

1. Kepner-Tregoe, Avoiding the Brain Drain, 2001.
2. Gilbert Nicholson, Screen and glean (screening of prospective employees), *Workforce Magazine,* October 2000.
3. H.R. Nalbantian et al., How Fleet Bank fought employee flight, *Harvard Business Review,* 82, 116, 2004.
4. Carol Orsag Madigan, Fail-Safe Hiring, *Business Finance,* July 1999.
5. Jo Ellen Moore and Lisa A. Burke, Top-notch retention strategies, *Pay for Performance Report,* December 2002.
6. Kenneth F. Clarke, What businesses are doing to attract and retain employees — becoming an employer of choice, *Employee Benefits Journal,* March 2001.
7. T. Shawn Taylor, Mismatching workers, jobs a costly mistake, *Chicago Tribune,* July 6, 2004.
8. Shelley Langan, Finding the needle in the haystack: the challenge of recruiting and retaining sharp employees, *Public Personnel Management,* December 22, 2000.
9. Jo Ellen Moore and Lisa A. Burke, Top-notch retention strategies, *Pay for Performance Report,* December 2002.
10. Jim Sirbasku, Growing companies must utilize solid interviews, *Los Angeles Business Journal,* Aug. 19, 2002.
11. Jeannette Cabanis, Your career — the project of a lifetime, *PM Network,* April 1998.
12. Alan Horowitz, Hiring an IT leader?, *Computerworld,* July 17, 2000.
13. Alan Horowitz, ibid.
14. John Sullivan, Jumping through Hoops: A New Job Requirement, http://www.careerjournal.com/columnists/perspective/20021202-fmp.html.
15. Geoffrey James, Looking to fill an IT job? Avoid these 10 mistakes, *Computerworld,* July 24, 2000.
16. Kevin D. Carlson et al., Recruitment evaluation: the case for assessing the quality of applicants attracted, *Personnel Psychology,* Summer 2002.
17. John Gantz, How to win in the battle for IT Talent, *Computerworld,* July 17, 2000.
18. "Performance-based Selection," www.hrstrategy.com.
19. Jim Sirbasku, ibid.
20. Jim Sirbasku, ibid.
21. "Performance-based Selection," www.hrstrategy.com.
22. Max Messmer, Robert Half International Inc.
23. From materials created by Sockwell Associates, Charlotte, NC.
24. Alison Overholt, True or false: you're hiring the right people, *Fast Company,* February 2002.

25. Robert S. Benchley, The value of human capital, *The Chief Executive,* February 2001.
26. Preston Cameron, Managing knowledge assets: the cure for an ailing structure, *CMA Management,* May 2002.
27. AON Consulting, United States @ Work, 2000.
28. Carol Orsag Madigan, Fail-Safe Hiring, *Business Finance,* July 1999.
29. Phillip Perry, Holding your top talent, *Research Technology Management,* May/June 2001.
30. Radford 2000 Benefits exchange.
31. Radford, ibid.
32. Kenneth Brownson and Raymond L Harriman, III, Recruiting staff in this era of shortage, *The Health Care Manager,* June 2001.
33. Tom Silveri, Orientation, *Workforce,* September 2001.
34. T.R. Block, and J.D. Frame, *The Corporate Project Office: A Key to Managing Projects Effectively,* Crisp Publications, Menlo Park, CA, 1988.
35. Human Resource Executive Online Survey, Retention: An Increasing Challenge?, November 1999.
36. George F. Farris and Rene Cordero, Leading your scientists and engineers, *Research Technology Management,* Nov./ Dec. 2002; M.K. Badawy, what we have learned about managing human resources, *Research Technology Management,* September-October 1988, pp. 19–35; W.M. James, Best HR practices for today's innovation management, *Research Technology Management,* January-February 2002, p. 57–60; R.T. Keller, Cross-functional project groups in research and new product development: diversity, communications, job stress, and outcomes, *Academy of Management Journal,* 44(3), 549–555, 2001; R. Cordero, G.F. Farris, and N. DiTomaso, Technical professionals in cross-functional teams: their quality of work life, *Journal of Product Innovation Management,* 15, 550–563, 1998; M. Baba et al. The Development of Globally Distributed Teams: An Ecological Approach, Working Paper, Wayne State University, July 24, 2001.
37. Rodney L. Robertson and Donald D. Tippett, Linking project team performance with team health, *Engineering Management Journal,* March 2002.
38. Glenn M. Parker, *Cross-Functional Teams,* Jossey-Bass, 1994.
39. Shelley Langan,, ibid.
40. Kenneth Brownson and Raymond L Harriman, III, ibid.
41. Allen DeMers, Solutions and strategies for recruitment and retention: a manager's guide, *Public Personnel Management,* March 22, 2002; International Personnel Management Association (IPMA), Best Practice: IT Staff Retention, Online, available: http://www.ipma-hr.org/public/bestp_toc. cfm, accessed: March 12, 2001; Meta Group 2000, IT Staffing and Compensation Guide, Online, available: http://www.metagroup.com/cgi-bin/ inetcgi/index.html, accessed March 20, 2001; International Telework Association and Council ITAC, Telecommuting Alive and Well or Fading Away?, http://www.telecommute.org/aboutitac/alive.shtm, accessed February 27, 2001 (organizational information Web site); International Telework Association of America ITAA, Building the 21st Century Information Technology Workforce, Online, available: http://www.itaa.org/workforce/studies/ upgrade.htm, accessed March 16, 2001.

42. Carol Orsag Madigan, ibid.

43. Alan Horowitz, ibid.

44. Ritu Agarwal, Crafting an HR strategy to meet the need for IT workers, *Communications of the ACM,* July 2001; U.S. Department of Commerce, America's New Deficit: The Shortage of Information Technology Workers, Office of Technology Policy, Washington, D.C., Sept. 29, 1997; R. Walton, From control to commitment in the workplace, *Harvard Business Review,* 63(2), 77–84, 1985.

45. AON Consulting, United States @ Work, 2000.

46. Ritu Agarwal, ibid.

47. http://www.themanager.org/Knowledgebase/HR/Recruiting.htm and http://www.hr-guide.com/data/CIT.

48. Leah Carlson, Overcoming telework's tech challenges, *Employee Benefit News,* 18, 53, June 2004.

49. Gene Slowinski et al., After the acquisition: managing paranoid people in schizophrenic organizations, *Research Technology Management,* May/June 2002.

50. Gene Slowinski et al., ibid.

51. Walter L. Tamosaitis, P.E., and Margaret G. Schwenker, Recruiting and retaining technical personnel at a contractor-operated government site Savannah River Site, *Engineering Management Journal,* March 2002.

52. Seymore Adler, Beware of the empty T-shirt in the new economy, *Customer Service Management,* Sept./Oct. 2000.

53. R. Cordero, G.F. Farris, and N. DiTomaso, Technical professionals in cross-functional teams: their quality of work life, *Journal of Product Innovation Management,* 15, 550–563, 1998.

54. Walter L. Tamosaitis, P.E., and Margaret G. Schwenker, ibid.

55. Kenneth Brownson and Raymond L Harriman, III, ibid.

56. Ritu Agarwal, ibid.

57. Rewarding employees with psychic income pays long-term dividends, *Benefits Quarterly,* Third Quarter 2001.

Chapter 6

The Care and Feeding of Project Management Personnel

Career Pathing and Professional Development

Chapter 5 laid out some turnover statistics that show why it is better to keep your project management talent than to find new talent. As we have shown, training and development, as well as the provision of meaningful opportunities for personal and professional growth, will play a large role in making a company an "employer of choice" for project managers. One of the key questions the smart project managers will ask early in the hiring game or soon after arrival is: "What's my future here?" (Or, reflecting the new mobility in the workforce, "What does this work experience add to my future prospects?") Companies sometimes worry that the investment they make in developing personnel will be wasted if those individuals leave the company. However, a more important question might be: What if you *do not* train or develop your project management personnel ... and they *stay*?

Planning for Careers in Project Management

Companies that regard project management as important nurture the people who are responsible. They ensure that project managers have a

135

clear and desirable career path that includes training, promotion criteria, recognition of achievement, and the opportunity to progress to the highest executive levels in the organization.[1] According to Christopher Sauer of Oxford University, developing a career structure is essential to the development of an organization's project management capability. The career path structure serves three purposes:

1. It allows the organization to match a project manager's level of competence or experience to the difficulty and importance of a project.
2. It assures project managers that the investments they make in developing their professional skills will be rewarded.
3. It provides an incentive for people to stay with the company because they can see a clear promotion path.[2]

Career planning is a challenging specialty that combines aspects of business, psychology, and education; and planning careers in project management is exceptionally challenging. Understanding what we mean by "career" is an essential starting point if we are to develop a path that meets both individual and organizational needs.

From a broad perspective, careers can be viewed as "a series of separate but related experiences and adventures through which a person, any person, passes during a lifetime."[3] An individual can pursue multiple careers, either in sequence or at the same time. We see this frequently in project management, where a technical or functional track is perceived as the career, and building project management expertise is considered a secondary endeavor supporting the primary career track.

Moreover, career includes both an individual's work and family experiences, as well as the interaction between the two. With project management being such a young and evolving profession, organizations are not totally clear on what their "needs" are and, consequently, individuals' work experiences and opportunities may have been limited in this profession until recently.

To survive in the competitive business environment, an organization must develop a career program that will respond to future strategic requirements for certain skills. By doing so, the organization provides opportunities for and encourages multifunctional experiences and allows its personnel choices and control over their lives. Typically, an employee will choose a career path that fits his or her talents, core competencies, and values, thereby ensuring satisfaction and growth — and reducing organizational attrition, which has positive financial and productivity impacts on any organization. Individual careers develop from an interaction between individuals' competencies and career goals and the work experience the organization provides. To the extent that the organization provides opportunities for the individual to use and develop his or her personal competence while moving through various jobs, functions, and levels, the individual will grow and experience career satisfaction.

The objectives of any career development program should be to:

- Improve skills
- Assess an employee's readiness for advancement
- Define professional skill areas
- Create an equitable salary structure
- Create a positive and open environment for career discussion
- Ensure frequent feedback
- Provide opportunity for advancement through a career path
- Encourage a "change to grow" environment

Developing a career development program for any profession can be challenging. In the project management profession, it is even more so because there are few models to draw upon, and the project management needs of an organization can be quite varied.

One of the first things an organization must do is take an inventory of the skills required for effective project management at all levels. (This is also, of course, the first step in developing competency requirements, as described in Chapter 3.) After developing a skills inventory, identifying the key attributes of those skills must be determined and a profile developed. Management must commit to meeting with employees at a minimum of twice a year to discuss opportunities and plans for advancing an employee's career goals. Most importantly, tangible actions must be taken that assist the employee with achieving his or her career goals. If this does not occur, the credibility of a career development program will be weakened.[4]

A career path includes at least three valuable elements: (1) experiential requirements, (2) education/training requirements (knowledge acquisition), and (3) documentation and tracking mechanisms. The experiential requirements detail the types of on-the-job activities that must be accomplished for each level in the career path. The education and training requirements detail the types of knowledge required for each rung on the career ladder. At the lower levels, these tend to be basic courses designed to provide exposure and practice to the rudimentary skills required of that level. The upper-level positions require more advanced, strategic types of educational experiences that enhance leadership, interpersonal, and communications skills. These might include topics that go beyond the realm of project management into personal business strategy, financial, and political development. Documentation mechanisms include the attainment of certificates, degrees, or other credentials that substantiate the acquisition of the desired set of skills.

To support the validity of a career path, the next step is to ensure the availability of the necessary experiential and educational opportunities. The experiential opportunities must be coordinated with the appropriate resource manager and the human resources department in the organization. The HR department is also valuable in the development of the training program. To be effective, information collected from the knowledge, behavior, and potential assessments is necessary to create a targeted training program. The educational program should be targeted to the requirements identified in the career path, and be designed in a progressive nature. That is, the training requirements of team members are prerequisites for project managers, etc. The most effective approach is to identify the learning requirements for each level and aggregate across all levels to get both introductory and advanced course requirements. Mentoring and coaching, in combination with other training and development, can help prepare the next generation of project leaders. (More guidance on mentoring is provided at the end of this chapter.)[5]

A broad range of experiences is required for future project managers. It is not possible to develop them by restricting their experiences to one function. Thus, rather than climbing up the ladder of the functional silo, project managers benefit from being exposed to a number of functions, perhaps moving back to functions they have fulfilled before, but in a more senior role. One writer has labeled this "the spiral staircase" career path.[6]

The first important criterion for project manager success is the desire to be a manager in general and a project manager in particular. Many organizations force people into the position even if they are not adept at it and do not desire to become one. True, the project management position may be the only way to promotion beyond the job of technical specialist; the step from technical specialist to project manager may be the assumed progression when there is no way to move up a technical ladder. It is far better, however, if alternative upward paths exist: one through technical managership and one through project managership (see Chapter 4 for a discussion of identifying these two sets of competencies in project management). With such dual promotional ladders, technical managers can stay in their departments and become core team members responsible for the technical portions of projects. Dual ladders also allow progression through project management, but project managers must be able to manage technical specialists while handling the behavioral and administrative tasks that motivate the specialists to do their best work.[7]

A project manager's multilevel career path can be developed around levels of competence in the following categories: education and experience, interpersonal skills, technical coaching ability, business acumen, customer focus, project complexity, role in managing projects, and the industry or work environment.[8]

The best project managers come from a variety of different career paths. A software development project manager, for example, would find it highly beneficial to come from a background of development programmer, team leader, and resource manager, three areas that help develop the technical, organizational, and leadership skills that are essential to being an effective project manager. A project manager would be further served by assisting a more experienced project manager for at least the first project. New project managers need mentoring. The mentor should be a seasoned project manager — or, as one project executive describes it, a "well-worn" project manager — with project successes (and failures) in his or her experience bank. The mentor's primary role is to help the new project manager learn how to do things right the first time.[9]

PM Career Paths: Two Best-Practice Examples

Nearly a decade ago, a benchmarking study of project management in large organizations declared that "best practice project management groups make project management a career track … [and] develop clear and precise job descriptions to differentiate different types of project manager roles." At that time, however, only 31 percent of the benchmarked companies said that their companies had clear promotion paths.[10]

Project management has undergone a dramatic shift over the past decade. Some observers date the change from a 1995 article by Thomas Stewart in *Fortune*, celebrating "project manager" as the career of the future. Certainly, it was the first time the title had ever received such lofty press attention. Since then, mainstream business media from the *Wall Street Journal* to *CFO* have carried an increasing number of articles on project management and project managers. But large corporations are like oil tankers — they take a while to respond to changes in direction. Project management may be a hot topic of conversation, but project managers in many corporate environments still feel one-down when it comes to recognition and rewards; relegated to a dead-end job description within a functional department. However, some companies have worked to become "best-practice" in the area of career development for project managers. The two examples that follow — one large organization and one small organization — provide excellent examples of what can happen when we start giving project management the attention it deserves.

Career Pathing for Project Managers at IBM

In the early 1990s, IBM looked at its corporate capability in project management — not at the project managers themselves, but at the organization — and decided improvement was critical. A consistent and broad understanding of how to manage projects throughout the company was lacking. Training was haphazard, with different programs going on in different parts of the company. With a common approach to educating project managers, the company hoped to have teams behaving in a common way. Because each project would not have to start by asking "Do we need to complete a Project Charter?" or "What content should be included in our Project Charter?", the company expected projects would get off to a quicker, better start.

IBM began by defining an approach to the education and career development of project managers. The first step was not only to define the skills, but also to define at what point in a career that skill was needed. They noticed that beginning project managers need to learn certain skills immediately and, in most cases, their level of proficiency needed increases as they mature in their careers. However, in some cases, a skill needed early in a career atrophies and is replaced by other skills. For example, senior project managers may lose some of their proficiency in scheduling because they depend on someone to take care of that for them. They found that the needed skills and skill levels go up and down throughout project managers' careers.

Next, the company created job codes for project managers so that everybody recognized that there was something significant about the people who do those jobs. At IBM, project manager is not an entry-level position. Project managers start in some technical area, whether coding or designing hardware or delivering services — even in HR or marketing. They begin by being involved in doing the work related to their background and progress, as their leadership skills grow, into team leadership positions. At that point, some people realize they like leading teams better than doing the technical work; others feel the opposite way.

IBM realized that, to some extent, project managers are a self-selecting group — although there are those who express interest in project management and their manager must tell them they are not cut out for it. While the company does not claim to have identifying a good project manager down to a science, it has identified a progression in terms of skills, from the core project management skills (scheduling and issue management, for example), and progressing beyond these into big picture issues — balancing priorities and making tradeoffs. The company married this concept of the progression of skills to some defined job codes and also to a program of education that supports skill development.

The company's project management education has three tiers. Tier One — basic or core skills — education from a vendor and modified the curriculum to include some internal content, so they learn not only generic project management but how we do certain things within IBM. When people complete that tier, they get a certificate in project management. Both internal and vendor-supplied courses are accredited, so they can be applied to a graduate degree at another institution. The "stage-gate" for moving on the Tier Two is to pass the Project Management Institute's Project Management Professional certification exam.

Tier Two and Tier Three focus more on experiences, on how the project manager applies learned skills inside IBM. At this level, topically focused workshop discussions with knowledgeable senior personnel take the place of classroom teaching. Tier Two also focuses on technical education. An IBM certification that focuses on their experiences within the company is the capstone of Tier Two.

Finally, top project managers — those in Tier Three — are required to show "giveback." People who are mature in their skills are not only required to keep up their own skills, but also to give back to the community by mentoring, sharing experiences, presenting at conferences, helping teams develop programs … sharing the intellectual capital.

Educational opportunities are structured to allow people to take the courses they need in the right general order or timing. In addition, "just-in-time" materials are developed from the courses and applied directly to current projects to reinforce the education.

Targeted educational events are offered for specific parts of the project management community, such as a conference for those who are IBM-certified, where they interact with others of similar experience and levels of knowledge. These exchanges are taped and webcast. These community-building events are important because one of the issues project managers have is that, unlike programmers or engineers, where 50 or so work together in a group, project managers tend to feel isolated.

A further community-building tactic is that IBM believes you cannot educate only project managers. Everyone on a team must know something about project management, so that they know why the project manager is doing what he is doing. Therefore, modules out of the core project management curriculum have been inserted into the educational programs of other professionals in the company.

This program blends aspects of social learning and classroom learning and strives to meet both personal goal achievement needs and corporate needs. Career is a "whole-life" project, and the career progression programs at IBM appear to address that project holistically: progressively throughout an individual career, and consistently throughout the company.[11]

Career Planning for Project Management Consultants at PM Solutions

In 2001, our own company, PM Solutions, a full service consulting organization of more than 100 employees, implemented a career development program for its employees, resulting in major changes in the way we discuss performance, current skills, and future goals. The results of an employee survey highlighted the employees' desire for a strong and proactive career development program. The three areas identified as needing the most improvement were (1) clearer definitions of roles and responsibilities, (2) more opportunity for promotion, and (3) more training opportunities.

The results of the employee survey validated the need for management to put in motion plans to address strong career development across the company. In addition to a career development program, there were other areas for improvement identified to complement building a robust career development program. These areas included:

- Defining the required skills for project management
- Developing a professional profile of a project manager with the requisite attributes
- Aligning training programs and on-the-job experiences to fill the "gaps" for the requisite skills required
- Creating a promotability program using the professional profile
- Revamping the employee appraisal process and replacing it with a merit review process
- Building a succession planning tool through the promotability program

Due to the rapid growth of the company, skill development had not been the focus of the company; keeping up with resource demands through hiring had been the major challenge. But it soon became apparent that, to prepare associates for new job assignments and to enrich their professional lives, the company needed to focus strongly on career development and begin to offer a positive career path.

The resulting career development program addressed improving process excellence and developing human capital to the point where associates could feel optimistic about career growth prospects. Since the program was implemented, feedback has been exceedingly positive, despite the fact that follow-through on the actual development plans has sometimes proven to be a challenge due to resource and budget constraints.[12]

To better define skills, functional positions were created such as Planner I and Planner II, and Project Manager and Senior Project Manager (see Tables 6.1 and 6.2). For each of the functional positions, skills in ten

TABLE 6.1   Program/Project Manager Career Growth Potential

Position	Organizational Level
Project Leadership Track	
Chief Project Officer	Enterprise
Strategic Project Office Director	Enterprise
Project Office Director	Divisional/Departmental
Portfolio Manager	Enterprise
Manager of Enterprise Project Managers	Enterprise
Manager, Project Managers	Divisional/Departmental
Global Program Manager	Enterprise
Enterprise Program Manager II	Enterprise
Enterprise Program Manager I	Enterprise
Enterprise Project Manager II	Enterprise
Enterprise Project Manager I	Enterprise
Program/Project Mentor I, II	Enterprise or Divisional
Program Manager II	Divisional
Program Manager I	Divisional
Project Manager III	Divisional/Departmental
Project Manager II	Divisional/Departmental
Project Manager I	Divisional/Departmental
Project Planning and Control Track	
Chief Project Officer	Enterprise
Strategic Project Office Director	Enterprise
Project Office Director	Divisional/Departmental
Manager of Enterprise Project Support	Enterprise
Manager, Project Support	Divisional/Departmental
Enterprise Project Controller	Enterprise
Project Controller II	Divisional/Departmental
Project Controller I	Divisional/Departmental
Project Planner II	Divisional/Departmental
Project Planner I	Divisional/Departmental
Project Estimator II	Divisional/Departmental

TABLE 6.1 (continued)   Program/Project Manager Career Growth Potential

Position	Organizational Level
Project Estimator I	Divisional/Departmental
Project Scheduler II	Divisional/Departmental
Project Scheduler I	Divisional/Departmental
Business Analyst	Any
Issues Management Coordinator	Any
Change Control Coordinator	Any
Risk Management Coordinator	Any
Specialty Positions	
Systems Analyst	Any
Knowledge Management Coordinator	Any
Methodologist	Any
Technical Advisor	Any
Budget Analyst	Any

different areas were determined. The progressive combination of the skills produced a career path for both project management consultants and administration personnel. This career path gave our associates a much better idea of what opportunities are available and what skill sets are needed to move to other functional positions. A sample list of roles and responsibilities, developed for project planners and administrators, is shown in Table 6.3.

In analyzing how associates were managed, PM Solutions realized that many of them were receiving performance reviews without the goals and measures to make them an effective tool. In addition, direct observation of an employee on a daily basis was difficult. The solution was to replace performance reviews with career development discussions, whereby both the associate and supervisor could discuss how to improve skills that are necessary to advance. Merit reviews separate from the skill discussions were instituted. In addition to addressing the skill needs of our associates, the managers and supervisors will benefit by improving their skills in leadership and associate development, which are key skill areas for higher-level positions.

The project management consulting field typically has had difficulty in addressing career growth issues. This new program, although a major change that the company continues to "grow into," has addressed many of the issues with which other consulting companies are struggling.

TABLE 6.2   PM Solutions Career Path for a Project Manager

Project Controller. A Project Controller brings knowledge of and experience with implementing and using project controls to the team. Professionals in this category are hands-on experts in using project management software to plan and schedule tasks, manage project and program interdependencies, roll up and/or integrate plans and schedules, analyze divisional/departmental resource projections, summarize and report status, and produce suggestions on how to make control process improvements.

Project Team Leader. A professional, the Project Team Leader has a proven track record in effectively applying the project management principles to project performance, attainment of the triple constraint and high team performance/motivation. The Project Team Leader has led small to medium project initiatives (generally six months or less in duration with up to ten core team members). Project team leaders may lead smaller project initiatives that integrate into a larger project led by a Project Manager.

Project Manager. An experienced manager capable of successfully directing the planning, development, and implementation of medium-large projects according to cost, schedule, and scope requirements. The project manager participates in project initiation activities, including plan and budget preparation; leads the project management team in successfully executing the project as planned and budgeted throughout the project life cycle; and oversees the project closure activities, including the collection of lessons learned.

Senior Project Manager. A recognized leader and manager capable of successfully directing the planning, development and implementation of large and complex projects according to cost, schedule, and scope requirements. The Senior Project Manager participates in all phases of the project (from concept to closure) and often has worked in a global environment or setting.

Program Manager. A recognized leader and manager well versed in the principles of project management, strategic and tactical planning, coordinating and integrating multiple large and complex projects into a comprehensive program. Program Manager is capable of working with the client in defining their business drivers and defining how the program and project objectives meet the benefit triggers for business success. A Program Manager may have multiple project managers as direct reports who are managing key sub-projects that integrate in their totality to satisfy programmatic deliverables.

Mentor. A project management professional with extensive project and program experience capable of working with project managers and project teams to help them put the processes, skills, and support structure in place to effectively establish and manage projects. Typically, mentors provide consulting services to program managers, project managers, program/project teams, and corporate managers. The Project Management Mentor is well versed in leading and managing program/project team members from diverse backgrounds, and within global and virtual settings. In program/project crisis, the mentor can be called in to fill in for an extended period of time for the project manager, senior project manager, or program manager.

TABLE 6.3 Project Coordinator and Project Planner Roles and Responsibilities

Level I Project Coordinator	Level II Planner I	Level III Planner II
A professional educated and trained in project management principles and knowledge areas (scope, schedule, cost, quality, risk, human resources, communications, and procurement). Project Coordinators have particular knowledge in the area's triple constraint: schedule, budget, and scope/quality development and monitoring. Project Coordinators are also involved with reviewing project deliverables and technical documentation.	A professional educated and trained in project management principles and knowledge areas (scope, schedule, cost, quality, risk, human resources, communications, and procurement). Project Planner I has a strong knowledge base in defining and tracking the project's triple constraint: schedule, budget, and scope/quality development and monitoring. Project Planner I has often become involved with creating and reviewing project deliverables and technical documentation and is capable of leading facilitation sessions for development of the project plan, schedule, and estimates, group reviews, and project charter definitions.	A professional educated and trained in the project management principles and knowledge areas (scope, schedule, cost, quality, risk, human resources, communications, and procurement). Project Planner II has a proven track record in effectively applying the project management principles both to the project's triple constraint (schedule, budget, and scope/quality development and monitoring) and to managing risks, quality, communications, and resourcing. Project Planner II often leads the creation of and facilitates the review of project plans, resource/cost/time estimates, risk analyses, project deliverables, and technical documentation.

The Process

Step 1: The Career Development Meeting

- Supervisors meet with associates for an initial meeting to fill out the Career Planning and Development Worksheet. Subsequent meetings are held every six months, with the merit assessment occurring on the anniversary date. HR will remind each supervisor of upcoming meetings. It is the responsibility of the supervisor to schedule and ensure that these career planning and development sessions occur on time.
- New hires, as part of their orientation, have an expectations exchange with their supervisor, at which time a preliminary Career

Planning and Development Worksheet is completed. The next session occurs in six months, followed by the merit session at the anniversary date.

■ The Professional Skills Inventory is used as a guide in assessing the skills of the associate. This guide is not meant to be all-inclusive.

■ The Career Development Worksheet is co-signed by the supervisor, associate, and Human Resources.

■ Prior to the merit session, Human Resources will e-mail the Personnel Action Request (PAR) to the supervisor with personal and salary information already inserted.

■ The supervisor, before conducting the merit session, forwards the Personnel Action Authorization form and Career Development and Planning Worksheet to their immediate supervisor for review and approval of the intended merit increase, if any. The rating, recommended salary action, and effective date must be included on the PAR. Final approval is given by the Vice President of the program area and the Human Resources manager. A copy of the approved PAR goes to the supervisor conducting the interview, to HR, and to payroll.

Step 2: Professional Growth Profile

■ Department heads assess their associates at least once annually using the Professional Growth Profile. This profile assesses each associate in a similar job to determine the comparative skill set. The skills assessed are exactly the same as those on the Career Development and Planning Worksheet. This profile is used also to ascertain associate readiness for short- and long-term career growth based on company needs. As the company grows, this will be used also as a succession-planning tool. Employees who consistently meet or exceed the requirements for their current positions know that opportunities exist for them in the roles described in the career paths described in Tables 6.1 and 6.2.

See Appendix E for examples of the career development and planning artifacts mentioned above.

Professional Development: Training, Coaching, and Mentoring

The concept of professional development brings to mind Marcus Buckingham's book, *Now, Discover Your Strengths*.[13] In it, he describes how great managers develop their people: They pay attention to the talents of their subordinates and find ways of giving them the opportunity to use that talent over and over again. In many ways, this is the opposite of the traditional concept of professional development, which has focused on what is missing in people. We need to develop ourselves, the logic goes, because there is an inherent weakness that we must overcome with more training and education. In this view of professional development, managers identify what is broken and urge the employees to "fix themselves."

But in Buckingham's view, great managers recognize talent and provide the opportunity to expand on that talent rather than focusing on what their people *do not* have. He recommends that organizations move toward a talent-based model rather than a deficit-based model.

Applying this logic to project management, one thing we quickly notice is that in the past, project management development has been almost entirely restricted to the project manager track. Yet an organization's project management capability also depends upon planners, schedulers, cost account managers, analysts, and others that make the administration of a project succeed. Each of these positions requires a discrete level of skill and knowledge. And those who succeed at these positions generally have the talent to do them well. They may or may not have the skills or desire to move into project manager positions — but in the past, our approach to these individuals has been to try to turn them into project managers. This goal may be ideal for some, but others will have to abandon what they do well, and feel good doing so, in order to follow the prescribed path to "success."

By contrast, the job descriptions, competency analyses, and career paths that we have described thus far in this book are all geared toward creating a professional development environment focused on maximizing the talents of all project management personnel. Supported by these processes and artifacts, managers can focus on opportunities that support the individual's development of their talents while, at the same time, adding to the skills and knowledge of that individual. When professional development is directed at getting better at what we do best, company performance can only improve.[14]

But what is the best way to facilitate that improvement? Certainly, by shifting employees of talent into the career paths and roles that most favor their development, one eliminates the wasted energy of trying to pound the square peg of technical brilliance into the round hole of project management finesse. But even within these roles and career paths, a multitude of options exists for training, educating, and developing innate talents.

Education and Training

From 1998 to 2001, money spent on learning as a retention tool increased 15 percent, according to Hackett Benchmarking and Research, and since then the market for project management training specifically has boomed.[15] New technologies have added the option of distance learning to the mix. The wealth of programs available is, of course, a benefit to companies seeking training vendors for project management personnel. But it also has created two business pressures previously rare in the PM training market: the pressure to prove the ROI of such training and increased difficulty in choosing training options. (See Appendix F for statistics from the Center for Business Practices' survey on the value of project management training.)

In a 2002 interview, Dr. Jimmie West, dean of the PM College, welcomed both the diversity of training options and the challenge to calculate ROI. The ROI issue, he asserted, brought more realism to project management training. As a result, the examples and case studies we use in the classroom have immediate transferability to the workplace. Once PM training was largely theoretical; but now, when students leave the classroom, they are looking for an immediate impact on the way they do their job. People now spend a shorter time in the classroom, which forces the trainer to focus on essential critical elements.

The new pattern for PM training is to have more, and shorter, courses. A general introduction can be followed by focused, brief courses on specific areas. This also leads to better customization of training content. A part of that customization is the balancing of classroom training, on-the-job experience (also known as "just-in-time" training), and distance or self-paced learning. According to Dr. West, distance learning has great potential application for teaching prerequisites to courses; for example, learning the theory behind project management and acquiring the basic concepts and language. Tom Edwards, vice president of training, education and development for Bell Atlantic Corp., describes computer-based training as effective from both cost and employee-development perspectives.[16]

Classroom training will never go away because the classroom is where students get to apply concepts and get feedback on an immediate basis from teachers and from fellow students, so that performance and understanding are validated. Sharing of information is much more free in real-time than it can be on the Web; it is a "richer" environment.

Just-in-time training also fits some specific needs. It is a motivational device; one can interject humor and fun into learning in a just-in-time environment. It can also be a powerful team-building experience. Just-in-time training also helps students retain what they learn. Traditional wisdom says that students attending a class forget 40 percent of what they learned within 30 days if their training is not put to immediate use.[17]

One benefit of computer-based training via CD-ROM or the Internet is timely delivery, which can, in fact, be more important than depth of content. Computer-based training succeeds, not because it is the most comprehensive, but because it delivers *usable* knowledge to the student on the day it is needed. A two-day project management class delivered the day before building the project plan is often worth more to the business than a week-long course delivered two months earlier.[18]

West recommends a progression from distance learning, to the classroom, and then following up in the short term with just-in-time training to refresh what has been learned. Using all three methods, one accommodates the various learning styles present in a diverse group of people. Differences in age, social relationships, family position, maturity, patience, and interests require different training approaches. People also have differing learning speeds and styles based on their cognitive styles. A single pace of learning cannot keep the attention of a diverse group.

The typical student attention span for a stand-up lecture is seven to ten minutes. Thus, effective training delivery must vary between lecture, hands-on, textbook, video, CD, computer, and other media to keep the attention of the student. One method that dramatically increases retention of training is to test the student immediately after teaching a module.

The ROI Question

Well-planned training investments *are* rewarded. According to a study sponsored by Saba and the American Society for Training and Development, companies that invested above-average amounts in training outperformed the market by 45 percent in the next year.[19] And the Center for Business Practices' Value of Project Management Training study reveals that organizations overwhelmingly improved in a number of areas as a result of project management training. The relationship between classroom and workplace performance is highlighted by the finding that 91 percent of the organizations showed a moderate to extreme improvement in the individual's on-the-job performance. They also show moderate to extreme improvement in a variety of business measures, including customer satisfaction, productivity, and cost-schedule-requirements performance.[20] Most companies are now at least making an effort to figure the ROI of training. Table 6.4 lists some common metrics that are tracked in these efforts.

Within the company, however, it can be a challenge to tie specific improvements to specific training modules, especially in the realm of "soft benefits" associated with process improvements. One of the conundrums of project management training is that, although quantitative ROI measurement is the first thing every executive asks for, and although it is drawn from comparison of fairly obvious factors (project performance metrics, variance analysis, schedule and budget compliance, risk avoidance), the problem is that one must have a fairly sophisticated project performance tracking in place to even get these numbers. How many companies that are just beginning to train for project management even

TABLE 6.4 Measuring Training Effectiveness: Some Common Metrics

Training Inputs	% of Companies Reporting
Total training expenditures	88
Number of employees receiving training	88
Number of courses	77
Payments to outside training providers	75
Total training time/days	74
Tuition reimbursements	72
Wages and salaries of training personnel	68
Trainee travel expenses	42
Course development expenditures	40
Cost of facilities and equipment	38
Training expenditure per employee	34
Training expenditure as a % of payroll	31
Course development time	29
Contributions to outside training funds	12
Lost wages and salaries of trainees	11
Training expenditure as a % of sales	8
Training Outcomes	
Customer satisfaction	69
Job satisfaction	38
Productivity	37
Return on expectations	35
Safety violations	28
Sales	22
Return on investment	20
Turnover	20
Cost/benefit ratio	18
Waste reduction	15
Grievances	12
Profitability	9
Absenteeism	8

Source: National HRD Executive Survey, www.astd.org, 1997.

know they need such systems? Even once performance tracking is in place, one cannot get a comparative measurement in much less than two years.

Keep in mind that a complete ROI study is appropriate for only about 10 to 20 percent of training programs. For example, if rolling out a new software package, the need to train the IT staff is obvious. Therefore, doing an ROI process would be pointless. Similarly, analyzing the returns on a low-cost noon-time seminar probably is not worth the effort. On the other hand, a good candidate for an ROI study is a training program that probably has a very long life cycle, is very closely tied to operational goals, is strategically focused, is very expensive and has a high visibility.[21]

That said, there are steps that every project office should take to pave the way for measuring the ROI of project management training.

Establish a Baseline

Using the data available to you as the head of the project management office, or the product development group, or the systems development group, one can establish a current baseline. Determine the percentage of projects running behind schedule or over-budget, or being de-scoped to fit by analyzing the data provided in project status reports and user feedback. Further analysis of those projects will indicate which ones are in trouble because of a lack of trained manager — those with the predictable risk that happened without a mitigation plan, those that are late because a crucial resource requirement was not anticipated. And staff turnover — or to put it more positively, the staff retention rate — is readily available from your Human Resources function. Another baseline that can be developed is Organizational Project Manager Competency: competency would be assessed, using the instruments discussed in Chapters 3 and 4, and a baseline established. Knowledge, skills, and traits development progress measured periodically thereafter can show the trend in improved competency, which can be linked to project performance or even to financial performance.

There are two quantifiable measures related to the corporate bottom line that are readily available, and even more important, relatively easy to measure: (1) project performance and (2) staff retention.

Project Performance

The bottom-line measure of success is often posed as a question: Are you delivering projects in accordance with expectations (schedule, budget, quality — the time-honored "triple constraint")? The ability to show an improvement in project performance as a result of training often hinges on being able to demonstrate that an individual project manager was able to apply his or her training to the project. Therefore, when sending a project manager to a training class, consider how that individual will apply the training and how the manager will know that it is having an impact. One method is to measure the individual's knowledge and competency before the class begins and then again after the class or series of classes, such as those that comprise a Master's Certificate Program.

Be prepared to actively review project charters, work breakdown structures, status reports, and other project artifacts. Look for behavioral changes such as scheduled project team meetings and timely status report generation, with project issues being resolved. Solicit feedback from project stakeholders, including users and team members; ask how they feel the project is going. And above all, discuss the project with the project manager; ask how he or she is applying what was learned in the classroom.

However, keep in mind that a project manager does not manage a project in a vacuum. Unless the rest of the organization has been exposed to management by projects and understands their roles and responsibilities to the project, the project manager cannot succeed.

Staff Retention

Another qualitative measure one can use is staff retention rate. Project managers have careers they are interested in enhancing — either while employed with you or with someone else. Providing project managers with the right opportunity to participate in skills development training is a powerful tool to retaining them. Consider the project managers' work schedules when scheduling training. These resources often cannot spend a week, or even two full days, away from their respective projects. To address this challenge, consider offering courses more than once, perhaps even during off-hours. This allows the project manager who cannot attend the session Tuesday morning because he has a project review scheduled at that time to possibly attend the same session on Thursday evening.

Establish a process to monitor these metrics during the period that the training is being offered. If there is no improvement, conduct the analysis to determine why. Are the right people attending the right training? Are there other factors preventing project success that are not related to the training (i.e., organizational politics)?[22]

Set Training Targets

While most business leaders set financial targets, organizational goals, and objectives, few set measurable goals for employee training. First develop a list of tasks that you want your employees to be able to accomplish. Determine how the training is connected to a business need. Too often, training is put in place without enough forethought. It may be the right thing to do, but we would like to precede that with an understanding of how it helps the business if we do the training.

Make sure the program has clear objectives. Training programs should have a learning objective: some observable and measurable behavior at the end of the process. There are five types of learning objectives:

1. *Awareness:* a familiarity with terms, concepts, and processes.
2. *Knowledge:* a general understanding of concepts, processes, or procedures.
3. *Performance:* an ability to demonstrate skills on at least a basic level.
4. *Application:* "What do we expect you to do differently?"
5. *Impact:* "What business measure will you drive if you do this?"

Impact objectives are often hard data such as output, quality, cost, and time. Soft-data impact objectives include customer service, work climate, and work habits. What is often missing from training programs are the application and impact objectives.[23]

Now, measuring ROI on a qualitative basis is pretty readily accessible. Are we changing behaviors? Are they doing the things they need to do? For example, are project charters now a part of the company culture? If not, training has not had any impact. Are they doing risk management plans? Communication plans? We can collect artifacts that show the changed behaviors. Here they are: the lessons learned. If I see a quantitative leap in the project documents produced, I can assume increased attention to project management.[24]

ROI data alone does not address other key business impacts, such as increased employee morale, better communications, or increased customer satisfaction, enhanced corporate image, improved conflict resolution, increased sensitivity to human diversity, and increased employee loyalty. While less tangible, and therefore more difficult to convert to dollar figures, these "soft benefits" are important. They cannot be directly measured but they can be inferred or indirectly measured by associated outcomes. One way to approximate the value of soft benefits is to ask experts within your organization to give a monetary figure for these intangibles.

Most of the time, of course, improvements in job performance are only partially due to training programs. Variables other than the training — trainees' age and work experience, economic changes, shifts in managerial styles, customer attitudes — might influence the data, making it difficult to determine the actual effect of the training on the ROI results. One way to measure the effects of extraneous factors is to compare the results of a control group with the results of the trainee group. The experimental group receives training; the control group does not. Trend-line analysis, forecasting, participant estimation, supervisor estimation, management estimation, customer input, expert estimation, subordinate input, and other factors are additional ways to isolate training's effect on performance.[25]

Who Should Be Trained?

There are four audiences for training and each one needs a different depth and focus:

1. *Executives* need awareness training to give them an appreciation of what project management can do for them, and to teach them how to ask the right questions to get the right information so they can make good decisions.
2. *Practitioners* (project managers) need training designed around their present level of capability. One does not design a uniform training program — one designs a program that meets the needs of the population. Train all levels, from novice PMs to experts who need refreshers. Assess the practitioner audience for areas of strength and weakness and design around that.
3. *Matrix organization functional managers* need training in three areas: (a) their role in a project environment (as resource owners), (b) the role of project management in the organization, and finally, (c) an overview of what project management is all about. A related audience is ancillary managers, such as HR and finance, who support projects. The need for functional managers to receive project management training was highlighted in a recent field study published in the project management journal. One of the findings was that, even when project managers are knowledgeable about risk management, poor risk management results when functional managers do not have any formal risk management training.[26]
4. *Team members* on the project need to understand both the big picture and their supporting roles. Encourage "would-be" project managers to participate in the training as well. Use training to grow the skills one will need to address the staff transition that will occur, to ensure there will a pool of trained staff upon which to draw.

Executives and project managers should be trained simultaneously. The executives are change agents and project champions. If project managers know that executives are going to be asking them questions they might not be able to answer, they pay more attention. It improves performance at the same time it raises expectations on the part of executives, so the two trainings reinforce each other.[27]

Most individual workers believe they need training. Most corporate executives also believe training is a high priority but often, middle managers need to be educated on its importance. Managers send a strong message about the value of employees via policies on who pays and when the training is delivered. When management wants employees to pay for the class and use vacation time to attend, the messages that employees receive about trust, power, and career are not positive ones.

So, because training is important to the business, one should take care of fees and time. There should be some availability of time during the workweek to study and to attend classes if required. Some experts suggest a policy where the business "loans" training costs to the employee and then forgives the costs based on successful completion or contingent on continued employment.

As product management author and consultant Dennis Smith says, "If you spend 10 percent of your gross sales on a factory machine, you would spend what is required on maintenance and upgrades. You probably spend more than that on your employees: isn't keeping them productive at least as important?"[28]

Plan to reinforce the training with follow-on activities to maximize the effectiveness of the training. Implement a mentoring program that supports project managers benefiting from the experiences of others who have gone through the training. Ask your instructors to conduct follow-up sessions: bring the entire class back together to talk about their experiences applying the classroom instruction in the real world.[29] Figure 6.1 and Figure 6.2 provide examples of training and education plans for developing project managers and other project personnel.

Select Vendors with Care

Training is a large investment and demands the selection of cost- and results-effective vendors. Select a vendor that can deliver your task-training, is a credible business, and has instructors and course developers who have experience in your industry. After reviewing their training offerings, negotiate changes to their standard curriculum so it meets your needs. In addition to experience, look for a personality match with the trainer and your business. Ongoing relationships are important and, with time, the trainer will become more effective as he or she learns about your business.

What about Conferences?

There are very few conferences where participants are still lively and full of ideas at the end. More typically, excitement peaks in the first workshop

Project Manager Training and Education Requirements

Development Activities	Type	Learning Activities	Verification
Course Completions	IL	PM Essentials	Course completion certificates
Course Exams	IL	Risk Management	
PM Knowledge Assessment Profile (PMKAP)	IL	Contracting and Negotiation Skills for Project Managers	Passing scores on exams
Mentor Certification	IL	Cost and Schedule Management	Associate's Certificate awarded
Master's Certificate	IL	Leading Project Teams	Completed courses within 12 months
Professional Certification	IL	Managing Multiple Projects	
Appropriate Job Assignments	IL	PM Practicum	
	SP	Estimating Techniques	
	SP	Advanced Risk Techniques	
	SP	Conflict Management	
	SP	Stakeholder Communication	

FIGURE 6.1   Example of a project manager education and training requirements description. (IL = Individual Learning; SP = Simulated Project)

Education and Training Requirements

COURSES:	PM Essentials	Risk Management	Cost & Schedule	Managing Multiple Projects	Leading Project Teams	PM Practicum
LEVELS						
Team Member	X					
Project Manager	X	X	X		X	X
Program Manager	X	X	X	X		
Project Office Director	X	X	X	X		

FIGURE 6.2   Example of education and training requirements by position. Requirements at entry levels are prerequisites for higher levels.

and fades completely by the closing session. This is because most of us are driven to attend conferences on topics about which we already know a lot. HR departments that will only approve expenditures for education directly related to an employee's job reinforce this inclination. Consequently, CFOs learn about finance, and project managers study project management. It is rare that people leave conferences with their heads brimming with new thoughts and ideas.

Ideally, what a conference should do — what any time away from the office should do — is revitalize employees, allowing them to think about work in a new way. Sometimes, attending conferences on the same old subjects only reinforces how bored, overworked, or unappreciated a person is. There is value in learning for learning's sake; for such things as art appreciation courses, philosophy roundtables, and conferences about the future. By letting employees' own interests — as opposed to narrow corporate guidelines — direct their learning, companies will get back more creative and stimulated employees.[30]

It is important to sometimes step back from the task-oriented issues of training ROI to remember that, over the long term, people whose love of learning is nurtured in the workplace are happier, more creative, and more valuable to the organization. They are motivated from within to acquire new skills or knowledge or to build on existing skills or knowledge. They feel good when they are learning new things. Research shows that people whose love of learning is nurtured have the ability to self-regulate efforts to persevere, despite challenge and frustration; they have increased feelings of autonomy and challenge. They feel a sense of possibility. They are more resourceful. Not only that, but they are likely to be more physically and mentally healthy than their less-engaged peers.

Companies can support individuals — and improve training results — when they are mindful that individuals are more likely to take ownership for their learning when:

- They are given a compelling, meaningful reason to do the task.
- They have options to make the task more interesting.
- Social networks exist to support the learning (so that individuals fulfill social needs as they connect with one another through a topic or project of interest). The project management community of practice is an example of such a social network, as are online threaded discussions with other practitioners, professional associations, and the like.[31]

Other Professional Development Issues and Strategies

It is crucial to demonstrate that the company is willing to invest in enhancing individuals' competencies. A development plan should include both provision for formal training and progression to more challenging assignments. Assignments should be selected not only to be achievable but also to stretch project managers. This will both develop them and be likely to result in effective project outcomes.[32]

Companies now realize that it takes a blended approach to grow the project talent they need. In the Center for Business Practices Value of PM Training Study, companies report that they provide growth and development opportunities for employees through skills training (43 percent), career paths (29 percent), and professional education (25 percent). In another report, members of the CIO Executive Council discussed their companies' career development efforts. Samantra Sengupta, CIO of the Scotts Co., "walks the halls a lot and sits down with people at all levels" to identify what they need and desire. Based on such feedback, she created a three-pronged managerial path based on workers' preferences in technology, management, and architecture. Smurfit-Stone developed an integrated job model that connected four different areas to salaries, skills, merit increases, and annual reviews. Linda Brigance, CIO at FedEx Asia Pacific, recommends that firms should not automatically turn project leaders into management leaders because the latter must also possess leadership skills such as guiding and motivating others. Business training can be an important component of career development for technical personnel. Another important concept for career development is cross-training; Nixon Peabody CIO Barbara Kunkel, for example, lets a certain staff member stand in for her when she is away.[33]

Whatever the strategy chosen, making an effort to professionalize the role of project manager is valuable to the individual, and is absolutely essential to the success of the organization. At the inception of a professional development program, the organization should develop a baseline of its current project performance level. This baseline serves as a benchmark against which the organization can measure its progress toward improved performance. A program such as the PM Solutions career path/professional development approach outlined in this chapter needs the support of the organization to carry it beyond the classroom and into the work environment. An expectation that communicates to the individuals in this professional development area that their behavior in the workplace is expected to contribute to improved corporate performance must be clearly established. Therefore, measurements of performance must go beyond the traditional assessment of the classroom experience for the learner. They need to include metrics such as increased use of a standard methodology; increase in knowledge of the practitioners; improvement in cost performance, schedule performance, customer satisfaction, and employee satisfaction; in addition to others. Table 6.5 shows a Project Management Performance Expectations worksheet used by PM Solutions. It serves as both a guide to individuals for personal development and a formal set of cues to management for advancement along the career path(s).

TABLE 6.5 PM Solutions Team Career Competencies

PM Solutions Team Career Competencies Matrix Project Management Career Path	Minimum Expectation to Enter the Job Classification							
	Business Analyst I / Proj. Coordinator	Business Analyst II / Planner I	Sr. Project Analyst / Planner II	Proj. Controller	Project Manager / Proj. Team Leader	Program Manager / Sr. Project Manager	Mentor	Account Manager / Product Integration Manager

Core Competency Levels: Definitions

1 EXPOSED: The employee is not expected to demonstrate skill in the competency at the present staff level. The employee may begin to develop the competency through training, day-to-day activities, and project assignments. The employee should be aware of the self-development required to meet expectation, as defined in the employees' development plan.

2 DEVELOPMENT: The employee's competencies is in its primary development phase. Development is supported by the identification of specific training and activities, as defined in the employees' development plan. The employee is expected to display significant progress in the basic knowledge of the competency.

3 PROFICIENT: The employee exhibits the competency in a skillful and consistent manner. The employee confidently takes on opportunities to exhibit or use the skill. The employee should progress to the mastery stage with additional time and experience.

4 MASTERY: The employee demonstrates the competency in a highly proficient and consistent manner. The employee exhibits mastery of the competency in a wide variety of situations and circumstances. The employee is regarded by PMI management, other employees, and customers, as an authority in the competency area.

5 EXPERT/MENTOR/TEACHER: The employee demonstrates the competency with a high degree of knowledge. The employee exhibits mastery of the competency in a wide variety of complex situations and circumstances. The employee is regarded by PMI management, other employees, and customers, as an expert in this area. The employee is capable of leading customer, branch, regional, and national activities, which provide the employee with an opportunity to teach or mentor others.

Company Knowledge

PM Solutions Team Organization Management-Structure: Demonstrates the knowledge, understanding, and acceptance of the PM Solutions Team mission statement; knowledge of the PM Solutions Team corporate organizational structure, including the key executives and their basic areas of responsibility; the structure, resources, and key executives of local branches and the appropriate regional organization; the various central and corporate service groups, their executives, available resources, functions, offerings, and facilities for internal as well as client-oriented requirements.	2	3	3	4	4	4	5	5
PM Solutions Team Organization Management-Practices: Demonstrates a working knowledge of the people, tools, policies, processes and procedures governing access to and utilization requirements for the various functions, services and facilities of these groups, including product, service, and administrative areas.	1	2	3	3	4	4	5	5
New Service Offerings: Stays abreast of industry trends and recommends new best practices and services for PM Solutions Team to focus on; participates in development and positioning of new services.	3	3	3	3	4	4	5	5
Networking-Establishment: Establishes and maintains relationships with associates from the industry and community.	3	3	3	3	4	4	5	5
Networking-Execution: Actively works to build reputation of PM Solutions Team and self.	4	4	4	4	5	5	5	5
Achieving Client Satisfaction-Understanding: Demonstrates understanding of client's business and seeks ways to give client a competitive advantage.	2	2	3	3	4	4	5	5

TABLE 6.5 (continued) PM Solutions Team Career Competencies

	Minimum Expectation to Enter the Job Classification							
PM Solutions Team Career Competencies / Matrix Project Management Career Path	Business Analyst I / Proj. Coordinator	Business Analyst II / Planner I	Sr. Project Analyst / Planner II	Proj. Controller	Project Manager / Proj. Team Leader	Program Manager / Sr. Project Manager	Mentor	Account Manager / Product Integration Manager
Technical Knowledge Core Skills								
Quality of Work-Methodology: Conducts work using appropriate methodology.	3	3	3	3	4	5	5	5
Business Development: Understands the full range of PM Solutions Team's capabilities and applies them to customer's need. Recognizes and explores opportunities, converting them into revenue-generating engagements. This includes the ability to investigate and define customer needs and requirements, and to develop solutions in conjunction with sales personnel.	1	2	2	3	4	4	5	5
Integration Management: Develops a project plan using historical information, organization policies, and a methodology that clearly guides the project's execution and control. The project plan documents assumptions, risks, communication and quality requirements, change process, and provides a baseline for which progress can be measured.	1	2	3	4	4	4	5	5

Competency	1	2	3	4	4	4	5	5
Integration Management: Formally manages change to the project. Changes are identified, investigated, and evaluated. Implementation recommendations are presented for approval from the proper project stakeholders. Documentation is thorough whether changes are implemented or not. All approved changes are reflected throughout the project plan.	1	2	3	4	4	4	5	5
Scope Management-Project Planning: Develops a project plan through consistent planning processes. The scope of the project should include scheduling, cost, quality, resources, procurement and communications in the project and the risks that may impact them.	1	3	4	4	4	4	5	5
Scope Management-Project Implementation: Executes a project plan by performing the planned activities and thorough documentation throughout the project life cycle.	1	3	4	4	4	4	5	5
Scope Management-Project Definition: Manages the project definition from writing of a Statement of Work to signature by the Customer and PM Solutions Team.	1	3	4	3	4	4	5	5
Scheduling Management: Demonstrates an ability to manage projects through consistent processes to ensure their timely completion. This includes: identifying the specific activities that must be performed to produce the various project deliverables, sequencing and identifying dependencies between activities, determining fixed and resource-driven activity durations with resource work estimates, developing a realistic schedule with client acceptance, and controlling changes to the schedule through formal processes.	1	3	4	4	4	4	5	5

TABLE 6.5 (continued)   PM Solutions Team Career Competencies

PM Solutions Team Career Competencies Matrix Project Management Career Path	Business Analyst I Proj. Coordinator	Business Analyst II Planner I	Sr. Project Analyst Planner II	Proj. Controller	Project Manager Proj. Team Leader	Program Manager Sr. Project Manager	Mentor	Account Manager Product Integration Manager
			Minimum Expectation to Enter the Job Classification					
Cost Management-Financial Monitoring: Demonstrates the ability to monitor project cost and report variations from budget to management for corrective action. Ensure customer invoices are correct and generated in a timely manner.	2	3	3	4	4	4	5	5
Cost Management-Budgeting: Develops an estimated project budget from resource work estimates; allocate the overall budget to individual activities.	1	2	3	4	4	4	5	5
Cost Management-Fee Management: Demonstrates an understanding of the various types of fees and financial arrangements and the ability to apply each; understands and is responsible for the profitability of the project. Some internal concepts to be understood are NTS Plus, Direct-billing for PM Solutions Services, Third party payment, Cross Charges, Resource Sharing, General Ledger Adjustments, Revenue Sharing, Leasing, Maintenance contracts, NFSO internal rate structures.	1	2	3	4	4	4	5	5

Risk Management: Demonstrates an ability to identify, analyze, and respond to project risk through formal and consistent processes. This includes: analyzing which risks are likely to affect the project and documenting their characteristics; evaluating risks and risk interactions to assess the range of possible project outcomes; developing risk mitigation activities to keep the project on course; and controlling changes risk over the life of the project.	1	3	4	4	4	4	5	5
Procurement Management-Products and Services Procurement: Identifying what to procure and when; documenting vendor, product/service and vendor-relationship requirements and critical success factors; negotiating the vendor contract, including resolution of any open issues; understanding both client and PM Solutions Team acquisition processes, requirements and restrictions; defining and implementing contract close-out; and engaging the right PM Solutions Team organizations as appropriate or required.	1	2	3	4	4	4	5	5
Procurement Management-Vendor Relationships: Identifying prospective suppliers, obtaining quotes, bids or proposals as appropriate; evaluating and selecting vendors based on defined success criteria; managing vendor relationships; administering the vendor contract including open issue escalation as needed.	1	2	3	4	4	4	5	5
Use of Software Tools: For their particular job level, is proficient in all applications (i.e., Word, Excel, Access, Microsoft Project, Mapping S/W, Quick Locate, Visio.) Demonstrates ability to create and modify project tools, such as forms, templates, schedules, databases, reports, etc.	1	3	4	4	4	4	5	5

TABLE 6.5 (continued) PM Solutions Team Career Competencies

PM Solutions Team Career Competencies / Matrix Project Management Career Path	Minimum Expectation to Enter the Job Classification							
	Business Analyst I / Proj. Coordinator	Business Analyst II / Planner I	Sr. Project Analyst / Planner II	Proj. Controller	Project Manager / Proj. Team Leader	Program Manager / Sr. Project Manager	Mentor	Account Manager / Product Integration Manager
Understanding of Current Technology: Demonstrates a general understanding of current technology in order to clearly follow the work of the project team.	2	3	3	4	4	4	5	5
Awareness of Technology Trends: Demonstrates an understanding of the trends driving change in the industry; effectively communicates trends with emerging technologies to clients; helps to position PM Solutions Team to capitalize on new technologies.	1	2	3	3	4	4	5	5
Understanding of Project Process and Tools: Demonstrates an understanding of project processes for planning, controlling, and closing projects and the tools associated with each process. Planner II and above should educate and mentor in this area.	2	3	4	4	4	4	5	5
PMI's PMP® Certification-Bachelor's Degree Track: Is working toward, has attained, or is maintaining project management professional certification.	1500 HRS EXP	3000 HRS EXP	4500 HRS EXP	PMP Taking Test	Certified PMP	Certified PMP	Certified PMP	Certified PMP
PMI's PMP Certification-Non-Bachelor's Degree Track: Is working toward, has attained, or is maintaining project management professional certification.	1500 HRS EXP	3500 HRS EXP	5500 HRS EXP	7500 HRS EXP	PMP Taking Test	Certified PMP	Certified PMP	Certified PMP

	1 Classes	1-4 Classes	Associate Certificate	MC	MC	MC	MC	MC
PM College Master's Certificate of Project Management: Is working towards, has attained, or is supplementing a Master's Certificate in project management.								
Communication Skills								
Writing-Effectiveness: Expresses ideas and summarizes findings and recommendations in a concise and easily understood manner.	2	3	4	4	4	4	5	5
Writing-Protocol: Displays understanding of the proper protocol for written communication (e.g. client v. internal correspondence).	2	3	4	4	4	4	5	5
Speaking-Clarity/Authority/Command of Subject Matter: Articulates ideas with conciseness, clarity, authority and confidence.	2	3	4	4	4	4	5	5
Speaking-Conveys Technical Information Effectively: Demonstrates ability to translate technical information into a business and project context and vice versa.	1	2	3	4	4	4	5	5
Listening: Listens to others and works effectively to understand all project stakeholders' perspectives. Works much more strongly "to understand" than "to be understood."	2	2	3	4	4	5	5	5
Interviewing: Prepares comprehensive project stakeholder interview plans; asks probing questions which promote comments; interprets responses accurately and records results of the interview.	1	2	3	4	4	4	5	5
Conducting Meetings-Preparation: Prepares and communicates an agenda and objectives (prior to meetings).	2	3	4	4	4	4	5	5

TABLE 6.5 (continued)   PM Solutions Team Career Competencies

PM Solutions Team Career Competencies Matrix Project Management Career Path	Minimum Expectation to Enter the Job Classification							
	Business Analyst I Proj. Coordinator	Business Analyst II Planner I	St. Project Analyst Planner II	Proj. Controller	Project Manager Proj. Team Leader	Program Manager Sr. Project Manager	Mentor	Account Manager Product Integration Manager
Conducting Meetings-Execution: Keeps meeting within scheduled timeframe; resolves issues and achieves defined objectives.	2	3	4	4	4	4	5	5
Conducting or Attending Meetings-Follow-up: Ensures that all participants are clear about decisions made, and provides comprehensive minutes and action item documents.	2	2	3	4	4	5	5	5
Preparing Reports, Proposals and Presentations: Writes client proposals, reports, manuals, and presentations, ensuring that the document is technically accurate, organized appropriately, uniform in terms of style, and communicates accurately and clearly.	2	3	3	4	4	4	5	5
Delivering Presentations: Plans, organizes, and delivers appropriate, formal oral presentations relating to client work and internal PM Solutions Team matters.	2	3	3	4	4	4	5	5
Group Facilitation: Leads small group meetings or discussions so that the objective of the meeting is clearly accomplished.	2	3	4	4	4	4	5	5

Administration and Logistics: Updates databases regularly; completes timesheets and expense forms in a timely manner; responds to e-mail and v-mail in appropriate timeframes.	3	3	3	4	4	4	5	5
Use of Software Applications: Is proficient in all applications required for his or her particular job level.	3	3	3	4	4	5	5	5
Managing Client Relationships-Building: Ensures that the client has an accurate understanding of the project and project status.	2	2	3	4	4	4	5	5
Managing Client Relationships-Communicating: Identifies client needs and communicates them to all team members.	2	2	3	4	4	4	5	5
Managing Client Relationships-Maintaining: Maintains ongoing relationship with key client contacts.	2	2	3	4	4	4	5	5
Interaction with Client Team: Maintains excellent (internal to PM Solutions Team) communications about client with the Account Manager and management.	4	4	4	5	5	5	5	5
Achieving Client Satisfaction-Communicating: Prepares thoroughly for client meetings.	2	3	3	3	4	4	5	5
Communications Management-Communications Planning: Determining the information and communications needs of the project stakeholders.	1	3	4	4	4	4	5	5
Communications Management-Information Distribution: Making needed information available to project stakeholders in a timely manner.	2	3	4	4	4	4	5	5
Communications Management-Performance Reporting: Collecting and disseminating performance information (e.g., status reports, progress measurement, and forecasting).	2	3	4	4	4	4	5	5

TABLE 6.5 (continued)   PM Solutions Team Career Competencies

PM Solutions Team Career Competencies Matrix Project Management Career Path	Minimum Expectation to Enter the Job Classification							
	Business Analyst I / Proj. Coordinator	Business Analyst II / Planner I	Sr. Project Analyst / Planner II	Proj. Controller	Project Manager / Proj. Team Leader	Program Manager / Sr. Project Manager	Mentor	Account Manager / Product Integration Manager
Communications Management-Administrative Closure: Generating, gathering and disseminating information to formalize review/completion of phases or project completion.	2	3	4	4	4	4	5	5
Analytical Skills								
Problem Solving-Approach: Deals confidently with complex problems, distinguishing the essential from the nonessential.	1	2	3	3	4	4	5	5
Problem Solving-Resolution: Defines problems precisely; identifies multiple solution options and recommends solution with the greatest potential for success.	1	2	3	3	4	4	5	5
Analysis: Understands the phases of implementing a PM Project Office in order to accurately articulate the needed processes for proposed project solutions.	2	3	4	4	5	5	5	5
Design: Understands the Design phases of the Project Office in order to successfully design and implement the processes of the proposed project solution.	2	3	4	4	5	5	5	5

	1	2	3	4	4	5	5
Cost Management-Financial Responsibility: Demonstrates an ability to complete projects within approved budgets through consistent processes. That includes determining which resources, equipment, and materials at what quantities each should be used to complete project activities.	1	2	3	4	4	5	5
Problem Solving/Decision Making							
Judgement-Decision Making: Arrives at appropriate decisions given the available level of information and circumstances.	3	3	3	4	5	5	5
Integration Management: Executes the project plan by directing the project team, measuring and evaluating performance, resolving issues, and controlling changes. Coordination and documentation of activities is performed on a regular cycle.	1	2	2	3	4	5	5
Scope Management-Project Coordination: Demonstrates the ability to coordinate the various elements of a project including scheduling, cost, quality, resources, procurement and communications.	2	3	3	4	4	5	5
Quality Management: Understands and demonstrates an ability to ensure that the project will satisfy the client's needs for which it was undertaken. This includes: identifying which client requirements are relevant to the project and determining how to satisfy them, evaluating overall project performance on an regular basis through formal project status reviews to provide confidence that the project will satisfy the customer requirements, monitoring specific project results, and identifying and implementing processes to eliminate any causes of unsatisfactory performance.	1	2	3	4	4	5	5

TABLE 6.5 (continued) PM Solutions Team Career Competencies

Minimum Expectation to Enter the Job Classification

PM Solutions Team Career Competencies Matrix Project Management Career Path	Business Analyst I Proj. Coordinator	Business Analyst II Planner I	Sr. Project Analyst Planner II	Proj. Controller	Project Manager Proj. Team Leader	Program Manager Sr. Project Manager	Mentor	Account Manager Product Integration Manager
Change Management-Identify: Demonstrates an ability to recognize and identify events constituting a change in scope; clearly communicates the nature of the change.	2	3	4	4	4	4	5	5
Change Management-Execute: Evaluates the impact of the change upon the project, PMI, and the customer; and executes a sound change management process, including the negotiation of scope and fee modifications.	1	2	3	4	4	4	5	5
Deliverables Management: Ensures project specifications, budget and time constraints have been met and customer satisfaction has been met or exceeded via appropriate project status reviews and/or closure.	1	2	3	4	4	4	5	5
Best Practices: Consistently utilizes best practices, and contributes to their evolution.	2	3	3	4	4	4	5	5
Innovator: Demonstrates the ability to visualize the end results, risks associated with a project, and develops the most appropriate processes and tools for a successful project execution.	1	2	3	3	4	4	5	5

Integrator: Demonstrates the ability to see the "big picture" of projects and the way they fit into the overall plan for the client's organization. Demonstrates the ability to coordinate and communicate multiple project efforts inside and outside the project organization.	1	2	3	3	4	4	5	5
Communicator: Demonstrates the ability to decipher and send the appropriate project information to the appropriate project audience in a form that is understandable.	2	3	3	4	4	4	5	5
Decision Maker: Demonstrates the ability to make key decisions for different projects at different times in their life cycle. Key decisions might include the allocation of resources, the costs of performance and schedule tradeoffs, and changing the scope.	1	2	2	3	3	4	5	5
Results Orientation								
Initiative-Self-starter: Persistently follows through till completion.	2	2	2	3	3	4	5	5
Creativity: Demonstrates imagination; has the ability to conceptualize and to "think on feet."	2	2	2	3	3	4	5	5
Quality of Work-Deliverables: Delivers high quality work products; pays attention to details of deliverable (e.g., proofreads, double-checks, performs QA).	3	3	4	4	4	5	5	5
Quality of Work-Personal Pride: Takes pride in the results of his or her work.	4	4	4	4	5	5	5	5
Timeliness of Work-Effective Work Prioritization: Balances assignments effectively.	2	2	2	3	3	4	5	5

TABLE 6.5 (continued)   PM Solutions Team Career Competencies

PM Solutions Team Career Competencies / Matrix Project Management Career Path	Business Analyst I / Proj. Coordinator	Business Analyst II / Planner I	Sr. Project Analyst / Planner II	Proj. Controller	Project Manager / Proj. Team Leader	Program Manager / Sr. Project Manager	Mentor	Account Manager / Product Integration Manager
				Minimum Expectation to Enter the Job Classification				
Productivity-Effectiveness/Efficiency: Works effectively and efficiently and completes tasks within the defined guidelines/parameters and budget.	2	2	2	3	3	4	5	5
Capacity for Work: Exhibits the stamina to persevere and is a hard worker.	3	3	4	4	4	5	5	5
Achieving Client Satisfaction-Responding: Deals promptly with customer requests.	2	3	3	3	4	4	5	5
Achieving Client Satisfaction-Excelling: Exceeds client expectations.	2	3	3	3	4	4	5	5
Cost Management-Control: Manages the overall project budget against actual results. This includes managing any project reserve budgets, and controlling changes to the project budget through formal processes.	1	1	2	3	4	4	5	5
Self-Management Skills								
Motivation: Maintains an enthusiastic, positive attitude and strong commitment to quality toward all assigned projects and tasks.	3	3	3	4	4	5	5	5

Professionalism: Demonstrates reliability, confidence, integrity, loyalty and a professional appearance.	3	3	3	4	4	5	5	5
Judgment-Confidentiality/accountability: Appropriately guards confidentiality of communication, assumes accountability and possesses accurate sense of personal capabilities.	3	3	3	4	4	5	5	5
Timeliness of Work-Effective Time Management: Effectively uses time management skills and executes tasks within the defined work schedule. Keeps management informed of status of work.	3	3	4	4	5	5	5	5
Productivity: Manages personal utilization: Seeks out additional productive work when personal utilization is below target.	2	2	3	3	4	4	5	5
Response to Pressure: Effectively manages competing priorities and demands.	2	3	3	4	5	5	5	5
Interpersonal Skills								
Teamwork-Flexibility/Objectivity: Exhibits flexibility and objectivity in working with others to meet common objectives; shares information with peers; maintains a positive attitude toward organizational goals. Demonstrates a willingness to change and adapt as conditions and the needs of the team change.	3	3	4	4	5	5	5	5
Interpersonal Skills: Works well with others: Displays cooperative, supportive, sensitive attitude and creates rapport with co-workers and clients.	3	3	4	5	5	5	5	5
Interpersonal Skills-Flexibility: Adjusts to the situation and works with others to meet common objectives.	3	3	4	4	5	5	5	5

TABLE 6.5 (continued)   PM Solutions Team Career Competencies

PM Solutions Team Career Competencies Matrix Project Management Career Path	Minimum Expectation to Enter the Job Classification							
	Business Analyst I Proj. Coordinator	Business Analyst II Planner I	Sr. Project Analyst Planner II	Proj. Controller	Project Manager Proj. Team Leader	Program Manager Sr. Project Manager	Mentor	Account Manager Product Integration Manager
Interpersonal Skills-Receptivity: Is receptive and open to new suggestions and ideas.	3	3	4	4	5	5	5	5
Human Resource Management-Teamwork: Demonstrates the ability to work in a team environment to make the most effective use of the people involved with the project. Work and play well together.	2	3	4	4	5	5	5	5
Leadership								
Leadership-Character: Demonstrates confidence, caring, resourcefulness, integrity, endurance, maturity, openness, inclusiveness, rigor, discipline and a sense of humor in dealings with clients and other PM team members.	2	3	3	4	4	4	5	5
Leadership-Style: Demonstrates ability to adapt leadership styles according to project environment. Adept at persuasive, collaborative, and consensus styles of leadership. Comfortable in working with little, no, or unclear authority.	2	2	2	3	3	4	5	5
Leadership-Stakeholders: Develops ongoing relationships with key stakeholders in other parts of the organization.	2	3	3	4	4	4	5	5

Teamwork: Contributes to team behavior: Voluntarily assists others to obtain results. Provides positive and constructive, humane, substantive feedback to project team members.	3	3	3	4	4	5	5	5
Staff Management-Strategy: Cultivates the motivation of team members. Promotes an environment of teamwork and accomplishing work through others.	1	2	3	3	4	4	5	5
Staff Management-Executing: Issues clear and realistic instructions and facilitates resolution of conflict among team members. At the E05 level and above, manages high sustainable PRODUCTIVITY by project teams, while ensuring the health of the project team.	1	2	3	4	4	4	5	5
Mentoring-Execution: Assists, encourages, teaches, explains and leads others. Continuously sets a positive example for others to follow.	1	2	3	3	4	4	5	5
Providing Leadership: Is assertive and does not defer to the client for leadership in the engagement. Provides leadership to the client that is appropriate for the circumstances.	1	2	3	4	4	5	5	5
Difficult client situations-ability to be successful in highly politicized client situations. Demonstrates the skill to bring project stakeholders together and either resolve politically generated problems or identify (to the satisfaction of the client) that what is being asked is not part of the PM engagement. As a project management professional: proactively aware and sensitive to the client's organizational structure, political climate and personalities as well as the client's objectives. Responds to these dynamics while maintaining the integrity of the Statement of Work/Project Plan.	1	2	2	3	4	5	5	5

TABLE 6.5 (continued) PM Solutions Team Career Competencies

PM Solutions Team Career Competencies / Matrix Project Management Career Path	Minimum Expectation to Enter the Job Classification							
	Business Analyst I / Proj. Coordinator	Business Analyst II / Planner I	Sr. Project Analyst / Planner II	Proj. Controller	Project Manager / Proj. Team Leader	Program Manager / Sr. Project Manager	Mentor	Account Manager / Product Integration Manager
Networking-Expansion: Assumes leadership role in professional and community organizations.	2	2	3	3	4	4	5	5
Leader and Motivator: Demonstrates the ability to solve conflicts as they arise, guide people from different backgrounds to the project's end result while motivating participants not directly under his or her authority.	2	2	3	3	4	4	5	5
Climate Creator: Demonstrates the ability to create an environment early in the project life cycle that has a supportive atmosphere where the client and project team members can work together and not against each other. That supportive environment helps to prevent misunderstandings and conflicts.	1	2	2	3	4	4	5	5
People (Personnel) Development Skills								
Teamwork-Contributes to Team Behavior: Voluntarily assists others to obtain results. Provides positive and constructive, humane, substantive feedback to project team members.	1	1	2	3	4	4	5	5

	1	2	3	4	4	5	5	5
Staff Management-Cross-Functional Teams: Demonstrates the know-how to assist the team establish a mission and set goals and objectives. Helps cross-functional team members balance their responsibilities to the team and their functional departments.	1	2	3	4	5	5	5	5
Staff Management-Nurturing: Provides constructive and positive feedback and encourages and requires autonomy, team behaviors, ownership, and responsibility in all staff members. Protects team from undue and counterproductive interference.	1	2	3	3	4	4	5	5
Mentoring-Growth: Perceived as a trusted counselor/guide helping peers and less senior members enhance their skills.	1	2	3	3	4	4	5	5
Staff Development-Staffing: Structures staff assignments to provide challenge and professional growth.	1	1	2	3	4	4	5	5
Staff Development-Nurturing: Motivates staff to achieve full potential and counsels staff on career progress and development. Provides well-structured feedback to project team member's functional management.	1	2	2	3	4	4	5	5
Staff Development-Recruitment: Participates actively in recruitment process.	1	2	2	3	3	4	5	5
Human Resource Management-Personnel Management: Develops and implements the staffing plan for a project conforming to all PM Solutions Team HR guidelines. This includes hiring, transferring, third party resources, and resource sharing from other PM Solutions Team locations to staff the project as appropriate. Also included is the use of the PM Solutions Team Employee retention procedure throughout the life of the project.	1	2	3	4	4	5	5	5

TABLE 6.5 (continued) PM Solutions Team Career Competencies

PM Solutions Team Career Competencies Matrix Project Management Career Path	Minimum Expectation to Enter the Job Classification							
	Business Analyst I Proj. Coordinator	Business Analyst II Planner I	Sr. Project Analyst Planner II	Proj. Controller	Project Manager Proj. Team Leader	Program Manager Sr. Project Manager	Mentor	Account Manager Product Integration Manager
Human Resources Management-Project Planning and Implementation: Identifying, documenting, and assigning roles and responsibilities with reporting relationships; getting the right people assigned to and working on the project; developing individual and group skills to enhance project performance.	1	2	2	3	4	4	5	5
Human Resource Management-Cross-Function Teams: Experienced in managing group process issues, facilitating team member participation, conflict resolution, consensus building, and providing performance reviews to the management of other PM Solutions Team staff contributing to the project.	1	2	3	4	4	5	5	5
Experience and Certifications								
Years of Industry Experience: Has the required number of years experience in the industry. These are just guidelines and not hard and fast timeframes that must be met.	0–2 Years	2–4 Years	3–5 Years	4–6 Years	6–8 Years	8–10 Years	10+ Years	10+ Years

Education (D = Desired, R = Recommended)							
Associate's Degree: Is working toward or has attained an Associate's Degree in an industry related subject.	D	R	R				
Bachelor's Degree: Is working toward or has attained a Bachelor's Degree in an industry-related subject or management program.		D	D	R	R	R	R
Master's Degree: Is working toward or has attained a Master's Degree in Business Administration or Project Management.		D	D	D	R	R	R
Continuing Education Points/Year: Has attended seminars, workshops, and events to accumulate the minimum number of continuing education points per year.				25	24	25	25

Mentoring and Coaching

Mentoring is the best source to better understand work standards and behaviors that fit the company culture. Effective mentoring involves a relationship with a respected executive-level person to gain their evaluation of your professional and personal goals, their insight into the development of action plans, and their experience on how to develop relationships or handle specific situations.

"A mentor can teach you what you won't learn in college: the ropes," said Sheila Wellington, president of Catalyst, the research and advisory organization that works to advance women in business. "Getting the inside track on the people and politics of your office can take years to master on your own. Mentors clue you in, open doors, and "talk you up" with senior management." When all things are equal, it is the guidance, feedback, and visibility that come from having a mentor that may make the difference between a career that languishes in the mid-management pipeline and one that reaches its full potential — for men as well as women — according to Catalyst.[34]

Because it so important, why leave mentoring to chance? Rather than relying on executives and project personnel to find each other and form mentoring relationships privately, the company should set up a program to train mentors and pair them with developing employees. Mentoring is a perfect match for project management development. For project managers, mentoring — whether or not we called it that — has always played an important role in professional development. As members of "the accidental profession," project managers more often than not learned how to manage projects by managing projects, and by observing other project managers in action. And mentoring still remains "the most effective way to bring new project managers up to speed quickly."[35]

Frank Toney, Ph.D., of the Executive Initiative Institute, identifies mentoring as both a skill the project managers should master for success and as one of the few reliable routes to competence in the project-based workplace. Lynn Crawford, of the University of Technology at Sydney (Australia), a leading project management thinker who was instrumental in developing Australia's government-mandated competency measurement system for project managers, recommends mentoring and other social learning modes (such as communities of practice) as important learning tools for project management.[36]

Who Should Be Mentored?

According to the *Mentoring Guide*, good candidates include:

- First-time project and program managers
- Newer project managers who have had basic project management training
- Technical staff making the transition to management
- Project managers working with a new project management process
- Project managers moving into a program manager role

The mentee's role is simple: to be open to learning and growing professionally.[37]

The role of the mentor includes facilitating that growth by providing information, guidance and constructive comments, and evaluating mentee's plans and decisions. The mentor supports and encourages and, when necessary, highlights shortfalls in agreed performance. Also important to the mentoring relationship — often referred to as a partnership — is confidentiality.

Mentors must be willing to give freely of their time. In addition, they must have the necessary skills and appropriate knowledge to be perceived as valuable to a protégé, and they must be able to share what they know effectively with the protégé. That is why good communication skills are critical.[38]

Mentee and mentor pairs should be encouraged to draw up a mentoring agreement to help clarify their respective roles and expectations. The agreement, while not binding, determines the framework of the relationship. Although mentoring relationships thrive on commitment, it is wise to acknowledge that not all partnerships work out. Thus, most mentoring experts recommend that the program have a specific process and criteria set up to allow for no-fault dissolution of the partnership. (See Table 6.6, "Best Practices in Project Management Mentoring," for more ideas on setting up mentoring programs.)

Beyond mentoring, professional coaching combines self-focused personal value measurements, personality-type testing, and style-preference identification with feedback on personal and professional behaviors from a broad group of people. The professional coach is most likely educated in a behavioral field, such as psychology, and combines education training with years of experience working with other clients to provide extremely valuable insight. Their counsel will help leverage strengths and eliminate behaviors that might derail success. Professional coaches are an expensive benefit to provide but demonstrate a strong commitment to developing talent on the part of the organization.[39]

The PM Solutions professional development plan provides for coaching by a more-experienced project manager. Appendix I shows the Coaching Guidelines we have developed.

TABLE 6.6   Best Practices in Project Management Mentoring

Seven rules for establishing an effective mentoring program: clear program goals; voluntary participation; limited duration; strong upper-management support; specific objectives for each partnership; regularly scheduled meetings between mentors and protégés; and an evaluation system to rescue partnerships that may be in trouble. (Kathryn Tyler, Mentoring programs link employees and experienced execs, *HR Magazine*, April 1998.)

Ten steps to being a master mentor: be willing to reveal your own challenges and frustrations to your protégé; remove the mask of position as you demonstrate enthusiasm for the learning; display enthusiastic curiosity — learning, like planting, requires warmth; avoid "why" questions — they can be heard as judgment and create defensiveness; ask questions that make your protégé think — questions that ask for comparison, evaluation, and reflection; listen as if your protégé was a "hero" you always wanted to meet and interview; do not rely on power symbols — an imposing desk, making the protégé do the approaching, or a reserved manner — all of which telegraph distance; support without rescuing — before your help, ask if your help will build greater competence or just more dependence; protégés watch your moves, not your mouth — be a courageous role model. Learning requires humility, curiosity, and risk taking. Let your protégé see these qualities in you. (Chip R. Bell, Mentoring: a key to employee loyalty, *PM Network*, November 1999.)

Four stages in the development of mentoring relationships. Stage 1: The mentor and recipient become acquainted and informally clarify their common interests, shared values, and professional goals. Stage 2: The mentor and recipient communicate initial expectations and agree upon some common procedures and expectations as a starting point. In the very few cases where a major disparity is found to exist between the needs and expectations of the two individuals — and where neither party can accommodate to the other — the pair is able to part company on a friendly basis before the actual mentoring and inevitable frustration begins. Stage 3: Gradually, needs are fulfilled. Objectives are met. Professional growth takes place. New challenges are presented and achieved. This stage may last for months or years. Stage 4: The mentor and recipient redefine their relationship as colleagues, peers, partners, or friends. (Rita Peterson, *Mentor Teacher Handbook*, 1989.)

While most mentoring programs are aimed at new employees, Office Depot and AIG team established employees with mentors so they can pick up extra skills. AIG has taken an "extreme team approach" throughout the company, where project leaders serve as mentors. During performance reviews, mentoring performance is included in project leaders' evaluations. (Mentoring speeds the learning curve, *Information-week*, April 9, 2001.)

When introducing mentoring, do not imply that managers are being replaced or to allow managers and supervisors to abdicate their responsibilities in developing their employees, even when the individuals are also benefiting from a mentor's guidance. Managers may be mentors to individuals who do not report to them, but still must be involved in coaching and developing employees about performance on the job. (Peggy Simonsen, *Promoting a Development Culture in Your Organization*, Davies-Black Publishing, 1997.)

TABLE 6.6 (continued)   Best Practices in Project Management Mentoring

At DuPont, managers and executives maintain formal arrangements with staff members outside their supervision to discuss work-related issues at least once a month. Protégés choose from a list of volunteer mentors whose skills and experience the protégés seek to tap in their quest to climb the corporate ladder. (Frank Jossi, Mentoring in changing times, *Training*, August 1997.)

Successful organizations expand their definition of mentoring beyond the traditional one-to-one, to include the concept of group mentoring. In group mentoring, four to eight carefully selected learners who share a common purpose or goal are both mentees as well as mentors to each other. The group is guided by a senior mentor who offers insights, shares personal experiences, and provides guidance, but does not run the group. The group runs the group. (Linda Allan, Mentoring: the need to move to newer models, *Canadian HR Reporter,* March 1999.)

In the early phases of the mentoring program at Hewlett- Packard, the project manager assigned mentees based on experience and skill assessments, without looking at personality. This did not always work. Now they have matching receptions where everybody can meet face-to-face before requesting a mentor, to learn each other's personalities. That is working out better. (Kathryn Tyler, Mentoring programs link employees and experienced execs, *HR Magazine,* April 1998.)

In excellent mentoring, the types of questions that the project manager asks of the mentor are similar to these:

Is there a better way to _____ ?

What should I watch out for if I _____ ?

Is this a good way to _____ ?

How do others _____ ?

Excellent mentors often reply with explanatory answers or with questions that help the project manager see the situation more clearly, such as:

Have you considered _____ ?

Do you know how to _____ ?
What are your choices _____ ?
What do you think will happen if you _____ ?
What have you done in the past _____ ?

(Diana Mekelburg, Excellent PM mentoring, *People on Projects,* June 2001.)

Personal Development Plans

We have said a lot about the organization's role and responsibility in creating professional development plans. But professional growth is also personal growth — a commitment to self-improvement. People who continuously seek feedback, work on their listening skills, polish communication skills, build relationships, and demonstrate control of their personal lives will rise above their peers. Yet many individuals rather passively accept (or grumble about) whatever growth programs are on offer by the organization.

Instead, individuals should be encouraged to construct a personal development plan. The essence of this plan is to know oneself and the environment, build a road map to adapt and grow, and take personal ownership for change. An effective plan will help a person understand the culture within their current business environment, increase the velocity and effectiveness of their actions, and supply power to sustain performance. Constructing a personal development plan requires openness to feedback, maturity to change behaviors, and willingness to practice new techniques.

Personal growth comes through self-evaluation and appraisal against personal standards, role models, group norms, peer behavior, and corporate or team culture. Input to the plan comes from both personal evaluation and relational sources, including supervisors, peers, clients, mentors, and friends. Reading is another critical resource for gaining new insights. Experiential education — conferences, seminars, and the like — are also an important source for personal and emotional growth.[40]

Notes

1. Jolyon Hallows, *Information Systems Project Management*, AMACOM, 1998.
2. Christopher Sauer, Li Liu, and Kim Johnston, Where project managers are kings, *Project Management Journal*, December 2001.
3. M. Beer et al., *Managing Human Assets, The Groundbreaking Harvard Business School Program*, The Free Press, 1984.
4. Deborah Bigelow and Jim Oswald, An effective career development program, *Best Practices Report*, August 2001.
5. M. Freeman and R. Gould, The Art of Project Management: A Competency Model For Project Managers, white paper accessed June 2004 at www.BUTrain. com.
6. J. Rodney Turner, Anne Keegan, and Lynn Crawford, Learning by experience in the project-based organization, *Proceedings of PMI Research Conference*, PMI, 2000.
7. Robert J. Graham and Randall L. Englund, *Creating an Environment for Successful Projects*, Jossey-Bass, 1997.
8. James J. Schneidmuller, Creating a professional project management organization, in Joan Knutson, Ed., *Project Management for Business Professionals*, Wiley, 2001.
9. Neal Whitten, *The EnterPrize Organization*, PMI, 2000.
10. Frank Toney and Ray Powers, *Best Practices of Project Management Groups in Large Functional Organizations*, PMI, 1997.

11. Jeannette Cabanis-Brewin, IBM forges a path for project managers, *Best Practice Report*, August 2001.
12. Deborah Bigelow and Jim Oswald, An effective career development program, *Best Practices Report*, August 2001.
13. Marcus Buckingham, *Now, Discover Your Strengths*, FreePress, 2001.
14. Jimmie West, Professional development: do I need it?, *Best Practices Report*, August 2001.
15. Carroll Lachnit, Training proves its worth, *Workforce*, September 2001.
16. Tyya Turner, TeleCom 101: training employees for 21st-Century service, *Tele.com*, March 22, 1999.
17. Dennis Smith, Making training pay: a trainer's perspective, *Best Practices Report*, August 2002.
18. Dennis Smith, Making training pay: a trainer's perspective, *Best Practices Report*, August 2002.
19. Joe Cothrel, Karina Funk, and Crystal Schaffer, Learning to Innovate, accessed June 2004 at www.Participate.com.
20. Center for Business Practices, *The Value of Project Management Training: A Benchmark of Current Business Practices*, CBP, 2003.
21. Ben Worthen, Measuring the ROI of training, *CIO Magazine*, February 15, 2001.
22. Karen R.J. White, Maximizing training effectiveness, *Best Practices Report*, August 2002.
23. Jack Phillips et al., *Human Resources Scorecard*, Butterworth-Heinemann, 2001.
24. Jeannette Cabanis-Brewin, Training ROI: A Red Herring? Interview with Jimmie West, Ph.D., *Best Practices Report*, August 2002.
25. Robert W. Rowden, Exploring methods to evaluate the return from training, *American Business Review*, January 2001.
26. Shlomo Globerson and Ofer Zwikael, The impact of the project manager on project management planning processes, *Project Management Journal*, September 2002.
27. Jimmie West, A Manager's Guide to Developing a Project Management Training Program, white paper, posted at http://www.pmsolutions.com/articles/index.htm.
28. Dennis Smith, Making training pay: a trainer's perspective, *Best Practices Report*, August 2002.
29. Karen R.J. White, Maximizing training effectiveness, *Best Practices Report*, August 2002.
30. Shari Caudron, Breaking out of the learning box, *Workforce*, October 2000.
31. Ben Dean, Ph.D., Learning about Learning, *Authentic Happiness Coaching e-newsletter*, September 2004. Accessible at http://www.authentichappinesscoaching.com/newsletter/LearningAboutLearning.php.
32. Christopher Sauer, Li Liu, and Kim Johnston, Where project managers are kings, *Project Management Journal*, December 2001.
33. Martha Heller, Six tips for effective career development programs, *CIO*, June 15, 2004.

34. A college degree alone doesn't spell career success, *Business Wire*, May 22, 2002.
35. Jeannette Cabanis-Brewin, Mentoring: a core competency for project managers, *People On Projects,* June 2001.
36. Frank Toney, Ph.D., *The Superior Project Manager,* CBP/Marcel Dekker, 2001.
37. PM Solutions, *Mentoring Guide,* 1999.
38. Patricia Buhler, A new role for managers: the move from directing to coaching, *Supervision*, October 1998.
39. Mark Morgan, Career-building strategies: are your skills helping you the corporate ladder?, *Strategic Finance*, June 1, 2002.
40. Mark Morgan, ibid.

Chapter 7

Performance Management on Projects: More Carrot, Less Stick

Why measure individual performance?

From the company's point of view, it is the old saw that says "what gets measured gets managed." Prior to the knowledge economy, the concrete inputs and outputs of business functioned as a way to measure human performance. Workers used materials to create objects, thus measuring materials used and objects produced gave the business a way to calculate something about worker productivity. But as we move into the realm of the information economy, the productivity equation becomes more complicated. Knowledge workers — and, as noted previously, this label fits nearly everyone in the project management field — use primarily information and processes to add value to work products that are often abstract: an organizational change project, for example, or a new product rollout plan. Yet, more than ever, business needs to know "How are we doing?" — and in a knowledge-based organization, "people performance" is the central metric.

From the individual worker's point of view, it is human nature to want to know how other people perceive us. In the workplace, this very natural desire for feedback, direction, and praise also serves a critical business purpose. However, performance measurement, when done right, is not something that is "done to" employees — it is a supportive, encouraging, and liberating process that aids people in growing in their careers and increases job satisfaction. The act of measuring performance itself can be a performance enhancer when the employee feels the process is fair and consistent. Unfortunately, instead of capitalizing on what comes naturally to human beings, many performance measurement and review programs turn the process into a punitive, illogical, or empty exercise. This chapter discusses how performance management ties in with the competency identification and career-planning strategies discussed in the previous chapters. We also discuss why linking individual performance measures with overall organizational performance helps motivate everyone to do his or her best.

What Is Wrong with Performance Management?

Performance management — the process of establishing both employee objectives and metrics by which performance against those objectives can be measured — should provide a formal, structured way to discuss work performance, identify performance gaps, and rate performance. Career and development planning elements are logically linked with this process. The "pay-for-performance" trend also links compensation to performance goals, as opposed to traditional reward structures based on rank or seniority.

While many performance management approaches exist, none of them is the "silver bullet" to achieving outstanding performance. However, research does tell us that there are some performance measurement and appraisal systems that *do not* work very well. Unfortunately, these are the ones in common use. A recent survey by the human capital research and consulting firm Watson Wyatt underscores some of the principal problems with how we measure work performance. The study found that less than 30 percent of U.S. workers agree that their company's performance management program actually does what it is intended to do: improve performance. Even fewer workers — about 20 percent — say that their company helps poorly performing workers improve. The survey of 1190 workers found that only 61 percent of employees feel their performance appraisal was accurate; only 54 percent say employees with better reviews get better raises and bonuses, showing a clear linkage between performance measurement processes and rewards. And less than 40 percent say the system establishes clear performance goals and generates honest feedback.

These statistics led Watson Wyatt to conclude that performance management programs "represent a lost opportunity for most companies." In fact, according to their studies, if designed and implemented properly,

TABLE 7.1   Performance Management Problems

Managers say:
  The process is too complicated.
  There is too much complex paperwork.
  It takes too long.
  It is always [emotionally] difficult to conduct the meetings.
  The process is out of context with activity in the workplace.
Employees say:
  Skills/knowledge in using the performance management process are
    poor *(for both themselves and their manager)*.
  I have no control over or involvement in setting my performance
    objectives.
  Lack of collaboration in managing and assessing performance *(i.e., "my
    forms arrived in my 'in' tray for my signature")*.
  Why have an "excellent" box if no one is allowed in it?
  I do not really feel I get or can give honest feedback.
  It is biased and subjective, as in "My team leader gives an unfair review
    if he does not like me."
Managers focus on the wrong things:
  Rating performance rather than planning
  One-way flow of words rather than dialogue
  Forms rather than communication
  Maintaining current activities rather than aligning individual effort to
    team and organizational objectives to ensure delivery of organizational
    goals

Source: Adapted from Graeme Dobson, Better Practice in Performance
Management, http://www.users.bigpond.com/dobsong/My%20Work/Better%20
Practice%20in%20PM.doc.

performance management can have a strong, positive impact not only on individual performance, but also on financial results — up to a 20 percent improvement in shareholder value.[1]

Of course, if great performance management were simple, every business would be reaping its benefits. Every manager would look forward to performance meetings with positive anticipation. Employees would be enthusiastic for their chance to be involved in the process. Instead, many people underutilize or avoid a structured performance management process. Table 7.1 lists some of the problems that managers, employees, and HR researchers have identified with companies' present performance processes.

The old "command-and-control" approach to management made managing performance a matter of employees being told what to do, and then told whether or not they did it right, usually once a year at the performance appraisal. In the past, the term "performance management" has been used interchangeably with the term "performance appraisal" to describe a process that focused on making judgments on individuals and filling out forms. Recently, however, companies have begun to realize that this kind of approach to human performance is counterproductive. Far from being objective, performance appraisals have often been subjective, even random, snapshots that have had little to do with determining if individuals are moving organizational objectives forward, and even less to do with developing future talent. Thus, what should be a cooperative effort between manager and employee becomes an awkward, stressful process that both parties avoid, or a time-consuming paper chase. The bottom line is that companies make huge investments in hiring talent, yet spend little time actually evaluating it, defining it, and cultivating it.

When performance measurement forms and meetings function as an isolated "add-on" requirement, the measures used tend to be superficial and the whole process becomes an exercise in bureaucracy that neither supports improved resource allocation decisions nor ensures that individual priorities are aligned with organizational priorities. A better way to view performance management is to frame it not as a way to judge past actions and reward or punish them, but as a supportive tool for professional development. Analyzing performance from this point of view, we can recognize that performance measurement's role is to answer the following questions:

- What *should* or *could be* happening?
- What *is* happening?
- How can desired and actual performance be measured?
- What is the performance gap between *what is* and *what should be?*

Viewed in this light, the performance appraisal can be seen as a good method of bridging the gaps and taking action that impacts performance, either by asking employees to keep doing what they are doing, or to change their behaviors in specific ways. In addition, it supports good training and development investments by identifying the most pressing issues to resolve for individuals and teams.

Special Challenges to Performance Management on Projects

Some work products are more difficult than others to measure. Usually there are cues to this hard-to-measure quality in the language we use to talk about the work: what, exactly, is an "elegant" engineering design, an "innovative" marketing plan, or "rapid" software development? Even so-called objective measures in cases like these are based on subjective judgments. But just because work is difficult to measure does not mean it cannot be measured — although workers whose output is difficult to measure may have a good deal of resistance to the implementation of a performance metrics program. Performance management expert Jack Zigon has identified several common sources of resistance:

- *"My job is creative"* (and therefore cannot be measured).
- *"I do not make standard widgets"* (so I cannot be measured).
- *"I am a professional"* (so I cannot be measured).
- *"I do not want to be measured"* (because I do not want you to realize I have not been doing my job very well lately, and I do not want to change my habits).[2]

All these are summed up in the attitude that project management author and consultant Randall Englund characterized as "We don't need no stinkin' processes" — an attitude he reports experiencing when seeking to implement project management methodologies among R&D personnel in the high-tech field.[3]

"What gets measured gets managed" is certainly true. But, as Franklin Becker of Cornell University has pointed out, it is also true that "what gets measured is eloquent of the real motives of management." Further, the most important things to measure may not be the easiest to measure.[4]

Beyond Numbers

Another common issue, according to Zigon, is caused by our insistence on trying to measure only using numbers. The underlying assumption seems to be that quantified measures are inherently more objective, and thus better, than any other kind of measure. This kind of thinking, he stresses, is limiting and results in measuring what is easily quantifiable — but not necessarily what is most important.

It is important to remember that our love affair with quantitative measurement is a relic of the Industrial Age and may not be well suited to a knowledge economy business. Back in the 1700s, Lord Kelvin announced that the measurement of an activity is basic to its control — a statement that formed part of the foundation for scientific management. The trouble is that management has changed. The weak link in our present ideas of metrics lies in the word "control." Kelvin's statement is true — if control is all you are trying to achieve. But in the context of dynamic, knowledge-based, information-economy business, control is a loser's game. Measures designed only to control employee behavior are motivation-killers for the individual; and from the company's point of view, they only tell us what already happened in the past rather than helping to prepare human capital to meet new challenges.[5]

An excellent example of using numbers to accurately measure the wrong thing is offered on Zigon's Web site. For a role that requires creating business reports, a finished report is a measurable deliverable. But how should it be measured? A report could be measured by its size, weight, number of pages, or even number of words. However, none of these easily measured aspects are as important as the "usefulness" or "clarity" of the report. "Usefulness and clarity" are descriptive measures that tell us a lot about the quality of the work performed — but they are not numbers. Such descriptive measures may be more difficult to arrive at; but if you are really interested in improving performance, they are invaluable. Because measuring performance of knowledge work is fundamentally different from measuring the manufacture of goods, the simplistic and purely objective measurement of input and output is inappropriate; there are too many system variables.

Creating Descriptive Measures

Descriptive measures include two components: (1) a person competent to judge the work performed and (2) a list of factors by which the quality of the work can be judged. Continuing to use the example of the "useful report," the judge might be the person who requested the report or the person who needs to make a decision based on the report's contents. The list of factors important to these two judges might be things such as adequate information on which to base the decision and justification supporting any conclusions. While these factors may not be quantifiable — that is, measurable in numbers — they should be *verifiable*.

Verifiable measures provide a way to measure those aspects of performance for which numbers do not work well. To continue with the above example, how would one verify that "adequate information for a decision" was contained in a report? Did the report include:

- A list of the options considered?
- A list of pros and cons for each option?
- A description of the values important to making the decision?
- The relative importance of each value? (and here a numeric scale can be employed)
- A recommended decision with reasons for the recommendation?

Answering yes to all or most of the above questions would verify that the work output — a written report, in this case — did in fact contain adequate information. If the person being measured produces such reports on a regular basis, as an important function of the role, judging each report on these factors and looking at the aggregate results over a period of six months would give a clear idea whether this aspect of that role was being fulfilled. If one factor is frequently missed, this is an area for development. Taking it one step further, one might look at how the decisions that were made based on the recommendations had worked out. Did assumptions prove correct? If not, why not? Is there something needed in the individual's training, education, research abilities, or access to information resources? Or was the execution of the decision lacking? In examining the results provided by descriptive measures, it becomes clear that one person's performance cannot be judged in a vacuum, but is linked to a wide variety of organizational issues.

Another technique for developing high-quality performance metrics is the *customer diagram*. This graphic describes the role's customers, and the products and services these customers need from the employee. When completed, the diagram shows the "links" between the employee and the customers and is a good starting point for developing results, measures, and performance standards. It is a process-mapping idea borrowed from Six Sigma practice that works well for understanding the outputs required from abstract process work such as project management.[6] The value of creating a customer diagram is that it helps clarify which products or results are worthwhile to the role's customers and which activities contribute to those value-added results.[7]

Best-Practice Performance Management

In contrast to the traditional performance appraisal, the emergent approach to performance management focuses on supporting people to manage their own performance. Performance expectations should be defined collaboratively and planned at the outset, with ongoing monitoring and review of progress, with a strong emphasis on continually striving to enhance performance and develop capability. This process must be linked to the defined competencies for the role as well as to development planning and opportunities. Following are some examples of practices in performance management that have proven successful in some companies.

Fixing a Broken Process

Get rid of the HR-speak and make sure the performance management processes use the language of the business. Recognize top performers and confront poor performers as soon as possible. Burn paper forms: user-friendly automation is better, faster, and cheaper.[8]

Frequent Appraisals

To keep employees motivated, some organizations reported increasing the frequency of their performance appraisal to one every six months. Work arrangements conducive to retention were those that gave people an opportunity to work on interesting and challenging projects and the ability to be rotated across jobs and technologies. The use of cross-functional teams and redesign of the workspace to accommodate teamwork were also reported as effective practices.[9]

Executive Support

Senior management can help performance by ensuring that project managers feel valued. Publicly praise good performance; advertise individuals' achievements; refrain from punishing understandable mistakes. These actions send the message that the company recognizes the difficulty of managing projects and encourages project managers to share problems before they become unmanageable. Ensure that project managers' authority and command of resources are commensurate with their responsibilities and accountability. Establish reporting processes and lessons learned forums that allow project managers to discuss problems openly so they can learn from experience. When project managers are less fearful of being penalized for mistakes, reporting and estimating become more honest. Another way to support the development of project managers is to increase the influence of project managers compared to functional managers in staff appraisal.[10]

Performance Metrics for Technical Personnel

These can be qualitative, such as self-evaluations and evaluations by experts, managers, peers, and customers who rank individuals on one or more dimensions of performance and evaluate the extent to which individuals accomplish previously agreed-upon objectives. Because individual metrics are imperfect, multiple measures are typically used.[11]

Turn the Tables

Rather than have managers evaluate the performance of their workers, workers are increasingly asked to evaluate their bosses. Experts suggest that this "upward feedback model" leads to better management, productivity, and morale. Some businesses have adopted 360-degree feedback evaluations that involve critiques from customers, peers, subordinates, supervisors, and the employee being reviewed. Experts note that supervisors are more likely to benefit from the program if they are able to adapt, are open to change, are interested in participating in additional activities to improve their skills, and feel accountable. Workers are more likely to review their supervisors if they know that their evaluations will remain anonymous.[12]

Effective Performance-Management Systems

These systems measure two components of performance: (1) deliverables or results (the "whats" of a job) and (2) knowledge, skills, and behavior (the "hows" of a job). As far as the "what" is concerned, a technically skilled software designer, for example, should be able to complete all assigned projects on time, within budget, without an unreasonable number of bugs or rework. The way to evaluate technical performance is to match actual behavior to agreed-upon specific measures of quantity, quality, timeliness, and cost, and then against those expectations. Measuring the "hows" is more challenging, especially for a supervisor who is not highly technical, as some project managers are not. One way to measure technical skill is to use the completion of training courses and certifications as outcomes. Another way is to get feedback from others, especially technical experts and end users or customers. Whatever measures are chosen, it is important to involve technical personnel in setting expectations, collecting data, and tracking progress throughout the year. This changes the role of the supervisor from evaluator to coach — someone who provides support, resources, and advice, breaks down barriers, and helps solve problems, rather than evaluating or judging technical expertise.[13]

Five Elements of Best-Practice Performance Management

The following phases or elements of performance management are recommended by Australian HR expert Graeme Dobson and can apply equally to a project manager responsible for managing the performance of team members or to a manager of project managers in his or her interactions with experienced project management staff. (See Figure 7.1).

1. *Performance planning.* This step sets expectations and defines measures, preferably collaboratively, or in a situation where team-based rewards or compensation is the norm, as a group. Involving employees in this process develops their understanding of the organization's objectives and of their responsibilities in achieving those objectives. At the end of the performance planning process,

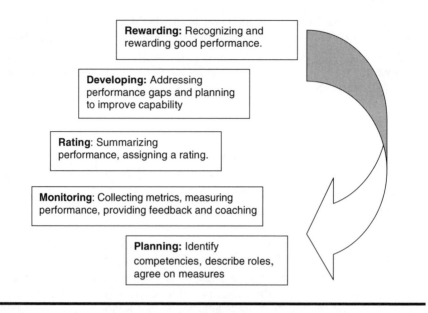

FIGURE 7.1 Five elements of performance measurement.
(Adapted from Graeme Dobson, Better Practice in Performance Management, http://www.users.bigpond.com/dobsong/My%20Work/Better%20Practice%20in% 20PM.doc.)

both the manager and employee should be able to answer the following questions in the same way:

■ What are the employee's key responsibilities for the following period (or duration of the project)?
■ How is successful performance defined and measured?
■ How do these responsibilities contribute to the success of team, project, and company?
■ How will the manager support the employee or team in the accomplishment of these responsibilities?

2. *Monitoring.* As the "day-to-day" aspect of performance management, this step includes collecting and analyzing performance metrics but, more importantly, the feedback and coaching that should be initiated by these metrics. Ideally, manager and employee work together, sharing information about work progress, potential barriers or problems, and how the manager can help the employee. If performance problems are identified, solutions are also developed to resolve the problem.

3. *Rating.* Generally, an annual process where manager and employee review and summarize performance, agree how this should be rated, and discuss development issues or career aspirations. The

focus should be on reviewing performance and determining what steps might be taken to support the employee in further growth and performance improvement. A review is simply written documentation of what already should be known through an ongoing coaching process, as well as an opportunity to formalize a record of growth, achievement, and opportunity.[14] Open communication between a manager and employee about performance is essential to increase productivity, improve staff morale and motivation, and allow coordination of work so that each employee is contributing to the objectives of the company. Broad, generally applicable metrics do not provide sufficient insight on the performance of an individual. To be meaningful, the measures must be specific to their roles in the organization.

4. *Development.* Do project managers or team members have the skills and knowledge required to perform effectively in their current roles? Are they being prepared for future roles? This capacity-building is just as important as measuring and judging present behavior. Monitoring performance will highlight development opportunities and performance issues. Performance management discussions can often help identify employees' career aspirations, which then becomes an input into training and development plans. This approach builds capacity to perform in future roles, which is a benefit to the individual and critical to the growth of the company. The development plan that is an output of performance evaluation discussions specifies how new learning will be achieved, either through work assignments that introduce new skills or higher levels of responsibility, or through training, coaching, or mentoring.

5. *Rewarding.* Individuals or teams must be recognized for their behavior in fulfilling their responsibilities and delivering the outcomes specified performance plans.[15] While the results of a performance review could form the basis for adjustments in compensation and for bonusing, remember that this is not the purpose of the review. Experts recommend that performance reviews should be completed on a different calendar than compensation changes. This helps keep the performance meeting constructive and upbeat.[16] Nevertheless, as one expert has noted, "If competencies are the 'wheels' for managing knowledge work, pay remains the engine." And technical personnel statistically prefer "pay-for-performance" systems, which they feel are more fair.[17,18]

In summary, performance measurement provides a framework within which effective performance can take place. The elements of that framework, according to Graeme Dobson, are:

- The essential job functions the employee is expected to perform (role descriptions)
- What "doing the job well" means in concrete output-focused terms (role competencies)
- How job performance will be measured and rewarded (performance measurement and efforts at employee motivation and retention — which include, but are not limited to, compensation)
- How employee and supervisor will work together to sustain, improve, or build on existing employee performance (professional development)
- How the employee's job contributes to the objectives of the team and the organization (integration of performance management with the organization's strategic goals and objectives — an integration that is facilitated in project-oriented companies by a Strategic Project Office responsible for both the development of project personnel and for project portfolio management)

"Performance Culture": Creating a Best-Practice Environment

One aspect of the Watson Wyatt survey cited earlier that might surprise some managers is that employees complain that performance standards are not set *high enough*, and that people are not held accountable to these standards. Only 54 percent of workers say their company sets high performance standards and only 44 percent feel that people are held accountable for their performance. Nineteen percent of all workers say their company deals effectively with poorly performing employees. That so many workers view these as problems says something very positive about the workforce: people want to be held to high standards; they want a system that not only rewards high performance but confronts poor performance. In short, today's employees long to work in a "performance culture."

A performance culture, as described by Dobson, is one in which individuals and teams are motivated to proactively fulfill their responsibilities; stimulated to perform their work and achieve superior results; inspired to communicate their progress and results; and willing to accept responsibility for those results. To establish a performance culture, he lists ten organizational qualities that should be sought after:

1. *Reciprocity.* Performance is a two-way street. The person managing performance provides direction, guidance, and resources as well as removing barriers to performance. In return, the person being managed fulfills his or her responsibilities.
2. *Equity.* Fairness must be maintained and promoted.

3. *Trust.* A performance culture cannot survive in an environment of mistrust.
4. *Transparency.* Individuals and teams must conduct themselves without deceit or hidden motives.
5. *Clarity.* People need a clear picture of what they need to do and what results are expected.
6. *Balance.* Accountability and authority; expectations and capability; pay and performance — all should be balanced to achieve optimum performance.
7. *Ownership.* When employees feel like owners, responsible behavior and thoughtful approaches both increase. The sense of ownership includes commitment, involvement, and empowerment.
8. *Consequences.* Despite a positive focus in the performance culture, sometimes negative consequences must accrue. If top performers see others slacking off without any eventual consequences, this undermines their sense of the fairness of the system. Of course, rewards and recognition are the consequences of excellent performance.
9. *Consistency.* Policy, procedures, resources, and consequences must be applied in a consistent way.

Finally, *leadership* is the most important ingredient in establishing this environment. Employees are astute observers of what is being said and done and frequently emulate their leaders, in word and deed (see Table 7.2).

Managers play an important role, and many managers will require support in the form of coaching or simple performance management tools until they are able to master performance management. First, they might need to unlearn old habits of treating performance reviews as occasions for judgment and even punishment, rather than as facilitative, collaborative meetings that spur future development.

Organizational structure, resources, and budgets must also support the new performance system; it is not enough to identify the areas in which an employee could use training or mentoring if resources for such support do not exist. Therefore, appropriate courses, self-paced learning materials, and support tools should be developed to support the performance management system.[19]

Performance Gaps

One principle that runs counter to the traditional view of performance appraisal is that discovering and analyzing performance gaps or opportunities is the whole point of the review meeting. Thus, it is not a "problem" when areas for improvement are identified. Often, the first instinct is to

**TABLE 7.2   Moving to Talent Management for Projects:
A Paradigm Shift in Performance Management**

From:	To:
Command and control	Commitment and engagement
Past performance	Future capability
"Carrot and stick"	Self-mastery and development
Manager judges and evaluates	Manager coaches, mentors, and guides
Driven by manager	Shared responsibility
Passive and reactive	Proactive
Activity focused	Outcome and accountability focused
Performance is "managed"	Employees supported in managing their own performance
Top-down	Two-way or 360-degree collaboration

Source: Adapted from Graeme Dobson, Better Practice in Performance Management, http://www.users.bigpond.com/dobsong/My%20Work/Better%20Practice%20in%20PM.doc.

drop underperforming employees, especially if they are managers; but firing and replacing managerial personnel is a costly process. In fact, it may take six months or more before the new individual produces any value.[20] According to Joseph Weintraub, a professor of management at Babson College, performance issues with managers often reflect "a lack of understanding of expectations between managers and their bosses." To diagnose this, he recommends asking the manager to write down the "three most important things that they get paid to do. Then the manager's boss would independently do the same exercise for the manager." Finally, when seeking to close performance gaps, be patient. It takes six weeks or longer for people to change behavioral patterns in the workplace.[21]

Talent Management ... Not Performance Appraisal

Taken together, skills and competency assessments, plus performance management that is linked to development opportunities, create a "talent management strategy" that ensures that the right people are in the right roles at the right time. One must address the skills and competencies required for people to do their current jobs well, and you must assess, select, and develop people for their next jobs. As people move higher in the organization, manager and leader competencies become more critical. The goal here is not only successful performance in current roles, but the assessment of potential for future roles and then structuring work opportunities that help develop that potential into capacity.

Questions to ask about performance in your organization include:

- What does success look like for employees and for the business?
- Are you merging performance-management and potential development?
- What distinguishes the best performers in a particular role?[22]

Aligning Individual and Organizational Performance

Even the best individual performance can be wasted or go unnoticed, however, when it is misaligned with company objectives. A genuine performance culture does not measure individuals by actions that do not improve the business, nor does it measure the company in terms that do not relate to long-term organizational health and growth. Organizational and individual performance should be linked to one another by a strategy and values focus that values customer relationships and human capital more than procedure, rules, fixed assets, and other nonproductive features of organizational life.

The quality and usefulness of an organization's strategic planning process can be judged, in part, by whether it leads to the development of measurable performance objectives. These objectives guide the future actions of organizational units, provide a blueprint for resource allocation, and serve as an important means of providing yardsticks for feedback on progress or problems. The budget then translates intentions into actions. Strategic goals are distilled to lower and lower levels of the organization until individual employees develop personal goals that further those of the project and of the organization as a whole.

Aligning organizational goals with both project and individual performance tracking makes explicit the linkages between strategies, actions, and results. The performance measures signal organizational priorities and allow individuals at all levels to understand their own responsibilities. That is why measures should capture improvements in an organization's core business processes and ensure that the right individuals are in the right jobs.[23,24]

This alignment of the organization around strategy requires a broad-based approach to measuring and managing the business. One such approach is the "Balanced Scorecard." The Balanced Scorecard, with its four areas of focus (financial; shareholders; customers; internal processes; innovation and learning) defines what management means by performance and measures whether management is achieving the desired.[25] When paired with a system for gathering metrics on project and individual performance, along with a method for prioritizing and selecting the right projects, such a clearly defined strategic framework clearly identifies what it takes to determine success and makes sure that all managers and employees understand what they are responsible for in achieving organizational goals. Because it presents indicators that managers and staff can influence directly by their actions, the balanced-scorecard approach to performance measurement encourages behavioral changes aimed at achieving corporate strategies.[26]

Performance measurement aimed at management improvement rather than simply documentation must establish this relationship between corporate strategy and the tactical initiatives — that is, projects — that are required to achieve the strategy.[27]

In summary, performance management works best when it unifies activity at the individual, team, project, and organizational levels. Best-practice performance management systems translate the company vision into clear, measurable outcomes that are shared throughout the organization and with customers and stakeholders. Aligning organizational, project, and individual performance helps to strengthen the project management culture; facilitates continuous planning and review; and provides tools for assessing, managing, and improving the overall health and success of business systems. A paradigm shift is taking place, from prescriptive, compliance-based performance oversight to a forward-looking strategic partnership involving all elements of the business. Alignment of performance measurement with other management processes such as strategic planning, budgeting, quality improvement, project management, and employee evaluation offers the potential for improving overall efficiency and effectiveness. Through alignment, leaders articulate a vision and direction, managers develop operational or project plans to implement the vision, employees and managers together monitor and evaluate results and work to close performance gaps, and the capability for future projects is built. Figure 7.2 shows the relationship between the development of competency standards and role descriptions and the fulfillment of organizational priorities by the "people on projects."

To go back to the question we posed at the beginning of this chapter: why measure performance? In one best-practice example, the use of a performance measurement system called the Performance Prism showed the following benefits to the organization after 18 months of implementing a corporate scorecard and measurement system: management and employees began to focus on the company vision; accountability occurs at all levels. A strong culture of cost-justification for new projects started to evolve and team members better understood how their roles were integrated, with the result that productivity increases are occurring throughout the company. Significant top- and bottom-line growth occurred.[28]

FIGURE 7.2   Linking role competencies to organizational objectives through the selection of relevant performance metrics.

That said, most experts in human performance recommend that managers remember that successful performance is a journey, not a destination; "high performance" is a moving target. Thus, performance — not measurement — should be the ultimate objective.[29]

Notes

1. U.S. workers give performance management programs a failing grade, Watson Wyatt Survey Finds, *PRNewswire,* April 19, 2003. Data from the survey is available at www.watsonwyatt.com.
2. Jack Zigon, *Performance Measurement Examples,* ZPG, 2003.
3. Randy Englund, interview, in *Best Practices Report,* November 2001.
4. Jason Oliviera, The balanced scorecard: an integrative approach to performance evaluation, *Healthcare Financial Management,* May 1, 2001.
5. Jeannette Cabanis-Brewin, Project Management Metrics: Moving Towards a Balanced Approach; interview with Richard Russell of the Balanced Scorecard Collaborative, *Best Practices Report,* September 2000.
6. Customer diagram templates available at http://www.isixsigma.com/library/content/c010429b.asp.
7. Jack Zigon, ibid.

8. U.S. workers give performance management programs a failing grade, Watson Wyatt Survey Finds, *PRNewswire,* April 19, 2003. Data from the survey is available at www.watsonwyatt.com.

9. Ritu Agarwal and Thomas W. Ferratt, Enduring practices for managing IT professionals: assessing existing business practices to determine staff recruitment and retention capabilities, *Communications of the ACM*, September 1, 2002.

10. Christopher Sauer, Li Liu, and Kim Johnston, Where project managers are kings, *Project Management Journal*, December 2001.

11. George F. Farris and Rene Cordero, Leading your scientists and engineers, *Research Technology Management,* November/December 2002.

12. Michele M. Melendez, Turning Performance Review on Its Head, *St. Louis Post-Dispatch,* June 6, 2004.

13. Jim Concelman, Development dimensions international: evaluating technical skills, *Dear Workforce*, June 2004.

14. Roger Herman, interview, in *Workforce Week*, September 2001.

15. Graeme Dobson, Better Practice in Performance Management, posted at http://www.users.bigpond.com/dobsong/My%20Work/My%20Work.htm. Accessed October 2004.

16. Roger Herman, interview, in *Workforce Week*, September 2001.

17. Howard Risher, *Aligning Pay and Results*, Amacom, 1999.

18. Linda Thornburg, Variable compensation software: an emerging market, *HRMagazine*, May 1, 2001.

19. Graeme Dobson, ibid.

20. Michael Watkins, *The First 90 Days,* Harvard Business School Press, 2003.

21. Paul Michelman, Will you help or heave your underperformers?, *Harvard Management Update,* March 2004.

22. Brian Ruona, Measuring employee output, *Dear Workforce,* March 2002.

23. Bass and Clay, ibid.

24. Nancy A. Bagranoff, Jan Ellen Eighme, and Harvey Kahl, Jr., Who moved my ledger?, *The CPA Journal*, October 2002.

25. Robert S. Kaplan and David P. Norton, Transforming the balanced scorecard from performance measurement to strategic management. I, *Accounting Horizons*, March 2001.

26. Graeme Dobson, ibid.

27. Jason Oliviera, The balanced scorecard: an integrative approach to performance evaluation, *Healthcare Financial Management,* May 1, 2001.

28. Robert Dieckman, Designing measurement systems to drive corporate performance, *The Ohio CPA Journal*, July 1, 2001.

29. Alan L. Milliken, Key ingredients of successful performance metrics in the supply chain, *The Journal of Business Forecasting Methods & Systems*, Summer 2001.

THE FUTURE — WHAT IS NEXT FOR PROJECTS AND PEOPLE?

III

Chapter 8

On the Horizon: New Organizational Themes and Structures

As corporations become more aware of the creative power of managing by projects, project management personnel gain more and more visibility and respect. New roles and opportunities for personnel skilled in project leadership are developing. This chapter provides an overview of some of these trends, with the caveat that both the marketplace and project roles are changing rapidly. By the time this book is on the shelves, more changes can be expected.

New Themes in Project Management Staffing

Project management, like any other business model or technique, is dynamic: it changes in response to changes in the social or technological environment. In recent years, new technologies — the Internet in particular — have had a dramatic impact on our society, and these changes are mirrored in new ways of organizing and communicating within the project environment. In particular, the increasingly virtual project environment has implications for project manager competencies and career paths, as does the evolving practice of outsourcing the project management process.

Virtual Teams, Organizations, and Communities

The virtual workplace has edged its way into our business environment for many reasons. According to a 3M survey, 50 percent of corporate work is conducted in teams and 25 percent of those workers collaborate remotely. The Gartner Group, Inc., predicted that more than 137 million workers would be involved in some sort of remote work by 2003. Two of every three Fortune 500 companies now employ telecommuters. Obviously, companies are doing this because there are business benefits. The primary benefit is that a virtual workforce can unite highly qualified people without location restrictions. Other reasons that an organization might want to consider being virtual rather than "traditional" are the ability to:

- Leverage skills throughout the organization.
- Provide customers with the "best and brightest."
- Balance work/home relationships for employees, engendering loyalty and morale.
- Save organization overhead costs (up to $1 million per month for one Fortune 500 company that recently downsized and consolidated office space in multiple metropolitan areas).
- Optimize employee time and energy for work by eliminating commuting time and hassles.

To this list of the drivers that businesses are responding to when implementing virtual-work programs, the events of September 11, 2001, added a new one: security. Companies contemplated with horror those few World Trade Center firms that lost nearly all their intellectual capital and all their work infrastructure in moments. The distributed workforce now counts among its virtues that it is a safer workforce, removed from the risks presented by crowded public places. Companies with teleworkers can keep going when disaster strikes — whether that is a storm, a power outage, an epidemic, or a terrorist attack.

In terms of preserving intellectual capital, virtual work has proved itself in another way as well. In a 1997 survey, AT&T found that fully one third of telecommuters would look for other work if they were forced back into the office. More than 70 percent reported that they were more satisfied with their jobs than before they started telecommuting, and 75 percent reported feeling more satisfied with their personal and family lives. So virtual work is also a powerful tool for recruitment and retention.

When telecommuting is well planned, companies report that people's strategic planning skills increase dramatically "because they have time to think."[1] People themselves report that they are as much as 40 percent more productive while working away from the office because they have fewer distractions. In a 1995 AT&T-sponsored survey, 58 percent of Fortune 1000 managers reported increased worker productivity. The State of California's Telecommuting Pilot Program experienced productivity increases of up to 30 percent. Home-based telecommuters take fewer sick and personal days, continuing to work with a cold or other minor ailment or injury that would have kept them out of the office, or making up in the evening time they had to miss caring for a child or going to the doctor. In fact, telecommuters work longer hours and more workdays than the average employee, according to data compiled by the International Telework Association and Council (ITAC).[2]

Therefore, the challenge of managing a virtual team has become a common part of the organizational climate and will doubtless continue to grow in importance. A "virtual team" can be defined as a group of people working together on a project, but at different locations within the organization. Virtual teams can also include team members who come from outside the organization, such as subcontractors. In some situations, every team member might work from a different location. In our own company, for example, it is common practice for a researcher in Philadelphia, a content editor in North Carolina, a Webmaster in Ohio, and a subject matter expert in New Hampshire to collaborate on a Web publishing project without ever meeting face to face. Such teams naturally require competencies in written and verbal communication as well as the use of communication technologies that project teams may not have needed 20 years ago. Not only that, but the project or functional managers who manage virtual workers also need to develop new competencies. Table 8.1 lists some of the essential factors for successful virtual teaming.

Organizational and Management Challenges

On the face of it, nothing could make more sense than "moving work to where people are, rather than people to where the work is," in the words of Jack Nilles, the NASA scientist who invented the word "telecommute" back in the late 1980s. Today, information technologies no longer present a barrier to effective virtual work; if anything, the technology is ahead of the organizational will to use it, according to many experts. And knowledge work — the backbone of projects — is ideal for the virtual setting but organizational policies and the managerial mindset often get in the way.

"How can I manage them if I cannot see them?" This question characterizes the attitude of many managers toward the virtual employee population, but it reveals a lot more about the manager than it does about the true challenges of virtual workplaces. Says Dr. Wayne F. Cascio of the

TABLE 8.1 Nine Essentials for Virtual Teams

For virtual teams to achieve success, team members must have:

1. A shared purpose, defined by the pursuit of an urgent, common goal
2. The need to work together in order for the team to be successful; everyone on a virtual team is or should be expert in something needed for the group to accomplish its work
3. A culture of information sharing and seeking
4. Confidence that others in the organization care about, and recognize the accomplishments of the team
5. Flexibility about when, where, and how they communicate with each other
6. Communication supported by appropriate technology
7. Understand the mission of the team and how each individual's work contributes to it
8. Good follow-up on communications
9. Strong interpersonal communication skills

Source: Adapted from Deborah Jude-York, Lauren D. Davis, and Susan L. Wise, *Virtual Teaming,* 2000; Jessica Lipnack and Jeffery Stamps, *Virtual Teams,* Wiley, 1997.

University of Colorado–Denver, a manager who, when equipped with appropriate results-based performance measures for a job, is unable to provide orientation, direction, and feedback via e-mail, telephone, videoconferencing, and intranet just isn't trying very hard. As Dr. Sylvia van de Bunt-Kokhuis of Amsterdam-based Compu-train puts it, "[Managers] have to make a transition from managing time (activity-based) to managing projects (results-based)."[3]

The keyboard will never take the place of a handshake or a hug, and an emoticon is not a smile. But many of the social benefits of face-to-face interaction can easily be replicated in cyberspace if employers make it a priority to establish interactive work opportunities for employees and to develop better online relationships between managers and remote workers. However, management will waste some of the value of the virtual worker if they try to make it "business as always, just elsewhere." Virtual work offers some challenges to our assumptions about how things get done, as well as opportunities to rethink knowledge management, infrastructure, and technology — opportunities that can affect the entire organization, not just those who work from home or from the field.

Work redesign may be necessary. It is tempting to simply look at existing roles and say that some are appropriate for virtual work and some are not. But a greater opportunity lies in looking at the nature of the job to consider more flexible options. The nature of some jobs or projects is cyclical, which could suggest a telecommuting schedule based not on days per week, but on a per-month or even per-quarter basis to better match the workflow. The development of training courses is an example. In the initial and final phases, the course developer must interact with internal clients and experts to define objectives, tasks, and outcomes. In between, there is a long period of "heads-down, grind-it-out development of the content." It makes sense to allow that middle portion of the project to be completed through telecommuting.[4]

A request to consider a particular position for telecommuting should spur companies to think more creatively about job structure. In many cases, job descriptions are accretions of tasks and responsibilities that have piled up over time, not the result of formal job design. Some job responsibilities can and should be broken off from others and converted to telecommuting.[5] (For an example of this kind of job redesign, see "Case Study: Virtually in Control" later in this chapter.)

Workplace Infrastructure

Of the seven critical success factors for virtual teams, technology is only one. (Others are human resource policies, training and development for team leaders and team members, standard organizational and team processes, organizational culture, leadership, and leader and member competencies.)[6] However, because technology provides the "office space" in which virtual work takes place, one should spend the same kind of effort in designing it that goes into a workplace made of bricks instead of clicks.

Learn ways of creating a truly collaborative environment. Many teams can log onto the technology, but do not know how to create an energetic sense of interaction. Virtual teams must learn to use the technology to create at least as much collaboration as one observes in co-located teams. If teams are using Web conferencing, but it is not as interactive and collaborative as in a meeting room, then they are not using the technology effectively. Virtual teams must become power users of the most critical collaboration technologies.[7]

Like "brick" offices, virtual organizations must contain both public and private areas that can be created through passwords and access lists. Virtual team boundaries tend to be multilayered, comprising a small core group, an extended team, and a network of external partners and stakeholders or subject matter experts. Companies regularly configure multilevel virtual spaces; Internet sites allow public access to published information, such as press releases and annual reports, while internal intranet areas require authorization with access to plans and results, so there's no reason why it can't be done to support virtual teams. Completely private places are where teams discuss their most sensitive issues, such as budgets and personnel matters.[8]

Pointers for Managers

Unless companies select telework-friendly managers, remote work programs will fail. Managers who supervise virtual employees should:

1. Attend their company's telecommuting training programs, even if they only work in the office. This is standard policy at Merrill Lynch.
2. Get to know their employees socially before they start working with them, either through an online virtual community or by meeting in person. Dorothy Leonard of Harvard Business School recommends holding one or more "kick-off meetings" before every project.
3. Supervise only remote workers. Managers with both telecommuting and office-based employees often give more attention to those in the office, ignoring their virtual employees.
4. Ensure that every telecommuting employee has the resources to stay involved in the project.
5. Learn to consider the amount and quality of an employee's work, without regard to physical presence. Come up with new and innovative ways to recognize and reward telecommuters.

Communication, always important in business, becomes paramount in a virtual work setting. In a focus group composed of 20 members of a single virtual organization, the most predominant challenges to the virtual world were identified as communication and trust.[9]

In a virtual team, communication comes in a multitude of forms: e-mails, phone calls, faxes, letters, memos, Web conferences, phone conferences, and, occasionally, face-to-face meetings. To be effective, the team should decide on how to manage the most common of these, such as e-mails and phone calls. Simple guidelines that help people manage these communications. For example, one team established criteria for using the term "urgent" to distinguish between e-mails. Overuse of "urgent" tended to degrade response times. Urgent e-mails were to be answered as soon as possible, but no later than two hours after receipt. Other e-mails were responded to within 24 hours. A response was required even if it was to acknowledge that the email was received and read by the recipient. Phone calls were handled the same way so that no issue was left unattended for more than 24 hours. As team members became more disciplined in using these forms, when an urgent e-mail was received, it was responded to promptly.[10]

No single form of communication will bridge the physical and social distance of distributed workgroups, so it is important for both managers and virtual workers to know when it is appropriate to use e-mail, voice-mail, teleconferencing or a personal meeting. Remote interaction requires a greater sensitivity to the strengths and limitations of different media: Face-to-face conversations are often best for creative brainstorming or sensitive negotiation, while e-mails are more effective for transmitting clearly defined pieces of information or brief, direct questions.[11]

Trust, the other leading identified challenge, is tied closely to communication. Trust comes in many forms:

- "I can count on you to do what you say you will do."
- "I trust that you will not share damaging information about me or others."
- "I trust you are committed to the mission of this team and will give it your best effort."
- "I trust you will share information that will help the team succeed."

There are many ways to build trust: sharing personal stories and prior experiences; a willingness to show both strengths and weaknesses; a demonstrated commitment to goals; acceptance of others who are different; openly communicating; and, most important, being honest. Research by Dr. Frank Toney of the University of Phoenix has shown that honesty is one of the most important characteristics of successful project managers — more important to success than technical skills, IQ, or educational background.[12]

On the other hand, trust is destroyed when managers share information outside the team without permission; withhold information that impacts the team's success; provide vague instructions and only critical feedback; use hierarchical channels in lieu of informal discussions; promote hidden agendas; use fear tactics and public criticisms. The ability to build and maintain trust with both on-site and virtual members of the organization will be a key competency for managers and project managers as virtual work becomes more prevalent.

Case Study

In a small start-up, AgInfoLink, Inc., a virtually run company that tracks beef from ranch to refrigerator case, the two previously identified challenges of trust and communication were confirmed and several other "lessons learned" were unveiled. For AgInfoLink, the keys to successful implementation of a virtual workforce were:

- *Place limited personnel near customers.* Proximity to customers was one of the most compelling reasons for having staff geographically separated. Face-to-face interaction with customers who were widespread throughout the country proved to be invaluable as staff could actually test technology in the field!

- *Get an intranet online as quickly as possible.* Store all company information online and keep it dynamic. Both organizations reported a strong intranet was developed to establish a unified environment for collaboration; to streamline the dissemination of corporate information; and to promote employee connectivity.
- *Have face-to-face orientations.* This establishes critical personal relationships and helps determine whether selected candidates could succeed in the virtual environment.
- *Mitigate the feeling of isolation that almost every virtual employee feels.* A "buddy program" was initiated at AgInfoLink.
- *Train employees in productive e-mail use.* The life of the organization happens on e-mail, so understanding the appropriate use of this vehicle is critical.
- *Stamp out the rumor wildfires that so easily spread in virtual environments.* Rumors start in the absence of information, so management should cultivate transparency and respond openly to questions and issues.
- *Realize the power of communication.* Daily, weekly, constant communications reduce anxiety, focus on issues, and help resolve problems. Electronic and paper newsletters should be supplemented with teleconferences and face-to-face meetings.

For this company, establishing and maintaining trust in parallel with developing strong communication channels and protocol were the main focus of executive management.[13]

Issues for the Project Manager and Team

To be successful in managing a virtual team, the project manager must practice the fundamentals of project management with more care and diligence than might be required in a face-to-face setting. For example:

- *Begin with a team charter that allows each team member to contribute ideas for inclusion.* The team charter also creates a means for team members to know what they are committing to in terms of expected behaviors.
- *Develop a formal communication plan.* A virtual team will rely more on clarity and frequency of communication than other teams.
- *Establish, maintain, and enforce reporting processes, specifying content, format, and frequency.* This type of practice will reduce or eliminate the information hoarding that hampers many virtual teams.

- *Find opportunities to build and sustain trust among team members.* Recognize members who consistently do what they say. Delegate responsibility where appropriate and hold those team members accountable.
- *Monitor the team dynamics.* Look for behaviors that support the health of the team as well as support the task-oriented aspect of the team.[14]

Successful virtual team leaders understand the fundamental principles of teambuilding and do not let time and place alter these precepts. The team leader, whether virtual or co-located, is accountable for the team's output. Top management and customers hold the virtual team leader accountable for the performance of the team. So accountability among team members and from team to project manager is of great importance.[15]

Virtual team leaders are also a primary force in planning for the team members' professional development and career progression. Because it is easy for virtual team members to feel isolated and unnoticed, it is even more important for the virtual team leader to actively assist them with their career planning and development. If members of virtual teams feel that they have been shortchanged in this important area, their motivation to work on such teams will diminish rapidly.

Virtual Team Best Practices

1. Select people who are self-starters, strong communicators, and have other good virtual-team skills.
2. Keep projects task-focused so team members will be able to gauge their progress and know if they are on target.
3. Keep team interactions upbeat and action oriented.
4. Standardize common protocols.
5. Create clear goals.
6. Celebrate reaching targets.
7. Create shared space — a virtual water cooler — where people can interact beyond the scope of work.
8. Identify the barriers to collaboration that you want to overcome.
9. Identify what people should do when a crisis occurs: whom should they contact? What is the decision-making hierarchy?[16]

Virtual team members need to possess six key competencies in addition to traditional team competencies that ensure success in collaboration and coordination and in autonomy roles: project management, networking, the use of technology, self-management, boundary management, and interpersonal awareness.[17]

These competencies allow team members to better perform in the virtual environment, which is different from the ordinary workplace in four key ways:

1. Team members are granted the autonomy and freedom to decide how to structure their workday and organize their tasks.
2. Virtual teams bring decision making closer to those who actually do the job, thereby allowing members to communicate to management what they feel are the solutions to problems facing the organization.
3. Virtual teams are based on the concept of collective-collaborative problem solving, where team members strive to create win-win solutions to difficult organizational problems.
4. Virtual teams are based on trust.[18]

Case Study: Virtually in Control

One example of an emerging way of organizing for project management is provided by a program our own company recently developed that we call "Remote Controls." Remote Controls is a services package that supports global and virtual project management initiatives by segmenting the planning and controls functionality within a project. Planning and controls — the somewhat less "touchy-feely" aspects of project management — lend themselves well to remote or virtual work. Moving the Project Controller/Planner functionality to a remote, technology-driven location allows for increased productivity, decreased cost of ownership, and increased flexibility. The remotely located Controller/Planner has few distractions, but is focused on the project at hand. A repository of best practices, both processes and technologies, in the project controls area is available to him or her. With the processes, technology, and knowledge available immediately when needed, the remote Project Controller/Planner is highly efficient. At the same time, this role is a source of job satisfaction for individuals who prefer to work in quiet concentration far from the "front lines" of the projects. Our Project Controllers/Planners are generally experienced people who have chosen to specialize in the Project Controller/Planner role as their career path. (See Chapter 4 for a complete discussion of the rationale for separating the roles of project manager and planner.) The consulting firm incurs the overhead, equipment, and employee-related costs, while avoiding travel expenses; the client can potentially reduce headcount by outsourcing the controls function. Another benefit is that virtual project personnel are not likely to "go native" and become more loyal to the client than to the firm. Thus, the consulting firm is able to build its own culture and encourage employees to grow within that environment.

Services and deliverables remain identical to on-site project work. Project controls services would include defining scope and project objectives, work breakdown structure (WBS) development, project schedule development, replanning efforts, and weekly project status reports. Deliverables would include project requirements document, WBS, project schedule, and status reports. In addition, the management reports services would include producing up to four biweekly management reports on the project status. These reports would include project dashboard, project costs, earned value, and project burn rate projections. Risk management, issue management, and change controls are also efficiently managed remotely. These services would include an initial project risk assessment, ongoing risk assessment, ongoing issue management, and management of the project change controls process. Deliverables include risk assessment, issue control document, and change control documentation. Remote planners can also track resource assignments. The resource assignment services would include monitoring project allocations and usage, resource contract dates, resource forecasting, and collection of timesheets. Deliverables include resource allocation and usage reports, and forecasting reports.

Beyond the Team: Community of Practice

"Any methodology worth its salt," says process improvement expert Michael Wood,[19] "seeks to harvest the wealth of knowledge that exists within the minds of those who actually do the work." Wood contends that knowledge workers who are organized into cross-functional groups representing the end-to-end processes that actually deliver value to stakeholders can readily define and resolve the value gaps in the process.

The cross-functional group that Wood describes is an apt description of the teams that accomplish project and program work in most organizations. Thus, an organization in which most work is accomplished by teams is already in a position to engage in continuous improvement of its own methodology and processes. All the project office needs to do is learn how to nurture those cross-functional groups and provide them with the infrastructure to put up their "harvest" for safekeeping and future use. What organizational structures are best suited for making the most of that harvest?

Australian project management researcher Lynn Crawford has suggested that communities of practice can be invaluable in facilitating knowledge creation, transfer, and learning between individuals and across organizational boundaries.[20]

Communities of practice are not new but the term has acquired new significance in the era of the knowledge worker and intellectual capital.[21]

TABLE 8.2 Communities of Practice

Communities of practice include some or all of the following characteristics	
Common language	Group has a professional language of its own (jargon, terminology)
Shared background	Members have shared background or knowledge
Common purpose	The group has a common purpose that gives it an internal impetus
Creation of new knowledge	The work of the group and the interaction of the members create new knowledge for those members
Dynamism	Social distribution of knowledge takes place in the group
Evolution	Group develops beyond mere social interaction
Unofficial	Group evolves rather than being created
Voluntary	Membership is generally voluntary
Narration	Swapping war stories is a key way in which members share domain knowledge
Informal	Group is often informal — there is no hierarchy
Fluidity	Newcomers arrive and old-timers leave
Similar jobs	Group members have similar jobs
Self-perpetuating	As groups generate knowledge, they reinforce and renew themselves
Self-managing	Groups benefit from cultivation but not from control

Source: Adapted from Paul Hildreth, Communities of practice. Available at http://www-users.cs.york.ac.uk/~pmh/work.html#Communities, 2000.

Communities of practice are groups of people informally bound together by shared interest and shared expertise — a simple enough definition and one that might apply to most voluntary groups in our society (see Table 8.2 for the characteristics of these groups).

Yet the importance of the community of practice to the development of technical and business knowledge began to be truly appreciated thanks to the Institute of Research on Learning (IRL; Palo Alto, California), founded in 1987 and associated with Xerox's Palo Alto Research Center, and to the work of social learning theorist Etienne Wenger.[22] A key finding of the IRL's work was that learning is social. In this context, communities of practice have become associated with the concepts of the learning organization and knowledge management.

The primary reason to implement a project office is to improve project performance across the organization. Standardizing on best practices is one way to accomplish that goal. Thus, the encouragement of best-practice sharing among all segments of the organization is a natural role for the project office to take. By recognizing the shared interests and goals of project management practitioners throughout the organization, the project office can play an important part in supporting, facilitating, and networking the informal communities that are "people repositories" of project knowledge around the enterprise.

Organizations such as Boeing, NASA, NCR, and Ericsson have provided support for project management communities of practice along these lines, even rewarding active participation in corporate communities of practice. Further, the development of communities of project management practice between organizations has led to initiatives that benchmark project management practices.[23]

The community of practice, like a distributed computing network, links and expands the "repository" of project management knowledge that is stored in practitioner's minds — the tacit knowledge that is otherwise so difficult to manage.

What do the experts tell us about building and maintaining communities of practice? In *Knowing in Community* knowledge management expert Richard McDermott[24] listed a number of critical success factors for communities of practice, to include:

1. *Focus on knowledge important to both the business and the people.* This echoes Wally Bock's advice to limit the focus of KM efforts to areas where one can make a difference. The topics addressed by the community must be ones about which people feel personally passionate.
2. Find a well-respected community member to act as coordinator, to keep people and create opportunities for people to share ideas. A coordinator need not be a leading expert but must be someone who connects well with people.
3. *Make sure people have time and encouragement to participate.* Some companies specifically allocate a certain amount of project time to community activities to ensure that the time and energy people invested in the community will count in their performance appraisal.
4. Involve thought leaders who either have an important specialized knowledge or who are well connected and influential members of

the project management community. These people legitimatize the community and draw in other members.

5. *Make opportunities for contact.* While documented reports, templates, tips, analyses, proposals, etc., are helpful to most community members, face-to-face contact is key to building a sense of commonality, enthusiasm, and trust.

6. *Allow people to participate at their own comfort level.* Even lurkers often get great value from a community where they can drop in quietly to find out who is working on what or learn about the field and make contact later.

7. Encourage real dialogue about real problems and cutting-edge issues. Do this by building a trustful and mutually helpful environment.

Further tips specific to developing communities of practice (CoPs) for project management include:

1. Give project personnel access to each other. The Internet is an ideal tool: listservs, chats, and discussion boards allow people dispersed across the company or the globe to share tips and experience.

2. Facilitate exchanges among technical experts who have vast company knowledge stored in their heads. Encourage them to become leaders in the project management "community of practice" within the organization to spread around that knowledge.

3. Use the resource library capabilities of project management software to catalog the competencies of employees to help match them up with the project teams that can best use their expertise; then expand these libraries beyond project management to encompass skills from other segments of the enterprise.

4. Encourage best-practice sharing between projects, between departments, and between project managers within and outside the organization. Best-practice sharing is also one of the simplest knowledge management tools; people who share an interest or a goal do it naturally. Companies can capitalize on this by providing infrastructure to spread the sharing around — networks, collaborative software, databases, libraries, etc. However, the most important success factor in best-practice sharing does not involve technology. It involves strong leadership, with attention to culture and change. The application of technology can make a good process better but will not be any substitute for organizational leadership that models an interest in knowledge management and process improvement.[25]

Managing with CoPs is a kind of catch-22; CoPs cannot be managed too much or they lose the spontaneous sense of affiliation among members that makes them so dynamic. Yet if the organization is to benefit from them, managers must still help them: first, by recognizing them and supporting them. Let them build an intranet, use the conference room, put a get-together on the expense account. Dedicated staff may be required.[26] For example, AT&T has an Information & Knowledge Exchange section on its Web site as an anchor for its communities of practice. It requires a full-time editor for each community that interacts with subject matter experts and distills, posts, and publishes high-value information, which is the knowledge base of community members.[27]

Some guidance and leadership of discussion databases in communities of practice are also desirable to obtain knowledge transfer and capture; make sure you have shared norms, provide some payback for participation (tangible or intangible), ensure active facilitation by a moderator, offer a "one-stop" solution for e-mail and discussion, and nourish the online community through other means as well (e.g., face-to-face meetings). Content must be good if these sites are to attract visitors; use logical, intuitive structure for views; use library scientists who understand the technology and technologists who understand library science; provide some editorial and publishing support to increase value and accuracy; and create automatic systems for archiving discussions.[28]

Technology makes today's virtual communities possible, and corporate support for communications technologies is one of the most important ways that management can encourage communities to develop and contribute. A portal is not, in itself, a community of practice but a tool that can help a community form. Portals are often used for knowledge management to create communities for geographically dispersed employees and to assist merger and acquisition activities. According to a recent survey by the analyst firm Meta Group, users say the greatest advantage of portals is that they can improve productivity by supporting remote online working. Other benefits include improved employee retention and increased sales. How important can such a portal be? One global media company spent $14 million worldwide on portal technology over four years. The Meta Group predicted a return of more than $29 million on this portal spending during the same period: 64 percent of the return will be accounted for by increased sales, 18 percent by improved information access — streamlining publication processes, improving global collaboration, cutting down on travel expenses, and making it faster to locate expertise — and 15 percent by making new employees more productive more quickly.

The other area of management support is in resource allocation. Put motivated workers in charge of new CoPs. Find people who are good at managing people relationships; networkers who know lots of people in the company. Their job is essentially to be facilitators. They must be able to enroll people into a new way of working. Sometimes people think a community implies "of the people, for the people, by the people," but pure democracy does not work, especially at the beginning. At the beginning, a community needs a community organizer. Otherwise, the urgent drives out the important, and nothing ever seems to get done.[29]

As all this surely makes clear, successful management of knowledge communities calls for new management practices and roles. The new roles include leaders-facilitators, content editors, and Webmasters. Other new roles include knowledge brokers or ambassadors who perform inter-community communication, and a "red-threads team" that articulates common principles learned from one assignment to the next.[30]

In fact, as communities of practice become more common and organizations more virtual, we will probably have to rewrite many of the job descriptions provided in this book to include these roles that support knowledge capture, transfer, creation, and management ... and thus support project management methodology and execution.

Case Study: Knowledge Transfer

Management in a high-tech manufacturing organization performed an audit and discovered that design teams were repeating common mistakes, resulting in tens of millions of dollars in rework and repair costs. A simple solution was formulated: create communities of practice (CoPs) across design groups to enable project personnel to more easily capture and share valuable knowledge, information, and best practices. Using existing collaborative software tools and databases, the CoPs focus on linking product engineers together so that they can collaborate and get assistance in real-time from experts across the organization. The CoPs filled the gap that sophisticated information systems could not; they allowed the engineers to ask each other: "What do I know that you need to know?" and "What do you know that I need to know?" These simple dialogues have resulted in significant savings and increased team satisfaction and innovation.[31]

This organization exemplifies the knowledge management strategy described in Table 8.3.

Outsourcing: Project Management Expertise as a Commodity

At one time, a debate raged within the profession as to whether or not project management expertise was portable — whether an experienced project manager could lead a nomadic existence, applying the discipline

TABLE 8.3   Leveraging Project Management Knowledge

To leverage knowledge, focus on the people who use it, not on the knowledge itself, not on the technological infrastructure for disseminating it.

1. To leverage knowledge, develop existing, naturally occurring communities. A group of project managers that shares practice tips informally and that may belong to the same professional association is such a potential community. Focus on knowledge important to both the business and the people.
2. Create forums for thinking as well as systems for sharing information. Do not rely on databases, but give the community ways to interact.
3. Let the community decide what to share and how to share it. Top-down "pushing" of information must be replaced by the community's need and desire to know and to share knowledge.
4. Create a community support structure. In most natural communities, an individual or small group takes on the job of holding the community together, keeping people informed, and creating opportunities for people to get together to share ideas. Community coordinators are usually a well-respected member of the community who function as "gatekeepers," evaluating new information and disseminating it. Use information technology to support communities, not to create them.
5. Use the community's terms for organizing knowledge. A shared language is one of the hallmarks of a community, especially a community organized around a work discipline. Organize information naturally, in ways that make sense to the users. A good taxonomy should be intuitive, reflecting the natural way members of a professional discipline think about the field.
6. Integrate sharing knowledge into the natural flow of work. Because communities create knowledge in the present moment, they need frequent enough contact to find commonality in the problems they face, see the value of each other's ideas, build trust, and create a common etiquette or set of norms on how to interact. When people work together or sit close enough to interact daily, they naturally build this connection. So community members need many opportunities to talk one-on-one or in small groups on the telephone, through e-mail, face-to-face, or through an Internet site.

Source: Adapted from Richard McDermott, Knowing is a human act: how information technology inspired, but cannot deliver knowledge management, *California Management Review,* Summer 1999.

in various organizations and industries. That debate is over, judging from the proliferation of professional services firms specializing in project management. Today, not only the management of single projects, but the entire project management function is often outsourced. Organizations that do not have a proficiency in managing projects, or that do not have as many project managers as they need and do not want to incur the overhead to recruit and orient new employees, increasingly turn to out-sourcing relationships.

Market pressures are responsible for this change. Companies no longer have a large enough staff to accomplish complicated projects on their own. According to research by the Center for Business Practices, 54.2 percent of organizations have only one to nine project managers on staff, and 25 percent have 10 to 25 project managers on staff. For most companies, it takes five to seven years of investment to develop a competent team of in-house project managers.[32] This is time and money that many companies no longer have. Yet companies also cannot afford to lose potential profit through missed delivery dates and failed projects.

No doubt this is why the Gartner Group issued a Strategic Planning Assumption that said that IS organizations with no strategy for blending internal and external resources to achieve "best-in-class" staffing would incur 25 percent higher labor costs than those with such a strategy.[33] Thus, many IS/IT organizations have now placed contractors in leadership roles (even supervising permanent employees) because of the required level of technical expertise and project-management skills. This is becoming an acceptable practice. Some contractors are also used as an interim solution to train permanent employees to backfill for the contractors at some point.[34] This trend is not just in IT; a wide variety of industries have followed suit.

R&D organizations increasingly contract out projects in whole or in part, or by bringing in contract scientists and engineers to work in teams with in-house staff. The organizations that develop their core technical competencies and outsourcing management practices are able to innovate faster and less expensively, particularly in those areas where they lack internal expertise. Moreover, outsourcing allows in-house staff to become part of a wider "invisible college" — otherwise known as a CoP — within the R&D community.[35] The pharmaceutical and biotech industries, where time to market is key, have also been found to ramp up projects faster by "installing" external project management expertise.

For those in the project management profession, this "have talent, will travel" trend is a very positive development, allowing skilled project managers, planners, schedulers, methodologists, and trainers the oppor-tunity to grow professionally from exposure to a wide variety of project settings. And, contrary to the widespread belief that outsourcing poses a threat to corporations' existing project management staffs, project man-agement outsourcing enables companies to leverage their in-house resources. By working with a skilled consultancy, in-house staff benefits from a valuable knowledge transfer that can enhance the existing staff's project management performance and broaden their network of colleagues in the discipline.

Not only project managers, but also other project staff are being swept up in this trend. A recent survey of several hundred Project Office Directors and senior-level executives revealed that 39 percent of respondents said that they currently outsource project management functions such as planning and controls, or are considering it. In addition, more than half (61 percent) of the responding companies use consultants for project management, primarily for augmented staffing.[36]

Some additional benefits of outsourcing the controller or planner role include:

■ Immediate access to professionally trained and experienced personnel, without the cost of recruiting, hiring, and training
■ Consistency across all projects in following prescribed methodology, processes, and reporting techniques
■ Objective assessment of project status (no political fallout when key projects are reported to be in trouble)
■ Allows internal project managers to take on additional, concurrent work without losing control over existing projects[37]

For companies whose project managers simply have too many responsibilities to complete them efficiently and effectively, outsourcing project controllers or planners is a viable option. These external resources can forge a trusted partnership with internal project managers, enabling them to achieve higher project success rates — a win-win for project managers and their organizations.

Overall, for the companies that utilize the skills of contract project managers and other project staff, there are many important benefits, including:

■ *Reduced costs.* Bringing in a project management outsourcing partner eliminates the need to invest in internal project management training and infrastructure development. It also eliminates the need to recruit and assimilate project management specialists for unique situations.
■ *A framework for continuous improvement.* Bringing in "ready-made" processes, staff, and support services will jump-start the entire project management function. Service firms coach and mentor internal staff as well. By reducing the burdens of managing projects in-house, companies can focus on improvement in other operational areas, such as research and development, software engineering, staff productivity, and quality assurance.
■ *Decreased employee turnover.* Turnover costs of a project manager average 150 percent of the employee's salary. This includes tangible

costs such as hiring and relocating new employees and intangible costs such as inefficiency and lost productivity while the job is vacant.

■ *Improved customer satisfaction.* When companies achieve new levels of efficiency and product and service quality, customer satisfaction improves. And customer satisfaction is the key to growing sales and profits.

■ *Knowledge transfer from external professionals to in-house staff.* The enterprise can enhance its internal project management competency with proficient outsourcing. Mentoring and coaching by the outsourced staff help build in-house expertise. When the client company uses documentation and benchmarking to capture and preserve new organizational learning, the benefits become long term. Outsourced project managers look at internal project management practices with fresh eyes and bring in new information about best practices. They do sector-specific research and bring in ideas from other industries that can "cross-fertilize" with their clients' base of expertise.[38]

■ *Outsourcing.* By outsourcing their project offices or project management improvement initiatives, companies can achieve a higher project success rate at a lower cost, enabling them to increase the value of project management competency within the organization.

■ *A healthier bottom line.* Having a team of established experts in place to take over the project management function enables companies to focus on improving profitability much more quickly than otherwise possible. Increasing productivity, decreasing operational costs, and improving product and service quality usually result in significant improvements to companies' profitability.[39]

Outsourcing Options

There are two basic project management outsourcing options to consider: (1) outsource the entire project office function or (2) use both internal and external resources to manage projects. Each has its own advantages.

Outsource the Entire Project Office Function

In this option, the outsourcing partner is brought in to install or develop, manage, and maintain the project office (an organizational center of excellence) at a program, organizational, or therapeutic area, or enterprise level. The partner provides the project management methodology and trains internal project staff in its use. They can also recommend and implement project management software and train staff in its use. A fully trained team of skilled project managers, planners, and control personnel are supplied by the outsourcing partner to plan, manage, and complete all projects in a timely and cost-effective manner. During the initial phase of the outsourcing contract, process reengineering, change management, and communications plans are developed to facilitate acceptance by the existing organization. The advantages of outsourcing the entire project management process include:

■ Project management best practices are immediately available.
■ Projects are led and managed by an expert team of personnel.
■ No up-front investments and recruiting costs are required.
■ The project office team is on hand to coach and mentor staff.
■ Changes to staff can be easily made to adjust to changes in requirements.

Use Both Internal and External Resources to Manage Projects

In this option, the outsourcing partner supplies a staff of professional project managers and project control personnel, as needed. The outside project team serves as a mentor to the internal staff. Using a blended resource approach ensures that experts are on hand to manage the more complex, unique, or difficult-to-staff projects. In addition, internal staff has access to coaching and mentoring from the outsourcing provider. The advantages to this approach include:

■ Steering troubled projects back on track immediately
■ Coaching and mentoring internal project managers and staff to improve morale and personnel performance
■ Boosting productivity and tightening efficiency with resource management tools and techniques
■ The company pays only for the outsourcing staff needed, and cultural resistance among inside staff is less likely

Making the Outsourcing Relationship Work

The key to getting the most out of an outsourcing relationship is to have a good plan in place beforehand and to work that plan — but remain flexible. The company must have a clear business goal and an understanding of the role the outsourcing partner will play in helping attain that goal. Performance metrics for the outsourced engagement must be in place so that the client company knows whether or not the outsourcing partner is doing a good job. The steps to creating a win-win outsourcing partnership include:

1. Develop a charter that describes the mission, responsibility, and business performance criteria for the project management organization and ideal outsourcing partner.
2. Assess the current project management environment and establish objectives within the following areas:
   - *People:* competency assessments and training
   - *Process:* project management and other methodology development (Drug Development Life Cycle, Software Development Life Cycle, or other industry standard)
   - *Technology:* software and tools for project scheduling, control, time management, and integration with accounting and human resource systems
   - *Benchmarks* for project performance
3. Define the future environment. Establish long-term objectives for the project management organization in the same areas as above. Determine the permanent role that an outsourcing partner will play in achieving those objectives.
4. Create a change management plan to help ease the transition of bringing an outside project team into the organization. Change management activities are important for overcoming any cultural resistance that one might encounter from one's staff.
5. Structure the contract with your outsourcing partner so that both parties are in agreement on the objectives, expectations, and challenges of the relationship. Institute an appropriate performance-based incentive plan into the contract.[40]

A New Role: The Outsourcing Relationship Manager

To successfully outsource project management expertise, here are some guidelines. Make sure that the scope of services to be provided is well-defined. Carefully draft the roles and responsibilities of the outsourcing partner and agree to service levels and business performance levels. Focus on a few metrics at a time and schedule ongoing performance reviews to ensure that expectations are being met. Make sure that you have contacts who are always available to address any problems or questions. Establish a structure where everyone in the organization has direct access to important information. Do not let valuable knowledge slip away with the outsourcing partner. Structure processes so that valuable lessons learned and procedures are documented and maintained in a central location that is easily accessible by all parties. Have the outsourcing partner train and educate staff in the project management model. And, most importantly, manage communication effectively. Effective communication is probably the most critical outsourcing success factor.[41] In fact, it is so critical in a situation where professional services are being provided and contracted for, that we recommend the creation of a special role dedicated to the development of sound outsourcing partnerships. (See Appendix A.) An Outsourcing Relationship Manager combines sound project management procurement practices with top-notch communication skills. Without such a dedicated role, miscommunications between client and provider, or between external and in-house resources, are likely.

New Opportunities and Visibility for Project Managers

Balanced Scorecards, Strategy Mapping, Business Process Fusion, Sarbanes–Oxley compliance .... There is a shakeup going on in how businesses are run, and the drivers for change come from many different quarters. Competitive pressure, social change, and regulatory requirements all create a business environment that at times feels chaotic. The good news is that constant organizational change and a demanding marketplace elevate the importance of project management to the attention of the highest levels in organizations. And as awareness rises, roles for project management experts are also rising.

As this book goes to press, a new magazine has been launched, extolling the role of the Chief Project Officer.[42] It is a rare title, but ten years ago, CIO was rare too and CTO (Chief Technology Officer) unheard of. Ten years ago, there was no such animal as a Project Portfolio Manager, but this position is now becoming more common. We list and describe these executive-level project management roles in Appendix A because we believe this is the direction in which project management is headed.

What is different now? A glance at the impact that the Balanced Scorecard has had upon businesses gives us some clues. The scorecard emphasizes the linkage of measurement to strategy. The tighter connection between the measurement system and strategy elevates the role for non-financial measures from an operational checklist to a comprehensive system for strategy implementation. For the first time, the details of the project portfolio (what Kaplan and Norton call the "strategic initiatives") become important to a company's strategic thinker.

Furthermore, the Balanced Scorecard reflects the changing nature of competitive advantage. In Industrial-Age competition, companies achieved competitive advantage from their investment in and management of tangible assets such as inventory, property, plant, and equipment. But in today's knowledge economy, intangible assets have become the major source for competitive advantage. In 1982, tangible book values represented 62 percent of industrial organizations' market values; by the end of the 20th century, the book value of tangible assets accounted for less than 20 percent of companies' market values. Thus, strategies for creating value shifted from managing tangible assets to knowledge-based strategies that create and deploy an organization's intangible assets: customer relationships, innovative products and services, high-quality and responsive processes, worker skills and knowledge, information technology, and supportive organizational climate. Kaplan and Norton have noted that "the value from intangible assets depends on organizational context and strategy [and] cannot be separated from the organizational processes that transform intangibles into customer and financial outcomes."[43] In our view, project management is the key process in making that transformation.

The requirements of the Sarbanes–Oxley Act (SarbOx) are having a similar effect. When top management of publicly traded companies became personally responsible for organizational risks, the details of the project portfolio — risks, budgets, successes, failures — became of intense interest to executives. According to one expert in project management and auditing:

> [This is] a huge, huge opportunity and challenge for project managers. ... What this does is effectively erase many of the barriers between project management and finance, and between projects and the highest decision-making levels of the corporation. Project managers need to be well along on the maturity curve to handle this ... A mature project manager can say what the 15 or 20 items are that might be problematic out of 2000 items in a work breakdown structure. Those "project breakers" transcend cost and schedule issues; they are big issues, issues that PMs once thought were outside their scope — such as regulatory compliance, the environment, internal politics, market timing ... risk processes throughout the enterprise are going to be under great scrutiny by regulators and by executive leadership, forging a link between the project level and the board level that has not existed before.[44]

From this comment, it is obvious that more than finance and project management are forced into cozier integration by the new rules. According to an article in the April 2003 issue of *Risk and Insurance* magazine, one of the most important implications of SarbOx is a bias in favor of "risk transparency." How can an enterprise adequately manage risks without knowing exactly what is going on? The strong pressure for project portfolio management inherent in the SarbOx rules changes has only begun to be felt. As noted in previous chapters, it is difficult to implement portfolio management in the absence of sound project management methodology, project knowledge management, and infrastructure — including enterprise project management systems and an organizational "home" to oversee project management processes, such as an enterprise-level project office. Implementing an enterprise project office brings up the issues of organizational maturity and personal competence. It is a puzzling chicken-and-egg question: can an organization achieve a high level of maturity in sophisticated project management practices such as portfolio and risk management without an enterprise project office in place? Can it create such an office effectively without a high level of maturity? The answer probably lies in the personal competence of project managers who are motivated to make a difference in their organizations.

Tug on one enterprise issue and you find that they are all connected to each other. This is important and pressing news for project managers. The integrative skills that are the soul of project management have never been more needed by organizations, the pressure to perform them effectively never more intense. We hope this book helps both executives and project management leaders to put the power of project management expertise to work, in a climate that supports success for all concerned.[45]

Notes

1. M. Warner, Working at home, *Fortune,* March 3, 1997.
2. Jeannette Cabanis-Brewin, ibid.
3. Jeannette Cabanis-Brewin, ibid.
4. Charlotte Garvey, Teleworking HR, *HRMagazine,* August 1, 2001.
5. Charlotte Garvey, ibid.
6. Deborah Duarte and Nancy Tennant Snyder, *Mastering Virtual Teams,* Jossey-Bass, 1999.
7. Jaclyn Kostner, interview, *Product Development Best Practices Report,* August 2000.
8. Jessica Lipnack and Jeffrey Stamps, *Virtual Teams,* Wiley, 1997.
9. Deborah Bigelow, Managing the virtual workplace, *Project Management Best Practices Report*, February 2002.
10. Joan Knutson, Teams at a distance, *People on Projects,* March–April 2004.
11. Laurie Putnam, Distance teamwork: the realities of collaborating with virtual colleagues *Online Magazine,* March 2001.
12. Frank Toney, *The Superior Project Manager,* Center for Business Practices, 2001.
13. Deborah Bigelow, ibid.

14. Beverly Gerber, *Virtual Teams, Work Groups,* Lakewood Publications, 1995; Jacklyn Kostner, The phantom of the office without walls, *PM Network,* August 1994.

15. Deborah Duarte and Nancy Tennant Snyder, *Mastering Virtual Teams,* Jossey-Bass, 1999.

16. Charlene Marmer Solomon, Managing virtual teams, *Workforce,* June 2001.

17. Deborah Duarte and Nancy Tennant Snyder, ibid.

18. Jerry W. Gilley et al., *The Performance Challenge,* Perseus Publishing, 1999.

19. Michael Wood, What Is a Process Improvement Methodology Anyway?, www.gantthead.com/articles.

20. Lynn Crawford and Terry Cooke-Davies, Managing Projects — Managing Knowledge: Sharing A Journey Towards Performance Improvement, paper presented at the *International Project Management Association Conference,* 2000.

21. Stewart, T.A. *Intellectual Capital: the New Wealth of Organizations,* Doubleday, 1999.

22. Etienne Wenger, *Communities of Practice,* Harvard Business School Press, 1991; E.C. Wenger and W.M. Snyder, Communities of practice: the organizational frontier, *Harvard Business Review* 78(1), 139–146, 2000.

23. Lynn Crawford and Terry Cooke-Davies, Managing Projects — Managing Knowledge: Sharing A Journey towards Performance Improvement, paper presented at the *International Project Management Association Conference,* 2000; Frank Toney and Ray Powers, *Best Practices of Project Management in Large Functional Organizations,* PMI, 1997.

24. Richard McDermott, Knowing in community: ten critical success factors in building communities of practice, *Knowledge Management Review,* May/June 2000.

25. Wally Bock, Knowledge Management 101, *Intranet Journal,* http://idm..internet.com/articles (article originally appeared in Bock's *Briefing Memo* newsletter at www.bockinfo.com); Cinda Voegtli, Know-All 10, archived on www.gantthead.com.

26. Tom Stewart, The invisible key to success, *Fortune,* August 5, 1996.

27. Jim Botkin, *Smart Business: How Knowledge Communities Can Revolutionize Your Company,* Reed Business Information, 1999.

28. Carla O'Dell and C. Jackson Grayson, Jr., *If Only We Knew What We Know,* Free Press, 1998.

29. Jim Botkin, ibid.

30. Jim Botkin, ibid.

31. Embedding KM: Creating a Value Proposition, www.apqc.org, May 2001.

32. Center for Business Practices, *Project Management: The State of the Industry: Research Report,* CBP, 2002.

33. M. Light and T. Berg, Gartner Strategic Analysis Report: *The Project Office: Teams, Processes and Tools,* August 1, 2000.

34. Wolfgang B. Strigel, Outsourcing: what works, *Software Development,* January 1, 2004.

35. George F. Farris and Rene Cordero, Leading your scientists and engineers, *Research Technology Management,* Nov./Dec. 2002.

36. Center for Business Practices, Project Control Functions: A Benchmark of Best Practices, CBP, 2004.
37. Robert Wourms, Attention Project Managers: Project Relief Is within Sight, unpublished article, May 2004; A New Way to look at PM Roles: Where do you fit in?, presentation, April 28, 2004, Great Lakes (Detroit) Chapter of PMI Symposium.
38. Marcia Jedd, Outside in, *PM Network,* November 2004.
39. Bob Wourms, IT organizations discovering new ways to stay nimble: project management outsourcing, *DM Direct Newsletter,* May 23, 2003.
40. Bob Wourms, Discover new way to stay ahead of the game: project management outsourcing, *Pharmaceutical Processing*, September 2003.
41. Mark Morgan, Career-building strategies: are your skills helping you up the corporate ladder?, *Strategic Finance*, June 1, 2002.
42. See http://chiefprojectofficer.com. Accessed February 2005.
43. Robert S. Kaplan and David P. Norton. Transforming the balanced scorecard from performance measurement to strategic management. I, *Accounting Horizons*, March 2001.
44. Greg Hutchins, interviewed in "Sarbanes–Oxley Fallout: Opportunities and Challenges for Project Management," by Jeannette Cabanis, *People on Projects*, July 2003.
45. Jeannette Cabanis-Brewin, Inside the SarbOx: The Future of Project Management, *developer.com*. Accessed Feb. 2005 at http://www.developer.com/mgmt/article.php/3072511.

APPENDICES

Appendix A

Sample Role Descriptions for Project Office Personnel and Other Project-Management-Related Positions

Introduction

The following position descriptions cover the gamut of project-management-related jobs in an organization that is committed to managing by projects, from executive staff members on the enterprise and organizational levels to specialty staff. The positions in one's own company probably represent a subset of those described here because few companies have fully implemented and committed to enterprise project management on an enterprise scale of this magnitude. Lest one think these are unrealistic organizational positions, we note numerous organizations that have dedicated resources much like our descriptions. Specifically, fully mature Enterprise Project Offices in fields such as construction, federal governments, and certain industry groups represent examples of such matured, projectized organizations. We offer these as downstream goals that may spark discussion and planning for the future.

On a more practical level, one can use these descriptions of the responsibilities, skills, and desired backgrounds for project personnel to craft a job description that is appropriate for one's organization, or to rethink the ways in which one has assigned responsibilities to existing positions.

These snapshots of project management jobs are based on a broad review of the project management job marketplace, as represented by hundreds of job descriptions actually used in companies in a variety of industries around the world, in addition to ideal job descriptions crafted by project management experts.[1] Also, we have refined them by limiting the sometimes unwieldy job descriptions of project managers and their colleagues to combinations of duties and personal characteristics that we have learned from experience are workable. So in addition to "wish list," what follows is a "reality check." Add to the list any responsibilities that are important or unique in a specific organization or in an industry — while being careful not to create "monster" jobs as discussed in Chapter 3.

Position descriptions have a dual purpose: They both describe the ideal candidate for the job (and can be used as a checklist when considering internal hires or seeking external candidates) *AND* they assist the person fulfilling the role in keeping focused on the right areas, in knowing when to say no, and in understanding how his or her job fits into the larger picture of the organization. This information can also assist project participants in identifying their own personal professional development needs, in relation to the knowledge, skills, and competencies required for their project role(s). Project managers or project executives can use these position descriptions as checklists for the selection of new project personnel, or to help confirm a participant's commitment to their responsibilities.

Finally, we offer this list as a kind of template to solve one of the most pressing human resource problems facing project organizations today: the difficulty of communicating about the work that needs to be done due to a lack of consensus on the names, descriptions, or required backgrounds of jobs in project management. A little more commonality in the language surrounding staffing projects and project offices will help the discipline match the right people to the right positions.

Each position description includes an overview or general description, a list of possible responsibilities and duties, a suggested set of skills and competencies, and suggested background experience and educational credentials.

Note: While we are working from the premise of an enterprise-level Strategic Project Office, readers who are staffing a divisional-level project office (such as one within IT) can still use these job descriptions, which are scalable to any type of PO. Readers who are creating or staffing a divisional PO should be able to "read between the lines" to scale the described enterprise-level functions back to the circumstances of their specific organization. For a graphic example of the differences between the three levels of project office, see Figure 1.1 in Chapter 1.

Executive and Enterprise-Level Roles

Chief Project Officer

(Other titles that might be descriptive of this role: Director of Project Management, Director of Programs and Strategy, Director of Enterprise Project Management, Director of Project Portfolio Management)

Role Overview:

Reports to a senior C-level executive, preferably the CEO. Provides leadership, direction, and oversight of all corporate programs and projects under development and execution. This role also provides executive oversight for all divisional projects and maintains responsibility for data integration and reporting for all projects and programs within the organization. Oversees development and management of the Strategic Project Office and plays a key facilitative role in project portfolio management. May include the role of Portfolio Manager. Responsibilities for the Chief Project Officer parallel those of a Chief Financial Officer as the office of the CPO provides corporate status, reporting, analysis of all programs or projects with analysis of corresponding impacts to budget, delivery timetables, and resources.

Suggested Duties and Responsibilities:

- Promotes the development and diffusion of project management culture throughout the enterprise
- Maintains effective communication with senior management, making them aware of critical issues confronting corporate programs or projects and of the action plans for addressing those issues
- In conjunction with corporate leadership, develops and manages the enterprise project portfolio management process, integrates the corporate project decision making with corporate strategy, and facilitates ongoing enterprise program/project portfolio decision making

- Identifies needed corporate process improvements and works with business partners to effectively drive change throughout the organization
- Facilitates program/project reviews of critical/key enterprise programs and projects
- Direction and oversight of all corporate systems for project planning, implementation, and monitoring, ensuring that all projects have clear goals, objectives, and timelines with measurable milestones consistent with corporate strategy and goals
- With the director of divisional project offices, organizes the project office structure to effectively achieve divisional and departmental project objectives
- With the director of the divisional project offices, oversees major periodic divisional portfolio meetings, driving results and resolving key project and program issues
- With the director of divisional project offices, oversees preparation of key management communications such as project steering committee presentations, status reports, budget reports, etc.
- With the director of divisional project office, oversees relationships between project personnel and functional managers
- With the director of the Enterprise Project Office, oversees education and mentoring for staff and management regarding project management
- Oversees and participates in the project portfolio management process, ensuring that the technical objectives of projects are integrated with commercial requirements
- Oversees the integration of project processes with other functional areas such as manufacturing, marketing, and finance to ensure the success of corporate strategies, products, and initiatives
- Maintains an understanding of contemporary project management techniques and industry practices, as they impact corporate objectives
- Ultimate responsibility for enterprise project problem/issue identification and resolution

Suggested Knowledge, Skills, and Abilities:

- Ability to analyze and synthesize information in a concise manner and to make recommendations on strategies to resolve policy and political issues
- Demonstrated ability to use professional management or technical concepts to solve complex problems and oversee key projects in creative and effective ways
- Strong knowledge of finance and accounting

- Strong partnering skills
- Ability to understand and deal with political issues in a highly matrixed environment
- Excellent communication skills (oral and written)
- Strong organization skills and the ability to manage multiple priorities
- Strong project management ability
- Strong leadership ability
- Strong negotiation skills
- Skills to interact effectively with clients and business partners (especially if programs/projects are developed for external client use)
- Strong skills in conflict resolution and problem solving
- Results orientation
- Strong analytical and interpersonal skills

Suggested Background, Experience, and Education:

- Extensive experience (ten or more years) in the management of large, complex programs/projects
- Seven or more years of experience in the relevant industry area
- PMP® or other project management certification or equivalent experience required
- College degree in finance, accounting, subject related to the industry area, or a technical subject preferred; CPA or MBA is a plus; MS, or Ph.D. in a business specialty or industry-related subject may be useful
- Product development and delivery experience
- Experience with relevant enterprise project management and enterprise financial systems

Project Portfolio Manager

(Other titles that may be descriptive of this role include Director of Strategic Project Management, Director of Enterprise Project Management, Chief Project Officer)

Role Overview:

The Project Portfolio Manager's responsibility is ideally enterprisewide but in practice is at present usually limited to projects in a particular division, such as IT or R&D. This position manages the corporate or divisional project portfolio by managing the process for identifying, selecting, and prioritizing projects that support corporate business strategy. This is done using a facilitative process where the Portfolio Manager (or PO Director) facilitates decisions with the leadership team by providing data, inputs, analysis, and facilitative assistance so the executives reach prioritization conclusions and ultimately "own" the organizational projects. This position reports to an upper-level executive; in a small company, it may report to the CEO. The responsibilities described below might also reside with a CPO or Director of Enterprise Project Management; on a divisional level, they might be rolled into the Project Office Director position.

Suggested Duties and Responsibilities:

- With a team of project stakeholders from all levels of the organization (C-level at the enterprise level; senior managers at the divisional level), responsible for developing formal criteria for identifying, evaluating, prioritizing, selecting, and approving the set of projects that form the corporate (or division) project portfolio. (This process should be generally consistent throughout the organization, integrated at the CPO level. That is, the CPO should form the corporate process, integrating corporate strategy; then corporate strategy should flow down to the divisional level; portfolio decisions by the division management should first account for delivering projects against corporate strategies, then balance specific divisional strategies into the workload.)
- With an executive committee, administers and facilitates the portfolio management process, including oversight of documentation and periodic reviews.
- With senior executives from the finance function, works to establish a system for quantifying project benefits so that project approval decisions can be made objectively. (This should be developed within the office of the CPO, then flowed down to the divisions, which may choose to tailor the process to meet their specific needs.)
- Assists Project Office Director in identifying project interrelationships that will affect priority and resource allocation decisions.
- With functional managers and project managers, oversees the process for collecting the project data on which portfolio decisions are based.
- Monitors projects in the portfolio (such as milestones, schedule performance, resource constraints, etc.) and updates executives on progress in the portfolio.

- With functional and project managers, analyzes the impact to the existing portfolio of changes in existing projects, or the addition of new projects outside the portfolio process cycle, and identifies strategies (resource allocation, project sequencing) for accomplishing all the desired projects.
- Oversees the distribution of project portfolio information to executive management, directors, and other key personnel.
- With the director of the project office and project managers, works to translate portfolio decisions into appropriate planning and execution of projects.

Suggested Knowledge, Skills, and Abilities:

- Strategic business knowledge; a long-term focus; ability to make recommendations regarding complex strategic decisions
- High-level organization, communication, and facilitation skills; credibility with executive management
- Willing to assume responsibility and ownership for making critical decisions or recommendations related to approving, rejecting, and discontinuing projects
- Negotiation and conflict resolution skills; ability to create an open environment where conflicts as to project priorities and funding decisions can be aired and resolved in an objective manner
- High-level understanding of technical concepts as related to the industry and products/services of the company
- Ability to instill trust, motivate, and work with other people
- Finance, accounting, and budgeting knowledge
- Ability to create and deliver executive-level summary reports and presentations

Suggested Background, Experience, and Education:

- Extensive experience (ten or more years) in the management of projects
- PMP or other project management certification or equivalent experience required
- MBA or equivalent educational experiences and experience in business and finance
- Experience and/or a related degree in the specific industry sector

INSIDE THE STRATEGIC PROJECT OFFICE

I. Leaders

Strategic Project Office (SPO) Director

(Other titles that may be descriptive of this role include Director, Project Management Office, Manager of PMO, Project Office Director)

Role Overview:

The SPO Director is responsible for the overall project management function, providing leadership, coordination, and management to SPO activities. Reporting to a C-level director (e.g., Chief Project Officer, or, for a department-level project office, the CIO, Chief Financial Officer, Chief Operating Officer), the person who heads the SPO creates and maintains a uniform approach to project management and serves as change agent for continuous improvement through improved/enhanced methodologies. Either personally or through "a manager of project managers," the SPO Director supports other project managers and leads the development and application of project management methodology and culture. He or she oversees enterprise project management strategy, training, communication, program/project control/analysis/reporting, process development, and tool development, and serves on the corporate committee for portfolio review. When no Chief Project Officer position exists, the position of Project Portfolio Manager can be combined with SPO Director and the SPO Director might serve on a corporate leadership team. Essentially, the SPO Director is a "relationship manager": one who serves as a conduit for communications and understanding between the project personnel who carry out corporate initiatives and the senior executives who make strategic decisions.

Suggested Duties and Responsibilities:

- Oversees implementation of processes and products to increase project management effectiveness
- Interfaces with senior managers to provide strategic and tactical advice on program/project planning and execution
- Appoints or approves the appointment of project managers
- Facilitates approval (through the Project Review Boards) for scope and objectives, schedule and resources, roles and responsibilities of all projects

- Oversees development and deployment of enterprise project controls tools, methodologies, and systems
- Coordinates recurrent enterprise program/project budgets and resource forecasts
- Facilitates resource, budget, timing, and deliverables issues resolution for all enterprise programs and projects
- Oversees coaching and mentoring of project team members in the use of project management tools and processes and develops training standards for project managers
- With Methodologist, ensures enterprise consistency through the development and implementation of methodology
- Oversees risk management process
- Maintains a master status list of all enterprise projects and provides "dashboard" reports and analysis to senior leadership
- Oversees the development of effective SPO program/project tools to aid in process standardization (project audits, reports, templates, knowledge management tools such as a "Lessons Learned" library, and intranet)
- With business development team, participates in business case and proposal development to ensure integration between the project planning effort and other functional areas, such as engineering, research and development, operations, marketing, and sales
- Oversees development of enterprise program/project business cases, plans, budgets, and resource requirements
- Facilitates resolution of enterprise multiproject resource and integration conflicts
- Accountable for SPO budget

Suggested Knowledge, Skills, and Abilities:

- Thorough understanding of budgeting, project management, and resource management
- Thorough knowledge of company's industry area
- Strong negotiation, facilitation, and influencing skills
- Strong analytical, interpersonal, and verbal/written communication skills
- Strong leadership skills
- Customer and results oriented
- Capable of developing solutions to complex, integrated business problems

- Extensive knowledge of project management tools and methodologies; extensive experience with using relevant project management and business management computer software
- Ability to influence executive-level associates and bring issues to resolution

Suggested Background, Experience, and Education:

- Seven to ten years of project management experience in a business environment, including successful oversight of large, complex projects or programs; at least five years of experience in company's industry
- Demonstrated success in management of other project managers or other experience on a management level within a project office
- PMP or other project management certification
- College degree in a discipline such as Computer Science, Engineering, Business Administration, or a discipline related to industry; an MBA or equivalent project management and business experience is desirable
- Experience with roll-out of project management and process improvement in an organization, including implementation of standards and methodologies
- Demonstrated ability to manage large, complex projects on time and within budget
- Ability to express complex technical concepts effectively, both verbally and in writing, to diverse groups of people

Manager of Project Support

(Other titles that may be descriptive of this role include Project Controls Manager, Project Support Manager)

Role Overview:

A second tier of management within a large corporate SPO might include this position, which provides line management oversight. This manager reports to the Enterprise SPO Director and manages the day-to-day project controls operations in the implementation of SPO objectives.

Suggested Duties and Responsibilities:

- Ensures adherence to enterprise policies and procedures and SPO methodologies, guidelines, and practices
- Oversees maintenance of enterprise program/project controls tools, techniques, methodologies, processes, and procedures
- Manages integration of enterprise project controls tools with corporate financial, procurement, quality, and reporting systems
- Establishes communication plans and roll-out strategies for implementation and continuous improvement of processes, based on metrics and feedback from SPO members
- Maintains the enterprise program/project portfolio information database
- Coordinates development of the annual enterprise program/project budget
- Integrates divisional project controls reporting for enterprise reporting and analysis
- Ensures consistent application of an effective project management methodology and tools across the enterprise
- Performs corporate dashboard reporting with regard to resources: resource leveling, utilization forecasts, and integrated program/project analysis

Suggested Knowledge, Skills, and Abilities:

- Management skill as it relates to the administration of departmental goals and objectives
- Ability to express complex technical concepts effectively, both verbally and in writing, to diverse groups of people
- Strong leadership, facilitation, negotiation, and mentoring and personnel management skills
- Thorough knowledge of project management principles and practices
- Strong knowledge in the use and application of project controls systems and tools
- Understanding of the use and application of business information and reporting systems
- Thorough knowledge of company's industry
- Knowledge of the strategic and operational issues of the project or business unit

Suggested Background, Experience, and Education:

- College degree in business or related discipline, plus three to five years of experience in company's industry
- Five to ten years of project management (or project controls, depending on the organization) experience in managing multiple, large, and complex divisional or enterprise programs/projects
- PMP or other project management certification
- Experience in resource capacity planning and accounting processes
- A previous project office role utilizing project management software
- Previous experience integrating enterprise project controls software with business information and reporting systems
- Methodology or process implementation background

Manager of Project Managers

(Other titles that may be descriptive of this role include Manager of Enterprise Project Managers, Project Office Human Resource Manager, Enterprise Program Manager)

Role Overview:

In large organizations, where multiple program/project managers are managing diverse enterprise projects, a Manager of Project Managers may be needed to oversee the assignment, development, and performance of initiative project managers. The Manager of Project Managers will be responsible for the "care and feeding" of this unique set of resources. Enterprise Program/Project Managers are highly experienced and successful in delivering large, very complex, programs/projects that may last several years. These projects may involve highly complex interrelationships within the organization, but may also include relationships to entities outside the enterprise: clients, partners, vendors, government agencies, regulatory agencies, and the citizenry. This manager reports to the Enterprise SPO Director and oversees the performance of enterprise program/project managers.

Suggested Duties and Responsibilities:

- Ensures adherence to enterprise policies and procedures and SPO practices; provides SPO interface with corporate Human Resources function

- With enterprise HR staff, participates in design and administration of systems for recruitment, rewards, retention, and professional development of SPO staff; oversees these activities within the SPO
- In coordination with enterprise HR staff, develops and maintains program/project manager career progression paths, performance measurement systems, and performance incentive/rewards systems
- In coordination with enterprise HR staff, develops and maintains project manager competency measurement programs to ensure project managers are assigned programs/projects commensurate with their traits, skills, and knowledge
- Enhances core project management disciplines by ensuring that project managers and project leads are enabled to consistently deliver projects on time, within budget, and with high levels of customer satisfaction
- Establishes communication plans and roll-out strategies for implementation and continuous improvement of processes, based on metrics and feedback from SPO members
- Coordinates formal and informal program/project manager training
- Appoints or approves the appointment of project managers
- Ensures consistent application of an effective project management methodology across the SPO
- Through program/project managers, oversees project activity ensuring critical tasks are identified and target dates are achieved; participates in planning sessions as necessary to assist in determining project approach and overall time lines associated with project requirements; ensures quality standards are met for projects overseen by the respective Project Review Boards
- Ensures that client needs are communicated clearly to other project managers and staff: ensures that client relations are maintained at the highest level through all phases of project planning and execution
- Ensures that program/project managers adhere to project management methodology and Project Office procedure and that appropriate tracking, reporting, and communication take place
- Serves as a mentor/advisor on issues related to corporate politics, external politics, client relations, governmental regulation, project quality, project risk, issues resolution, conflict management, and safety

Suggested Knowledge, Skills, and Abilities:

- Ability to express complex technical concepts effectively, both verbally and in writing, to diverse groups of people

- Strong leadership, facilitation, negotiation, mentoring, and personnel management skills
- Thorough knowledge of project management principles and practices
- Thorough knowledge of company's industry
- A technical background sufficient to understand the technologies and technical issues involved with the project and industry, to be able to anticipate and identify technical obstacles, and to make accurate technology decisions
- Knowledge of the strategic and operational issues of the project or business unit
- Demonstrated ability in conflict resolution, issues, and change management
- Strong understanding of internal/external political environment, with demonstrated success in managing diverse internal/external issues
- Understanding of legal issues and dealing with their resolutions for the enterprise programs/projects

Suggested Background, Experience, and Education:

- College degree in business or related discipline, plus five to ten years of experience in company's industry
- Ten or more years of project management experience, with three years of experience managing project managers
- Certification, education, or experience in human resource management helpful
- PMP or other project management certification
- Demonstrated success in the management of large, complex, highly interrelated programs/projects
- Previous successful experience working with mid- and senior-level executives
- Demonstrated ability working with clients, vendors, and government regulators (if applicable)

Project Management (PM) Mentors

Role Overview:

A PM Mentor is a project management professional with extensive project and program experience, who is capable of working with project managers and project teams to help them grow in the practice of the profession. Mentors are skilled at teaching and coaching project participants. They specialize in helping to put in place the processes, skills, and support structure to effectively establish and manage projects. Typically, mentors provide consulting services to program managers, project managers, program/project teams, and corporate managers. The PM Mentor is well versed in leading and managing program/project team members from diverse backgrounds, and within global and virtual settings. In a program/project crisis, the mentor can be called in to fill in for an extended period of time for an unexpected absence of the senior project manager or program manager. Mentors play an important role in standardizing the practice of the agreed-upon methodology, in building a project management culture, and in spreading the project management "gospel" throughout the organization by troubleshooting projects in functional areas enterprisewide. This role is for experienced and highly skilled senior project or program managers with superior or advanced interpersonal skills. Mentors report to the Manager of Project Managers and work closely with the Manager of Project Support to assist the entire SPO staff in professional development or to effectively deliver enterprise or divisional program/projects.

Suggested Duties and Responsibilities:

- Serve as a subject matter expert for project management processes and tools
- Work closely with or supervise Methodologists in the development of project management methodology and tools
- Offer consulting support to new and ongoing initiatives
- Work closely with Project Managers and Business Systems Analysts to ensure that all projects are managed using corporate accepted tools, techniques, and methodology processes
- Serve as a senior advisor on project management issues enterprisewide
- Able to provide vision and direction for strategic planning within the SPO and across the enterprise
- Provide advice, counsel, and mentoring to program and project managers
- Provide conflict resolution to troubled projects

Suggested Knowledge, Skills, and Abilities:

- Superior/advanced competency in project management processes
- Full proficiency with project management tools

- Excellent counseling, facilitation, conflict resolution, and interviewing skills
- Able to provide visionary leadership to SPO staff
- Skilled at internal/external consulting and relationship management
- Well-versed in industry and in organizational politics

Suggested Background, Experience, and Education:

- Extensive experience (ten or more years) in the management of projects, including demonstrated ability to manage large, complex projects or programs on time and within budget
- Extensive experience in relevant industry area and understanding of strategic issues that impact the company and project management
- PMP or other project management certification
- College degree in finance, accounting, subject related to the industry area, or a technical subject preferred; advanced degree in a business specialty or project management may be useful
- Experience with relevant enterprise project management and enterprise financial software
- Demonstrated success in the mentoring or management of other project managers or other experience on a management level within a project office
- Experience with roll-out of project management and process improvement in an organization, including implementation of standards or methodologies
- Ability to express complex technical concepts effectively, both verbally and in writing, to diverse groups of people

Program Manager

Role Overview:

In large organizations with many project managers, project managers may be awarded "grades" based on their span of control; a Program Manager role is a top-grade role to which project managers might aspire. Thus, many of the duties, skills, and background traits listed below are repeated in the role description for Project Manager. However, this position manages complex, strategic projects that span organizational boundaries, so Program Managers should also have experience managing multiple high-risk projects, including projects involving external vendors and multiple business areas. This grade is a logical training ground for Manager of Project Managers, Manager of Project Support, Strategic Project Office Director, and CPO positions for the program manager with business acumen. When groups of related projects are organized into programs, this position may manage multiple project managers whose projects provide specific deliverables, all of which must be collectively managed to provide the desired programmatic results.

Suggested Duties and Responsibilities:

- Manage and direct multiple medium- to large-scale projects
- Translate generalized customer business goals and objectives into concrete strategy and tactical plans
- Work on complex problems where analysis of situation or data requires an in-depth evaluation of various factors to achieve best results
- Exercise judgment within broadly defined policies and practices to develop corporate methods, techniques
- Work effectively with internal and external clients, third-party vendors, and senior management in accomplishing project objectives
- Evaluate complex situations accurately and identify viable solutions that create successful outcomes for the customer
- Work closely with the Program Sponsor and Program Review Board to facilitate decisions necessary for program delivery
- Oversee effective project oversight and reviews to effect program success
- Develop and maintain "lessons-learned" inputs to the project repository for utilization in future programs initiated by the enterprise
- Resolve political, resource, budgeting, change, and legal issues affecting the program
- Serve as a mentor/advisor/decision maker to project managers for the program for issues related to corporate politics, external politics, client relations, governmental regulation, project quality, project risk, and safety
- Oversee development of proposals and requests for proposals associated with the program
- Oversee vendor relations and procurement related to the program
- Oversee execution and delivery of projects related to successful program execution

Suggested Knowledge, Skills, and Abilities:

- Understanding of the strategic and operational issues of the project or business unit
- Ability to train, mentor, and develop project managers in project management methodologies and their application

- Liaison and consultative skills; negotiating skills within a context of high political sensitivity and conflicting interests
- Presentation and written communication skills, including proposal writing
- Ability to advise on complex matters to nonspecialists
- Demonstrated ability in managing internal and external client expectations on program requirements and deliverables
- Highly developed business acumen
- Skilled at requirements analysis and management
- Strong writing, mentoring, negotiation, communication, and meeting facilitation skills; ability to utilize a combination of formal authority and persuasion skill sets
- Strong integration skills; ability to coordinate all aspects of a project or program
- Strong leadership, organizational, and interpersonal skills
- Ability to manage in a matrix environment

Suggested Background, Experience, and Education:

- College degree in a technical discipline; education in finance/ accounting or an MBA helpful; related work experience can be substituted for educational requirement in some industries
- Must have held project management and leadership positions (reflecting increasing levels of responsibility) in an organization of comparable size; five to seven years of project management experience with experience in large, complex projects and management of distributed project resource teams; three to five years of experience in the industry with previous supervisory or coaching experience
- Proficiency in relevant computer applications
- PMP or other project management certification
- Demonstrated experience leading cross-functional teams within a formalized methodology

Project Manager

Role Overview:

This role manages cross-functional teams responsible for delivering defined project outputs on time, within budget, and with quality results. Project Managers plan, organize, monitor, and oversee one or more projects to meet defined requirements or business specifications. They work closely with the Manager of Project Support and others in project management to guide efforts toward achieving intended business results. They report to a Program Manager, Manager of Project Managers, SPO Director, Executive Sponsor, or other senior project management role. Project Managers have primary responsibility for defining, planning, tracking, and managing the enterprise project, for identifying key resources and providing the direction they require in order to meet project objectives. They also ensure appropriate management, customer, and supplier involvement throughout the life of the project. Selecting the right person for the role of project manager is crucial to project success.

Suggested Duties and Responsibilities:

- Determine project goals and priorities with management program manager and/or project sponsors, SPO Director, or CPO
- Select team members; may not have direct supervisory responsibility (such as hiring and performance/pay reviews) for project team members, but provides performance input to team members' functional managers and/or the SPO Director or Project Support Manager
- Support requirements of the enterprise program manager (if supporting a program) to provide necessary information and support for successful program delivery
- May be responsible for one or more projects
- Negotiate the performance of activities with team members and their managers if operating in a matrix environment
- Coach to clarify assignments and deliverables; mentor others in project management practices; review quality of work and manage integration of team members' work
- With Project Support Manager, strategize to optimize professional development for each team member
- Co-create a project charter with the team, including the definition of completion criteria
- Manage and communicate a clear vision of the project's objectives, and motivate the project team to achieve them; create a project environment that enables peak performance by team members
- Organize the work into manageable activity clusters (phases) and determine an effective approach to completing the work
- With Estimator(s), compile a complete and accurate estimate of a project, using reserves appropriately
- With Project Planner(s), prepare project plan and obtain management approval

- Analyze risks, establish contingency plans, and identify trigger events and responsibility for initiating mitigating action; oversee activities of Risk Administrator: gather stakeholder input and rank the top project risks in terms of total impact
- Work with Planner/Scheduler/Controller in tracking and reporting on progress to plan, cost and schedule reporting, and change control
- Analyze the actual performance against the plan and make adjustments consistent with plan objectives
- Manage relationships with project stakeholders, including internal and external clients and vendors, keeping the stakeholders informed of progress and issues in order to manage expectations on all project requirements and deliverables
- Involve functional expertise and specialist SPO staff in design reviews and key decisions
- Manage change to preserve business plan commitments; initiate review if objectives must change
- Establish and publish clear priorities among project activities
- Arbitrate and resolve conflict and interface problems within the project
- Manage the financial aspects of the project: budgeting, estimate to actual variance, capital project management, etc.
- With Librarian, oversee project documentation and updates to relevant knowledge bases; analyze lessons learned and share with other project directors and project managers
- With Analyst(s), analyze original estimate against actual hours and duration, and understand the factors that contributed to any variance
- Effectively coordinate the activities of the team to meet project milestones
- Provide input/justification for project costs and budget impact
- Work with Methodologist to ensure implementation of SPO standards, processes, and support services
- Proactively identify changes in work scope and ensure appropriate planning measures are taken with internal and external clients to reassess and amend the scope of work requirement, budget, and timeline
- Oversee the reporting activities of Planners and Analysts, determining when to escalate issues to appropriate levels of management
- Represent project at meetings and with external consultants and departmental and senior management to ensure that priorities are communicated and understood, and that progress/delays/issues are reported

- Determine what constitutes successful closure for all parties; gain acceptance and sign-off by all parties when closure is attained
- Resolve issues related to client relations, governmental relations, project quality, project risk, and project safety
- Manage vendor relations and procurement related to the project(s)

Suggested Knowledge, Skills, and Abilities:

- Knowledge of and competency in project management processes, including planning tasks and allocating resources, risk management, issues management, time management, financial management, HR management, working in teams, quality management, monitoring and reporting, documentation, and record keeping
- Ability to plan and facilitate meetings
- Knowledge of the strategic and operational issues of the project or business unit
- Strategic, conceptual analytical thinking and decision-making skills
- Adaptability and flexibility, including ability to manage deadline pressure, ambiguity, and change
- Negotiating skills within a context of political sensitivity and conflicting interests
- Presentation and written communication skills
- Ability to advise on complex matters to nonspecialists; ability to communicate effectively with senior management
- A clear vision of what determines a successful project for the customer and for the company
- A technical background sufficient to understand the technologies and technical issues involved with the project and industry, to anticipate and identify technical obstacles, and to make accurate technology decisions
- Personal integrity and courage to escalate issues about the project to management when necessary and to advocate for responsible solutions to project problems
- Extensive knowledge of project management methodology
- Exceptional interpersonal skills; the ability to work well with people from many different disciplines with varying degrees of technical experience; competence in clear, concise, and tactful communication with senior management, clients, peers, and staff
- Ability to build teams and generate a spirit of cooperation while coordinating diverse activities and groups; people management and negotiating skills within a team environment
- Ability to negotiate consensus among diverse groups and impact the activities of others not in own reporting structure

- Budget management skills; ability to analyze and review financing plans and related budgetary information to determine the impact on a project is required

Suggested Background, Experience, and Education:

- College degree, preferably in a technical subject; minor or advanced degree in business or industry-related subject is a plus; in some industries, work experience can be substituted for educational credentials
- PMP certification and/or other industry and project management certifications
- Three to five years of experience in using formal project management methodology, techniques, and tools
- Demonstrated expertise in creating and maintaining project deliverables such as project charter, project plan, status reports, project timesheets, estimates, communication plan, reports, risk management plan, budget (work hours and cost), milestone/deliverable charts
- Demonstrated experience in managing issues, scope, and quality while bringing projects to successful completion within the cost and time requirements
- Proficiency with project management software tools used by the enterprise
- Industry experience preferred
- Demonstrated expertise in teambuilding and leading teams

Note on Project Manager Career Pathing

In large organizations with many project managers, project managers might be awarded "grades" based on their level of experience and expertise. A "Senior Project Manager" has all the qualifications listed above. In addition, because this position manages complex, strategic projects that span organizational boundaries, Senior Project Managers should have managed two or more high-risk projects, including projects involving external vendors and multiple business areas. Typically, large projects and high-risk projects would be given to more senior PMs. This grade is a logical training ground for Director of Project Support, Director of SPO, and CPO positions for the project manager with business acumen. In organizations with groups of related projects organized into programs, this position might be titled Program Manager; or, this level of skill might be assigned the role of Project Management Mentor.

Project Team Leader

(Other titles that may be descriptive of this role include Project Leader, Project Coordinator, Team Lead)

Role Overview:

The Project Team Leader is usually a senior staff member appointed by the Project Manager to head up a sub-project group, and to supervise and represent a team within a large project. A Project Team Leader may be responsible for one or more project components. Team leaders should possess a subset of the skills and experience necessary to a Project Manager. This role is a natural step in the career path to project managership. At a minimum, the Team Leaders should display:

- Knowledge of the principles and practices of contemporary project management
- Understanding of the strategic and operational issues of the project or business unit
- Conceptual and analytical thinking skills
- Decision-making and problem-solving skills
- General knowledge of the use and application of project management tools and techniques
- Adaptability and flexibility, including ability to manage pressure, ambiguity, and change
- General management skills necessary to plan, organize, and prioritize workload
- Ability to work in teams
- Communication skills required for reporting on progress and leading meetings
- Ability to prioritize and manage well under deadline pressure

II. Team Members

Project Support Team Members

(Other titles that may be descriptive of this role include Specialist Team Member)

Role Overview:

The Project Team members are appropriately skilled individuals who report to the Manager of Enterprise Project Support. They are assigned full-time to the Strategic Project Office, but may be assigned to an individual project full-time, part-time, or variably, based on the needs of the project. Naturally, the exact roles of team members will vary by project and by industry. We have attempted to create descriptions of the specifically project management-related roles that might be based in a Strategic Project Office. Specialist Team Roles within the project management discipline can include such roles as Controller, Scheduler, Risk Management, Methodologist, Systems Analyst, as well as a number of other, less-common titles, as described below. At a minimum, all team members, even those whose involvement in the project is on an as-needed basis from another functional area, should possess:

- Skills for working in teams: communication (oral and written), collaboration, problem solving in a team context
- Understanding of contemporary project management principles and practices
- Understanding of the strategic and operational issues of the project or business unit

Project Controller

(Other titles that may be descriptive of this role include Project Controls Manager, Controls Manager, Project Controls Specialist)

Role Overview:

Project Controllers have the primary responsibility of tracking enterprise or divisional program and project performance against budgets, plans, and schedules. Their primary area of responsibility is managing the integration of multiple programs and/or projects, providing data, analysis, and reporting to project managers and various levels of management. Project Controllers may have:

- Responsibility for integrating data from hundreds of programs and projects to provide many types of information and reporting, including; trend analysis, earned value analysis, divisional or enterprise resource forecasts, resource modeling, resource leveling, cost profiling, project prioritization, divisional or enterprise budgeting, periodic status reports to departments, to divisions, and to enterprise executives
- Control of costs and schedule and associated documents, especially those concerned with changes

- To work with other departments, implementation contractors, and consultants to support multiple project teams through the implementation of project management controls, assisting Project Managers in conducting variance analysis, performing assessments, project forecasting and projections, managing changes, and producing a variety of management reports

See notes below regarding reporting structure and career pathing under Project Planner. Project Controllers in large and complex organizations (or Project Planner/Controllers in smaller organizations) may have an assistant/administrative position, the Issue Resolution and Change Control Coordinator, with a subset of the following responsibilities, specifically those related to administration, data entry, and communication reporting to them.

Suggested Duties and Responsibilities:

- Develop and implement procedures, systems, and reports pertaining to program/project status and forecasts. Responsible for the cost/schedule control system, cost estimating capability, and the management reporting on these
- Provide input and review for development of schedule, work breakdown structure, estimates, and work packages during the different phases of a project
- Provide input and review project estimates
- Maintain accurate records of committed, expended, and forecast costs and monitor all organizational project costs to verify the Planned Value, Earned Value, Actual Cost, Cost Variance, Estimate to Complete, and Estimate at Completion.
- Maintain accurate time estimating and tracking for all organizational projects to verify the Planned Value, Earned Value, Actual Cost, Schedule Variance, Estimate to Complete, and Estimate at Completion
- Oversee management of scope changes, trends, and change notices initiated from the project management system and review time and cost implications
- Manage the transfer of cost data from financial, accounting, and procurement systems to the organizational project control system; review data transfer errors with the appropriate Project Planner or Project Manager and coordinate corrections with the accounting staff
- Operational responsibility also includes cross-functional integration of above items with other systems especially finance, purchasing, and contracts

- Develop timely, accurate, in-depth analysis of organizational cost and schedule data and provide corrective action recommendations; develop and implement project cost and schedule baselines; develop, track, and report subcontract accruals; track and monitor acquisition commitments; develop strategic planning schedules and provide support to project management in cost, schedule, performance measurement, forecasting, and variance analysis
- Apply appropriate metrics and tools for project control
- Recognize and evaluate actual or proposed changes to any aspect of a project scope or schedule
- Provide cash-flow analysis reports
- Identify cost-savings opportunities and develop programs to achieve long-term savings

Suggested Knowledge, Skills, and Abilities:

- Sound task management skills and demonstrated strong analytical ability
- Ability to assign and manage work activities and meet deadlines
- Strong oral and written communication skills
- Strong attention to detail and organizational skills
- Ability to work effectively as a member of a team and foster teamwork in others
- Demonstrated ability to handle multiple concurrent assignments
- Advanced computer skills and knowledge of the most current industry standard computerized project control applications, such as cost and planning software; working knowledge of computer relational databases, computer estimating systems, and budget control monitoring techniques
- Proficiency in project control techniques and principles, and the ability to perform comprehensive organizational forecasting and analysis
- Positive customer service orientation required, with both internal and external clients
- Strong interpersonal skills required, demonstrating a consistent commitment and ability to work with diverse workgroups and individuals
- Ability to work in a flexible team environment and independently with minimal supervision
- High-level numeracy, analytical skills, and management accounting knowledge
- Ability to write clear, concise reports for project reporting

Suggested Background, Experience, and Education:

- Experience summarizing results and producing project management reports
- Experience in budgeting, forecasting, scheduling (CPM), and analytical reporting, including baselines development and Earned Value Management systems
- Proficiency with project controls computer applications used by employer
- Five to ten years of experience in a project management role; five or more years in planning/scheduling/controls functions
- Industry experience
- PMP or other project management certification; certification in cost and/or contract management a plus
- College degree in a technical field with up to three to ten years of experience required, depending on size and complexity of project organization

Project Planner

Role Overview:

Planners assist Project Managers and Systems Analysts by developing, analyzing, and managing project plans, schedules, and resource forecasts. In organizations that run many projects concurrently, Planners focus on the project planning phases while working closely with Schedulers, Controllers, and Analysts to create schedules and keep the plan current and meaningful. In smaller organizations or project offices, the Planner role might include elements of the roles described in this appendix as Project Analyst, Controller, Estimator, and Scheduler; for this reason, the Planner role is often subject to overload. In this situation, individual and organizational needs should be carefully weighed (engaging the services of the Organizational Development Analyst) to create and fill Planner roles that both reflect the requirements of projects and the varying attributes (such as business acumen, technical skill, facility with analysis and figures, ability to negotiate with vendors and so on) that indicate whether a person would perform best as Planner/Scheduler, or Planner/Analyst, Planner/Estimator, or Planner/Business Analyst. Planners with strong leadership, facilitative, and interpersonal skills are good candidates for Project Manager. This is a role that could have multiple career paths, depending on the personal characteristics and education of the individual. Planners generally work on multiple projects and report to the Project Support Manager, while working closely with and under the supervision of the Program or Project

Managers they support. Entry-level Planners report to a Lead Planner in larger organizations.

Suggested Duties and Responsibilities:

- Prepare and keep current master project plans as well as sub-project plans for monitoring and tracking the requirements, and stay abreast of changes to the requirements
- Develop work breakdown structures; Critical Path Method (CPM) schedules; and resource, cost, and budget plans
- With Scheduler, create project timelines (if using Scheduler Role)
- With Project Controller, update master and sub-project plans with new information as changes occur; monitor dependencies affected by changes
- Provide key data to Portfolio Manager to update project status and impact on overall portfolio (e.g., timelines, budget, resources, delays)
- Responsible for communicating any schedule conflicts, resource constraints, and time constraints to the project team
- Work with staff from throughout the company as well as with Project Managers to develop detailed project plans (with all tasks, durations, resources, etc.) from concept through completion for approved projects with all the interacting departments
- Communicate and publish plans to appropriate involved individuals to ensure each person understands the overall scope of the project and when tasks are required to begin and end
- Utilize relevant project management software applications to manage projects
- Review each project periodically to ensure projects are on time and within cost projections
- Prepare an executive summary of all exceptions on projects, inclusive of tasks that are behind schedule, tasks that are competing for the same resource, conflicting priorities and exemplary performance, etc., for the executive review
- Provide planning and resource allocation services that support the project schedule
- Support the preparation of progress reports, standardized reporting procedures, and the monitoring of overall project performance
- Lead Planners may manage junior planners in multiple locations and handle hundreds of projects in a distributed environment simultaneously

Suggested Knowledge, Skills, and Abilities:

- Must have strong oral and written communication skills
- Full proficiency with relevant software tools
- Ability to work in a cross-functional team environment
- Must be a team player and demonstrate a teamwork approach to performance
- Good time management skills
- Sound understanding of project management in relation to time-frames, dependencies, and critical paths
- Ability to work with all levels of management and technical staff
- Analytical ability and problem-solving skills
- Ability to remain calm and productive in a high-pressure environment

Suggested Background, Experience, and Education:

- Five to ten years of project planning skills required for a Lead Planner
- Demonstrated knowledge of project management, with hands-on experience and proficiency using project management tools and computer-based scheduling systems
- Experience developing project-specific and high-level milestone deliverable master plans to meet defined business objectives
- Experience in helping develop work breakdown structures in creating project schedules and estimates
- Experience with program scheduling, to include an understanding of networks and interdependencies
- Previous hands-on project experience and experience working on industry-related projects
- Experience with project earned value principles
- Education may vary according to industry: for a Lead Planner, work experience in industry may substitute for a college (two- or four-year) degree in a technical field
- PMP or other project management certification helpful; other technical certifications as relevant to industry

Project Planners often lead small project initiatives (generally less than a month in duration with one or two people); are skilled in reviewing project deliverables and technical documentation; and are capable of leading facilitation sessions for group reviews and project charter definitions.

Lead Planners must have a proven track record in effectively applying project management. They may have led small-medium project initiatives (generally one to three months in duration with three to six people).

Project Scheduler

Role Overview:

The roles of Planner and Scheduler are frequently combined; but, in large organizations running many concurrent projects, they may be separated. The Scheduler is responsible for the development and maintenance of schedules for multiple, large or complex projects and programs. See notes above on reporting structure and career pathing under Project Planner.

Suggested Duties and Responsibilities:

- Create, manage, maintain, and update schedules in a complex project environment
- Develop policy and procedures to improve the adequacy and efficiency of the scheduling processes
- Perform critical path analysis and develop timelines for completion of tasks, measuring the deliverable work packages of the project against the project plan; develop work breakdown structure
- May manage junior schedulers in multiple locations and oversee multiple projects in a distributed environment simultaneously
- Keep Project Managers informed of impacts to project schedule
- Work with Analysts to ensure that schedule data is accurately interpreted; work with Planners to ensure that schedule changes and their impacts are accurately reflected in the master plan

Suggested Knowledge, Skills, and Abilities:

- Must have strong oral and written communication skills and problem solving abilities
- Good analytical skills and expertise with relevant software tools
- Ability to work in a cross-functional team environment; able to work with all levels of management and technical staff
- Must be a team player and demonstrate a teamwork approach to performance
- Good time management skills

- Sound understanding of project management in relation to time-frames, dependencies, and critical paths
- . Ability to remain calm and productive in a high-pressure environment

Suggested Background, Experience, and Education:

- Two to five years of project scheduling skills required for a Lead Scheduler
- Demonstrated knowledge of project management, with hands-on experience and proficiency using project management tools and computer-based scheduling systems
- Experience in developing project WBSs used to create project schedules and estimates
- Experience with program scheduling, to include an understanding of networks and interdependencies
- Previous hands-on project experience and experience working on industry-related projects
- Education may vary according to industry: for a Lead Scheduler, work experience in industry may substitute for a college (two- or four-year) degree in a technical field
- PMP or other project management certification helpful; other technical certifications as relevant to the industry
- High level of data manipulation and reporting knowledge required

Project Estimator

Role Overview:

This role works as a part of a team to develop detailed cost estimates during all phases of a project — in the proposal stage as well as for each scope change throughout the life cycle. The Estimator works with the Project Controller to continually keep project costs realistically forecast and recorded. Because poor estimation of costs is a primary contributor to project failure in many industries, the Estimator role is critical. It requires a skill set more consistent with cost management and accounting than with the facilitative role of Project Managers, yet it is a common error in organizations to expect both functions from the same person. An individual with business acumen or education might perform the role of both Estimator and Business Analyst in a smaller company; the Estimator skill set also overlaps with Project Control. One estimator can deal with many projects as early phases of the project typically require much higher levels of estimating support than do projects that are underway.

Suggested Duties and Responsibilities:

- Estimate labor requirements, required project equipment, supplies, contracted services, costs; prepare cost estimates and monitor expenditures
- Prepare estimates for proposed change orders and updates project plans and estimates with new information on change order approval
- With Business Analysts and Project Managers, work to accurately forecast costs of proposed projects
- Build systems to enhance organizational estimating capability
- Maintain estimating databases and integrate these databases with the enterprise project controls tools
- Integrate estimates with project schedules to achieve phased timing of costs and resources
- Support Risk Management Coordinator on quantitative risk assessments; provide inputs and analysis for prediction of project cost and resource risk

Suggested Knowledge, Skills, and Abilities:

- Excellent verbal and written communications skills, including the ability to interact effectively with customers and vendors
- Previous demonstrated experience in project cost and resource estimating
- High-level numeracy and familiarity with accounting and finance processes
- Ability to meet deadlines and work under stress
- Exposure to and general understanding of risk management tools and techniques
- Familiarity with enterprise project controls tools

Suggested Background, Experience, and Education:

- A minimum of two to five years of estimating experience in a related environment
- Proficiency with relevant computer applications
- High school graduate (minimum) or two-year degree with courses in accounting for entry-level Estimator
- Project management courses desirable; PMP required for advancement
- Experience working in cross-functional teams

Risk Management Coordinator

(Other titles that may be descriptive of this role include Risk Management Analyst, Risk Management Administrator, Risk Manager)

Role Overview:

Risk management has received increased attention in recent years as a neglected area of corporate planning and project execution. Creating a dedicated Risk Management Coordinator ensures that project risks will be adequately monitored and managed. Particularly when the Risk Management Coordinator supports multiple projects, there is less likelihood of a disconnect between projects creating an avoidable risk. Risk Management Coordinators work closely with Estimators, Business Analysts, Project Managers, and Project Controllers to assess, monitor, manage, and mitigate risk events throughout the project life cycle. They report to the Project Support Manager and work collaboratively with the Project Controllers or Planners of specific projects.

Suggested Duties and Responsibilities:

- Perform cost and schedule "what-if" analysis; prepare and effectively communicate corrective, mitigating, or improvement actions
- Identify project risk during project definition
- Perform risk assessment, qualification, analysis, and reporting
- Offer alternative solutions or mitigation plans
- Identify qualitative and quantitative impacts and recommend responses through prevention, mitigation, and contingency planning
- Communicate with others throughout the project organization about potential and identified risks and plans for corrective actions
- With Controller, monitor program/project risks, schedule, and cost variance

Suggested Knowledge, Skills, and Abilities:

- Facilitation, interviewing, and listening skills
- Experience in using advanced project risk assessment and analysis tools
- Experience in performing large, complex program and project risk assessments

- Knowledge of legal and regulatory requirements
- Organizational and problem-solving abilities
- Excellent written and verbal communication skills
- Thorough knowledge of industry
- Understanding of project management principles and practices
- Understanding of strategic implications and of initiatives being pursued through projects
- Research skills

Suggested Background, Experience, and Education:

- College degree in business, finance, or a related field
- Proficient in the use of advanced risk assessment software
- Three years of experience in project support, performing project scheduling, project planning, or project controls
- A breadth of personal knowledge and industry experience sufficient to be risk-aware
- PMP helpful; technical project management training a must
- Proficiency with the company-standard project management and productivity tools

Methodologist

(Other titles that may be descriptive of this role include Methodology Specialist, Process Improvement Coordinator, Manager of Methodology and Standards)

Role Overview:

A Methodologist keeps the SPO staff focused on the agreed-upon corporate standards for project management, while remaining alert to areas where improvements in process can be made. This requires a proactive approach to project management methodology, not simply a "policing" approach. Methodologists work with the CPO, the SPO director, Manager of Enterprise Project Support, Manager of Enterprise Project Managers, and Project Managers on projects for organizational improvement, including but not limited to defining, monitoring the use of, training in, and evaluating the effectiveness of project management methodologies. They may participate in organizational assessments such as those required to determine a project management maturity baseline, and set up benchmarking processes to identify best practices. This role also drives best practices usage within the organization to ensure processes are supported and trained for.

Suggested Duties and Responsibilities:

- Develop and maintain the organization's approved project management methodology, processes, templates, guidelines, and procedures
- Develop repository standards with Knowledge Management Coordinator
- Develop training requirements on methods and processes with Organizational Support Analyst
- Evaluate, select, and maintain process management tools
- Serve as a subject matter expert for certain project management processes and tools
- Proactively identify process improvement opportunities; drive continuous process improvement via post-project reviews
- Coordinate with project managers to ensure that all new projects/processes are developed and optimized according to the company's standard procedures
- Maintain repository for project experience and models to ensure accurate and consistent project management processes
- Mentor and provide guidance to project teams on formal project methodologies

Suggested Knowledge, Skills, and Abilities:

- Solid understanding of project management, including project control, planning estimating, resource management, change management, issue management, risk management, vendor management, and quality assurance
- Knowledge of project management best practices, benchmarking techniques, maturity modeling, and other concepts in process assessment and improvement
- Expertise in project management methodology design and management
- Excellent communication skills and the ability to conduct oral presentations
- Strong verbal and written communications skills, as well as listening skills
- Ability to solicit and collaborate with all team members, including stakeholders
- Strong knowledge and understanding of project needs, with the ability to establish and maintain a high level of trust and confidence
- Ability to facilitate large meetings ranging from ten to thirty people
- Research skills

Suggested Background, Experience, and Education:

- Five to ten years of project management experience as a member of cross-functional project teams; project office experience strongly preferred
- Experience in the use of structured project management methodologies
- Proficiency in the use of project management tools
- Experience mentoring other project managers
- College degree in a business or technical field, with a process-improvement focus; advanced degree in business, quality management, or project management helpful
- PMP or other project management certification required

Business Analyst

Roles Overview:

Business Analysts (BAs) are a primary interface between projects and business partners. They are responsible for understanding current and future processes, including processes for the entire enterprise. They define and document business needs and requirements, and generate project business cases. BAs work with Project Managers at project initiation to define costs and benefits of a proposed project prior to the project being reviewed for inclusion in the portfolio. They may participate in portfolio review meetings. Business Analysts report to the SPO Director. This role may include Risk Analyst/Administrator duties or Estimator duties in smaller organizations.

Suggested Duties and Responsibilities:

- With functional area representatives and Estimator(s), define benefits and costs of projects
- Analyze alignment of proposals to corporate strategies
- Document requirements to meet business needs of organization
- Write and present business cases
- Participate in project and portfolio reviews to maintain project's alignment with business cases

Suggested Knowledge, Skills, and Abilities:

■ Strong business background with thorough knowledge of company's industry, markets, and strategy
■ Skilled writer and communicator
■ Skilled at developing and presenting presentations
■ Knowledge of project management principles and practices
■ Strong business acumen and high level of numeracy
■ Extensive knowledge of financial and accounting practices

Suggested Background, Experience, and Education:

■ College degree in business, finance, or related field; MBA desirable
■ Project management education and training
■ Three to five years of experience in industry
■ Experience on project teams a plus
■ College degree in Accounting or Finance, plus a minimum of five years of experience in financial statement preparation, budgeting, and cost analysis

Project Office Administrator

(Other related titles include Administrative Coordinator, Organizational Support Specialist, Project Administrator)

Role Overview:

The administrative role in a project should not be minimized or overlooked. Many project managers are burdened by job descriptions that include administrative tasks that are necessary, even critical, but that do not require a staff member with a PMP to perform them. Any time that an experienced, highly skilled Project Manager spends on administrative duties diminishes his or her ability to achieve the level of management oversight that results in successful projects. Project Administrators are responsible for performing a variety of tasks in support of project management, including clerical support such as company correspondence, presentations and training materials, maintaining calendars, setting up meeting logistics, making travel arrangements, and various other duties as needed. The gathering and organizing of data is a common task. With experience and continuing professional development, they may lead or direct communications activities within the Project Office and grow into the role of Knowledge Management Coordinator.

Suggested Duties and Responsibilities:

- Develop and maintain procedures, tools, and practices that systematically control revisions to the scope, schedule, and cost of organizational projects to ensure that:
  - Changes are well defined and coordinated
  - Changes are approved at appropriate authority levels
  - Approved changes are fully documented and promptly communicated to affected parties
- Review submitted requests within the organization for changes and ensure required signatures/documentation are completed; coordinate and conduct change control meetings; update and maintain change control database; maintain change control supportive documentation and issue various reports to show status of change control
- Maintain and monitor issue logs for all projects within the organization
- Scribing of notes at project meetings; annotating, finalizing, and managing multiple sets of notes
- Provide proactive support to SPO staff
- Assist with project management training coordination and meeting planning and management
- Create and distribute minutes and document the resolution of action items
- Support communication plan and knowledge management administrative responsibilities
- A broad range of documentation and administrative tasks, including scheduling and maintaining calendars, and other tasks as required

Suggested Knowledge, Skills, and Abilities:

- Excellent verbal and written communication skills with attention to detail
- Effective whether working independently or as part of a team
- Ability to multitask; good prioritization, time management, and organizational skills
- An understanding of project management terminology and practices

Suggested Background, Experience, and Education:

- Three to five years of work experience, preferably in a related industry or project environment
- High-school graduate, or two-year college degree, or equivalent work experience
- Project office experience a plus
- Expert level skills with the relevant software applications

Organizational Development Analyst

(Other titles that may be descriptive of this role include Project Human Resource Coordinator)

Role Overview:

The Organizational Development (OD) Analyst assists programs and projects by identifying and addressing the human impact issues such as risks and resistance that endanger the successful implementation of a program, project, or change initiative. They identify and address communication and performance needs. OD Analysts act as training, communications, and change management experts, both within the SPO and by interfacing with other functional areas that may be impacted by a project to manage the transition and minimize the impact of a change. They report to the Project Support Manager or SPO Director, and work closely with the corporate HR function to implement policies for training, retention, performance measurement, and professional development of project personnel that will lead to successful projects.

Suggested Duties and Responsibilities:

- Assist Strategic Project Office Director and HR department in developing position descriptions and performance management plans for SPO personnel
- Design, develop, and deploy corporate project management training, education, and development programs
- Build, deploy, and maintain enterprise project management competency program
- Assist Methodologist with organizational assessments
- Assist Manager of Enterprise Project Support and Manager of Enterprise Project Managers with duties related to performance management and professional development within the SPO

- Provide meeting support through advanced facilitation skills
- Work with the SPO Director and management staff to design and implement project management training programs
- Assess organizational and human issues associated with implementation and change projects within the enterprise; provide recommendations for overcoming resistance and building morale

Suggested Knowledge, Skills, and Abilities:

- Understanding of contemporary project management principles and practices
- Understanding of the strategic and operational issues of the project or business unit
- Understanding of industry issues
- Superior/advanced listening, interviewing, facilitation, and conflict resolution skills
- Thorough understanding of organizational dynamics, including political issues and information flow
- Excellent communication skills, including writing, presentations, teaching, and coaching
- Ability to design training programs, including performance metrics

Suggested Background, Experience, and Education:

- College degree in human resource development or related field
- Project management training and education
- One to three years of project office or cross-functional team experience
- Certifications in organizational development or human resource management subjects a plus
- Experience developing training programs

Systems Analyst

Role Overview:

A Systems Analyst analyzes, designs, and develops information systems to support project management and acts as subject matter expert in project management technology, assisting other project personnel in effective use of these tools. In a small project office, this role might be combined with that of Project Controller if the candidate has the requisite project management experience.

Suggested Duties and Responsibilities:

- Customize, configure, and troubleshoot software to support project management methodology and practice
- Define appropriate technology deployment strategies to increase organization's maturity in project management tool use
- Identify project management software implementation and use best practices, document guidelines and procedures, and train the organization on the project management software applications
- Integrate project management software with enterprise management and reporting tools such as executive reporting, time collection, payroll, financial, budgeting, procurement, and reporting systems
- Develop and deploy enterprise project controls tools, procedures, and systems
- Maintain project controls tools with high levels of system availability
- Monitor compliance of SPO standards as institutionalized in software products
- Coach and mentor teams on project management tools
- Serve as a subject matter expert for certain project management processes and tools

Suggested Knowledge, Skills, and Abilities:

- Ability to understand and appreciate project management technology and best practices, as well as the ability to learn and apply new technologies and tools quickly
- Good communication skills, both written and oral
- Knowledge of business systems and how they integrate with the project controls tools
- Full proficiency in a wide range of project management and productivity tools
- Ability to work well in teams
- Ability to assist in preparation of technology training programs
- Teaching or coaching ability a plus, but not required

Suggested Background, Experience, and Education:

- Computer Science, Management Information Systems, or related college degree, or equivalent work experience and technical training
- Proficient in relevant software applications

- One to three years of project office or project team experience
- Project management certification or other technical certifications as appropriate to industry and tools used in company

Knowledge Management (KM) Coordinator

(Other titles that may be descriptive of this role include Documentation Specialist, Project Librarian, Project Information Coordinator)

Role Overview:

Formerly more often known as "Librarian" in organizations with sophisticated lessons learned repositories, this position is growing in importance due to the widespread recognition that project historical documents are only the first step in capturing, documenting, storing, and sharing the knowledge gained by the organization in the course of each project. Today, a KM Coordinator works primarily with Web-based tools to make project information widely accessible to project teams. He or she works closely with the Methodologist to make methodology components available to SPO staff, and with Planners and Controllers to capture and communicate project status, trends, and histories. Sharing administrative tasks with a Project Administrator, this role manages all project documents and maintains the corporate repository of project wisdom. This position reports to the Manager of Enterprise Project Support or an SPO Director but works closely with all members of the project office.

Suggested Duties and Responsibilities:

- Manage all project documents and coordinate documentation revisions and releases; ensure that project documents are archived for later retrieval
- Update project management Web sites, intranet, or community of practice tool
- Manage a historical database of project timeframes and estimates to improve the estimation process for future projects
- Implement and ensure controls for reproduction of "controlled documents" to minimize potential use of obsolete documents, and establish the process to cross-reference the documentation
- Develop lessons learned by applying developed project knowledge to augment corporate intellectual capital
- Support department objectives regarding appropriate methodology

- With Methodologist, provide contributions to knowledge management portions of project management manuals for all enterprise customers
- Assist in developing written processes, procedures, and flowcharts to support department activities
- Facilitate communication within the team by ensuring accessibility and completeness of information
- Maintain repository standards
- Maintain and perform periodic archiving of project records

Suggested Knowledge, Skills, and Abilities:

- Strong written communication skills and the ability to apply appropriate communication techniques to various individuals across the enterprise
- Knowledge of systems and tools for the organizing, archiving, and retrieval of documents
- Knowledge of project management principles and practices
- Research skills
- Able to handle multiple projects and deadlines
- Detail oriented and flexible

Suggested Background, Experience, and Education:

- Technical documentation abilities
- Three to five years of project administrative support experience
- Proficiency in the relevant project management, productivity, and KM tools
- College degree in library science, knowledge management, or technical communication preferred
- Project management training required; PMP needed for advancement

Communications Planner

(Other titles that may be descriptive of this role include Project Communications Coordinator, Project Office Communications Specialist, Communications Administrator)

Role Overview:

In a large and complex organization, a dedicated role for project and SPO communications is necessary to smooth over the many potential opportunities for disconnect and miscommunication in the fast-paced life of projects. Working with the Knowledge Management Coordinator and Project Administrator(s), the Communications Planner specializes in keeping SPO personnel informed and in touch with each other and with stakeholders elsewhere in the organization or externally. In smaller organizations and when the staff member is appropriately skilled, this role might be combined with the Knowledge Management Coordinator or a Project Administrator's duties.

Suggested Duties and Responsibilities:

- Help develop enterprisewide and project communications plan
- Determine communication strategies and medium for information delivery
- Interface with internal and external organizations for information delivery
- Ensure timely delivery of all project statuses
- Determine audiences requiring communications
- Identify and implement effective techniques to communicate project/program objectives, responsibilities, ideas, feedback, and other appropriate information
- Might publish SPO newsletter and contribute to community of practice Web site and intranet

Suggested Knowledge, Skills, and Abilities:

- Superior/advanced written communication skills
- Understanding of organizational dynamics and communication networks, formal and informal, within the SPO
- Excellent interpersonal skills
- Strong organizational and administrative skills
- Knowledge of communications delivery instruments
- Technical documentation abilities

Suggested Background, Experience, and Education:

- Three to five years of project administrative support, business communications, public relations, or marketing experience

- Experience working in a Project Office and on cross-functional teams
- Experience with planning and producing communications documents
- Proficiency in the relevant project management, productivity, and publishing tools
- College degree in technical writing, English, or business communication preferred
- Project management training required; PMP needed for advancement

Relationship Manager

Other titles that may be descriptive of this role include: Contracts Manager, Procurement Coordinator, Outsourcing Manager, Vendor Support Specialist.

Role Overview:

The growth of outsourcing as a strategy for success has meant a proliferation of partnerships, contracts, vendors, and relationships for the organization. Research shows that companies that fail at outsourcing arrangements generally do so because of failed relationship and contract management. The Relationship Manager manages contracts with vendors from project initiation to post-project review, to ensure that the partnership is successful.

Suggested Duties and Responsibilities:

- Work external contacts and vendors to facilitate project management; obtain and share information and develop consensus on issues related to partnerships and outsourcing contracts
- Maintain an adequate working knowledge of relevant subject matter to current assigned contracts, relationships, and projects

Suggested Knowledge, Skills, and Abilities:

- Must be able to work independently and handle multiple projects

Suggested Background, Experience, and Education:

- Project management experience required

- Computer literacy in word processing, spreadsheet, and graphics required with project management preferred
- Contracts management experience
- Extensive industry knowledge and familiarity with outsourcing best practices

Note

1. For contributions to our descriptions of executive and project manager roles, we are particularly indebted to the role descriptions and templates published on projectconnections.com, accessed in May 2003.

Appendix B

Excerpt from Project Management Maturity Model[1]

Project Human Resource Management

The overall purpose of human resource management is to identify the requisite skill sets required for specific project activities, to identify individuals who have those skill sets, and to assign roles and responsibilities for the project, managing and ensuring high productivity of those resources, and forecasting future resource needs.

Components

Organizational Planning

This refers to the activities of identifying, documenting, and assigning project roles, responsibilities, and reporting relationships for the project.

Staff Acquisition

This covers identifying, soliciting, and acquiring the necessary resources for the project.

Team Development and Buy-In

Team development is the act of creating synergy between project team members to enhance productivity, efficiency, and overall project success. Are there guidelines and standards in place to promote team buy-in to the project? They should feel a part of the process of requirements analysis, scope development, etc.

Special Interest Component — Professional Development

The overall purpose of professional project management development is to develop the level of professionalism that exists within the organization's project manager and project team member resource pool, as well as to develop how the organization supports and views the professional requirements for project management. This is viewed by the following subcomponents.

Individual Project Management Knowledge

Individual knowledge base refers to the knowledge acquired by the individual in project management — a degree, a certificate, an awareness of the need for project management education.

Individual Project Management Experience/Competence

This refers to the individual's actual experience in working on or leading projects. Examples of project experience include working as a project controller, planner or scheduler, estimator, project management process expert, methodologist, project administrative support (change control, action item, contract compliance, reporting, etc.), or mentor. Competency is measured by determining the effectiveness of an individual's work efforts, or an individual's ability to successfully lead the delivery of projects of varying size and complexity.

Corporate Initiative for Project Management Development

If the corporation acknowledges project management as a cornerstone for building corporate success, then they will incorporate environmental success factors, such as formalized professional developmental programs or project management career path (including training, compensation, motivation, etc.) for their project managers and project team members.

Level 1: Initial Process

There is recognition within the organization of the need for a human resource project management process consisting of identifying resource requirements and "reserving" them; however, there are no established practices or standards. This ad hoc process is used to determine how many people would be required to accomplish project activities and define who is available. In general, the "warm-body" concept applies, which means that there is an assumption that any person can serve in whatever capacity necessary. Documentation is loose and might exist in the form of a list of people working on a project. As such, informal project teams might exist in an ad hoc sense. Metric data exists only from the standpoint of who worked on the last project, but is not required.

Organizational Planning

There is an ad hoc process of determining how many people are required to work on project activities. An informal reporting relationship exists, such that project staff members know that they need to get their project assignments from the project manager.

Staff Acquisition

There is an ad hoc process of finding who is available to work on project activities and going to line management to ask to have certain resources for a project.

Team Development

There is an ad hoc process of trying to ensure that project team members work together in a professional manner, which may include occasionally trying to get complementary personalities on the same project team. Occasional team meetings can be held whereby the team may be included in an explanation of the direction of the organization to the level that deliverables, scope, WBS, and the like have been defined.

Professional Development

There are pockets within the organization that have recognized that the skills and abilities required to successfully lead a project are different than for other job functions, and thus could be considered a separate job function. However, there are no corporate standards or processes in place from which one can build the justification for a professional project management career path. Individual managers may recognize and give credit to specific individuals for their project-related accomplishments, but this is done on an ad hoc and individual basis.

Individual Project Management Knowledge

Some individuals within the organization may be recognized or acknowledged for knowing more than others about some project management aspects, such as an ability to use a scheduling tool, an awareness of a budgeting mechanism, or an ability to develop a general project scope statement.

Individual Project Management Experience/Competence

Some individuals within the organization may be recognized or acknowledged for successfully working on or managing a project. This success is considered unique to the abilities of the individual.

Corporate Initiative for Project Management Development

Some managers within the organization may have acknowledged or recognized the accomplishments of an individual who has worked on or has led a project with a successful outcome.

Level 2: Structured Process and Standards

There is a documented, repeatable process in place that defines how to define, acquire, and manage the human resources in the form of suggested inputs, tools and techniques, and outcomes. Formal teams are established on large projects that are held accountable to follow the human resource management process. Management expects the project manager to have a project management human resource plan in place for large projects. Project team evaluations are conducted and project managers are expected to provide line management with a performance report for the individuals at the end of the project. Processes are readily available and integrated with other project planning elements.

Organizational Planning

The project manager creates a basic overview of the types of skill sets that are required by the project and the approximate timeframe in which these skill sets are needed. Basic responsibility definition exists in the form of a responsibility assignment matrix by major deliverable. A project organization chart exists so that the individuals on the project know who reports to whom on the project. An informal analysis (which consists of the project team discussing these elements and defining their response, but no formal evaluation document produced for management) is conducted to define the organizational, technical, and interpersonal interfaces that exist within the organization. There is an understanding of the constraints that may be prevalent in attaining required resources, such as the type of organization (hierarchical to projectized), and individual preferences to work on one project or another. In addition to a project organization chart, there is a narrative description of the responsibilities for the key project personnel and a staffing plan that defines when resources will be needed. As the project progresses, measurement of planning versus actual will occur with regard to the staffing plan. Updated planning information will come from project integration and the staffing plan will provide corrective action, as necessary.

Staff Acquisition

Staff acquisition consists of identifying the individuals who have the requisite skill sets and time availability to work on the project. The project manager requests line management to reserve team members for a certain timeframe. A staffing requirements document will be submitted from cost management as an input for defining the staffing management plan. There is a "first-come, first-serve" process in place whereby whoever requests a resource first gets usage of that resource first. In addition, when a resource is assigned by line management to a project, line management documents that resource's labor category, so that the project manager can utilize that information for costing purposes. If there is another project or assignment of extremely high priority, a resource may be withdrawn from a project by organizational management for a short period of time. The staffing plan includes defining the parameters for the desired project team, including minimal experience, personal interests and characteristics, and availability to determine a good fit among project team members. However, the project manager must accept whatever resources are assigned by the line manager to the project. Project human resource management and the project office coordinate efforts in resource pool management.

Team Development

Project teams may or may not have had an opportunity to work together before; as such, the projects are begun with an informal kickoff in which the team members are briefed on the purpose of the project, their responsibility, and introductions to each other. There is a specified process for incorporating the team into scope development and the development of work plans, etc. In addition, there are guidelines in place for project initiation team meetings, scheduled status reviews, business reviews, technical reviews, and a plan for regular and ongoing project reviews. These reviews should include the team and will foster team buy-in. Regular status and progress meetings are conducted to keep project team members apprised of how the project is progressing, as well as to deal with issues that may arise. The project manager contributes to the performance evaluation of the individual team members. A rewards and recognition system is established whereby individual and team performance is acknowledged. A conflict management process is begun. Management enforces the process for team buy-in to ensure that teams are actively involved and integrated into scope planning and management of the project. A staff development plan is developed with the organization responsible for the professional development initiatives.

Professional Development

There is a general recognition within the organization that an individual's knowledge base, experience, and competence are contributing factors to the successful outcome of projects. As such, for large and highly visible projects, there is an expectation that the project manager will have a fundamental knowledge set about project management and that the individual project team will be made aware of what is expected of them with regard to project management planning components. The organization now has a track record that documents the value of an individual's knowledge base, experience, and competence as significant contributing factors to the successful outcome of projects. As such, the organization expects that most individuals working on projects will understand how to apply the fundamentals (triple constraint) of the corporate project management process. In addition, the organization has begun to define different project-related roles.

Individual Project Management Knowledge

It is expected that project managers on large or highly visible projects will follow a defined process for attaining the triple constraint (scope-schedule-cost) and will be able to document and track these elements. It is also expected that individual project team members will understand what is expected of them in fulfilling these elements (such as contribution to scope validation, identification of schedule activities, and estimation of associated hours for completing schedule activities). Most individuals working on projects are expected to understand how to define the triple constraint elements of scope, schedule, and cost, and what is required for tracking them. For large and highly visible projects, it is expected that the project managers will be able to develop a complete project plan and manage to that plan. Some individual project team members are beginning to recognize project-related areas of specialization, such as scheduling concepts, budgeting concepts, project management methodologies, etc.

Individual Project Management Experience/Competence

It is expected that project managers on large or highly visible projects have successfully managed other projects in the past through proper control of project outcomes, attaining a managed triple constraint and positive customer evaluations. It is expected that individual project team members have also had successful experience working on other projects and have demonstrated strong individual and teaming attributes, as well as timely delivery of high-quality deliverables. Most project managers within the organization have been project managers on previous projects and generally have a track record for successfully completing projects within the triple constraint parameters. Some individual project team members are beginning to demonstrate project-related specialties where they have strengths, such as planner/scheduler, estimator, or methodologist.

Corporate Initiative for Project Management Development

The organization acknowledges that it is necessary to have a defined project management process and has made an educational course available to project managers and project team members on large or highly visible projects to educate them on how to utilize this defined process. In addition, there is a recognition process in place whereby those who are successful on large or highly visible projects will be acknowledged and compensated for their performance. The corporation makes available to anyone who will be involved on a project a project management essentials course, and all are encouraged to take this course to ensure a basic understanding of project management concepts and applicability. The organization is also beginning to define specific project-related roles that would be assigned to specific project team members. As such, the corporation recognizes that these separate roles will require different training, compensation, and motivation.

Level 3: Organizational Standards and Institutionalized Process

All projects are expected to follow the human resource planning process, which has been institutionalized. External stakeholders and customers are considered an integral part of the project team.

Organizational Planning

A formal analysis is conducted to define the organizational, technical, and interpersonal interfaces that exist within the organization. Constraints that may be prevalent in attaining required resources — such as the type of organization, individual preferences to work on one project or another — are analyzed and a response is developed. There is a narrative description of the responsibilities for all of the project personnel.

Staff Acquisition

The project manager works with the project office and line manager in resource pool management and prioritization. The project manager may need to negotiate with line management for specific resources, or will have "preassigned" resources. On occasion, the project manager may need to look outside the organization for specific expertise.

Team Development

The project manager works with the project office and line management to establish collocation, as necessary. Project team peer evaluations may be conducted by the team for individual peer performance. A conflict management process has been developed and is being utilized on most projects. Management is integrally involved in the team buy-in process, and a fully integrated project team includes the business unit, technical groups, strategic groups as necessary, the client, etc. All stakeholder input is fully solicited and is consciously incorporated into project planning and execution.

Professional Development

The organization has a defined project management process in place, and all project managers are expected to follow the process in planning and managing their projects. The organization has established different project-related roles and expects that the individuals who are pursuing a project-related career progression will complete a gap analysis defining their current project management knowledge and experience and their desired state, thus determining what their needs are.

Individual Project Management Knowledge

All project managers are expected to have a solid knowledge base about how to plan and track projects, including following the defined project management methodology of the organization, which addresses all knowledge areas. In addition, project managers are encouraged to pursue a relationship with a professional project management association and work toward a certificate or degree related to project management. Project team members who are interested in the profession of project management are encouraged to define an area of project specialty (or overall project management) and work toward attaining the knowledge required to fulfill that role.

Individual Project Management Experience/Competence

Project managers are evaluated on their project performance, which includes their ability to meet the triple constraint parameters, customer satisfaction, and project team member satisfaction, to define a competency range that can be utilized for defining effectiveness. Project team members are actively pursuing the organizationally defined project roles and effectiveness measurements that are established to define competency in each of these roles. Client satisfaction surveys are periodically conducted to ascertain the abilities and impact of the project manager. This information is utilized to help determine competency and contributes to performance-related compensation.

Corporate Initiative for Project Management Development

The corporation insists that all project stakeholders (within the organization) attend a project management essentials course that covers the basic elements of project management and the specific roles and responsibilities of various project stakeholders (such as executive management or project sponsor). In addition, there are a series of project management courses geared toward the career progression of a project manager and there is at least one course for each of the recognized project team specialty areas. The organization recognizes that effective project management is a cornerstone to organizational success and that to create an environment for success, the organization is responsible for defining project-related professional tracks. As such, the organization has defined different roles (and associated compensation, training, and motivation) within a project that are considered project team roles at or below the status of project manager: project manager, project controller, planner/scheduler, estimator, and project administrative support. Those who are interested in pursuing a career in a project-related discipline should have a gap analysis and game plan to gain the knowledge and skills required.

Level 4: Managed Process

All projects are expected to follow the human resource planning process, which has been mandated. Management expects the project managers, project office, and line managers to work cohesively in resource pool management and prioritization. Decisions relating to each project are evaluated in light of other projects. Project team evaluations and performance reporting for the individuals at the end of the project play a significant role in individual performance reviews and measurements. Project teams work in conjunction with other corporate processes and systems.

Organizational Planning

Project organizational planning is integrated into the overall resource pool management and prioritization. An action plan is developed to deal with the organizational, technical, and interpersonal interfaces that exist within the organization. Constraints to resource planning are managed. There is commitment by all stakeholders to the definition of the roles and responsibilities in the staffing plan. Integrated decision making (which means that decisions are evaluated based on their impact to both the project and the organization) begins to occur.

Staff Acquisition

The project office has an effective resource pool management (including skills inventory database) and prioritization process in place that is used by the line and project managers in fulfilling project resource needs. Resource variance reports are developed for all projects.

Team Development

The organization adheres to a team development process to foster team concepts throughout the organization. A team development process is established by which teams on medium and large projects are expected to evolve. Team member training needs are identified and communicated to the project office and line management, who proactively works with the team member to meet those training needs. The project manager significantly contributes to the performance evaluation of the individual. The conflict management process is being utilized on all projects. The team buy-in process is engaged and used by the majority of projects. Management is actively engaged in the team — there is probably a project board in place that represents all stakeholders in the project. This project board is actively involved in the project on a regular basis (status, execution, planning, etc.).

Professional Development

Management supports the integration of the professional project-related tracks into the corporate human resource structure of the organization. Individuals are specifically hired based upon their project management knowledge and competence in the planning and execution of projects.

Individual Project Management Knowledge

Project managers on large or highly visible projects are expected to have a degree or PMP®-type certificate. Project managers on small- or medium-sized projects are encouraged to pursue a certificate, degree, or foundation set that demonstrates a solid knowledge base in project management. Project team members who have chosen to focus on a project-related specialty area are actively pursuing a related certificate or degree in that area.

Individual Project Management Experience/Competence

A project-related role competency measurement has been defined and individuals are given a continuum that can be utilized for performance measurement and career growth. Client satisfaction surveys are periodically conducted to ascertain the abilities and impact of both the project manager and the project team members. This information is utilized to help determine competency and contributes to performance-related compensation.

Corporate Initiative for Project Management Development

The organization is actively staffing and providing a complete training curriculum for each of the different project-related roles from project manager to project sponsor to scheduler, etc. Additional project-related positions are defined by the organization for those who have the ability and interest to go beyond the general management of projects (and thus are considered positions above that of project manager) to project management process expert, project management methodologist, and project management mentor/advisor. A compensation package for each role is in place and is based upon performance measurements as defined in the role competency. Individuals are motivated based upon the career progression within the project management track, the incentives built into the system for successful project performance, and the customer satisfaction.

Level 5: Optimizing Process

An improvement procedure exists whereby the project management human resource planning processes and standards are periodically reviewed and enhancements are incorporated. Project teams identify and support improvements to the process. At the conclusion of each project, lessons learned are captured, evaluated, and incorporated into the process to improve the process and documentation. Management is actively involved in the resource management and prioritization process and reviews and supports improvements. Functional line management of other corporate processes and systems are aware, support, and involved in overall resource pool management and prioritization for projects and maintenance requirements. Resource pool management and the prioritization process are integrated such that management can see how resources are being utilized to ensure high productivity of resources. Project team evaluations and performance reporting contribute to overall project efficiency and effectiveness for enhanced resource utilization and corporate career path standards.

Organizational Planning

Organizational planning is evaluated on a periodic basis and enhancements to the process are continuously incorporated. Performance metrics for human resources are utilized to define efficiency and effectiveness of resource utilization throughout the project. Stakeholder analysis effectiveness and efficiency is evaluated to ensure continuous involvement and sign-off throughout the project. Integrated decision making (whereby all decisions are evaluated with regard to their impact on other projects) occurs in all projects. Lessons learned are captured for effective organizational planning.

Staff Acquisition

Enterprise resource forecasting is evaluated for continuous improvement and enhancements. The project manager resource requests are evaluated against the resource pool constraints and prioritization to ensure maximization of resource utilization in effectiveness and efficiency. Resource variance reports measure performance metrics of efficiency and effectiveness. Enterprise resource forecasting is being utilized. Lessons learned about the effectiveness of acquiring resources are captured.

Team Development

The organization values investing in its people throughout the organization and actively ensures that project teams have all that is required to succeed on a regular basis. The question is continually asked (especially at project end): Are there ways in which we could get better team buy-in? This information is used to improve the overall process. Team member training needs are forecasted and acknowledged as a value-added investment for the organization. Project conflict management process is integrated into the overall corporate management system, and efficiency and effectiveness measurements are gathered. Team satisfaction is measured. Lessons learned about effective means of developing team synergy are captured.

Professional Development

Improvement procedures are in place and utilized. Lessons learned are regularly examined and used to improve documented processes. Projects are given high value within the organization; thus there is high visibility to the individuals who are actively involved in projects on a regular basis. Projects are directly tied to the success of the organization; thus there is a financial tie to success of the organization and the project-related positions that are responsible for successful project performance.

Individual Project Management Knowledge

An improvement process is in place to continuously improve the individual's knowledge base in project management. Lessons learned are captured and used to improve the monitoring and control efforts. All senior project-related personnel are either certified or degreed in their project specialty area and are serving as mentors/advisors to those who are pursuing a project-related career path. All nonsenior project-related personnel are actively pursuing a chosen project-related career path. Lessons learned about assessing individual project management knowledge are captured.

Individual Project Management Experience/Competence

An improvement process is in place to continuously improve the individual's ability to attain experience and improve competency in project management. Lessons learned are captured and used to improve the monitoring and control efforts. All senior project-related personnel are seasoned professionals with multiple years of experience working successfully in their specialty area. Lessons learned about the application of project management knowledge to practical application are captured.

Corporate Initiative for Project Management Development

An improvement process is in place to continuously improve the organization's ability to enhance the project management professional track and opportunities. Lessons learned are captured and used to improve the monitoring and control efforts. The corporation supports and sponsors project manager- and team member-related certificate programs (such as requiring all project managers to be PMP certified) and expects that individuals who define project management as their professional area complete the requisite corporate training curriculum. Senior project-related personnel are represented or involved in the executive corporate meetings and in defining the strategic direction of the organization. Lessons learned about the development of project personnel, turnover, and the correlation to successful project outcomes are captured.

Note

1. Excerpted from Crawford, J.K. (2002), *Project Management Maturity Model* New York: Marcel Dekker.

Appendix C

Sample Questions from Knowledge Assessment Instrument

Project Integration Management

1. If your manager asked the status of your project plan execution, what type of information would you provide him or her?
   a. Histograms for functional organizations
   b. Hammock condition analysis
   c. Manpower cost data
   d. Comparison of actual performance against plan
   e. Cost of administrative support tools
2. The project plan uses outputs from other planning processes and goes through several iterations. Its most critical contribution to project control is:
   a. Identifying the project manager
   b. Defining the quality control process
   c. Establishing the performance measurement baseline
   d. Creating a hierarchy of responsibility
   e. Describing reporting requirements

3. Project Integration Management includes:
   a. Plan execution
   b. Plan development
   c. Overall change
   d. Project definition
   e. Answers a, b, and c
4. A well-developed project plan commonly includes all of the following, except:
   a. Project charter
   b. Cost estimates
   c. Document control process
   d. Work breakdown structure
   e. Milestones with dates
5. Execution of the project plan may be significantly affected by:
   a. Size of the organization
   b. Organizational policies
   c. Technical complexity
   d. Detail of the WBS
   e. Both c and d
6. Preparation of a project plan may include the use of the Rolling Wave Planning concept. The Rolling Wave approach provides for:
   a. Adjusting scope of work
   b. Lack of resource availability compensation
   c. Progressive detailing of the project plan
   d. Delays in customer authorization
   e. Optimizing project schedules
7. Every organization should have a structured approach that can be used as a guide for the project team in developing the project plan. This approach is normally referred to as:
   a. Management by objectives
   b. Vertical hierarchy planning
   c. Precedence diagramming
   d. Project management assistance
   e. Project planning methodology
8. A(n) _____ is used to sanction project work to ensure that it is done at the right time and in the proper sequence.
   a. Project charter
   b. Configuration chart
   c. Arrow diagram
   d. Statement of work
   e. Work authorization

9. As a project is executed, the causes of variances and the reasoning behind the corrective actions should be well documented. These and other pieces of information would be included in the project closeout as:
   a. Evidence of errors
   b. Lessons learned
   c. Data distribution reports
   d. Project selection status
   e. All of the above
10. All work associated with a project must be carefully integrated with:
    a. Human resources
    b. Ongoing operations
    c. VP of planning
    d. Historical project records
    e. None of the above
11. Product Scope and Project Scope are not the same. However, they must be integrated. The major difference(s) between these two scope types is:
    a. One is financial-oriented and one is facility-oriented
    b. One is function oriented and one is work oriented
    c. One is short-term and one is long-term
    d. Both b and c
    e. Answers a, b, and c
12. Project planning, especially in the early stages, is frequently impacted by uncertainty associated with funding, functionality, or even resource availability. Project managers must learn to plan in this environment by effectively using:
    a. Historical project data
    b. Assumptions
    c. Gantt charts
    d. Monte Carlo simulations
    e. Detailed work breakdown structures (WBS)
13. A _____ is anyone who has an interest in or can affect the outcome of a project, and must therefore be considered as the project plan is developed.
    a. Participant
    b. Sponsor
    c. Stakeholder
    d. Contributor
    e. Developer

14. A specific set of limitations that can prevent a project team from exercising certain execution options are known as:
    a. Constraints
    b. Restraints
    c. Complex conditions
    d. Both a and b
    e. None of the above

15. Any documented process used to apply technical and administrative direction and surveillance to audit the items and a system to verify conformance to requirements is referred to as:
    a. Systems management
    b. Quality assurance
    c. Configuration management
    d. Change control
    e. Project management

16. Earned value is an important project scope, time, cost integration tool that is recognized for its significant contribution to the following project management activity:
    a. Performance measurement
    b. Vendor selection
    c. Fiscal control
    d. Product valuation
    e. Return on investment

17. Subsidiary change control includes:
    a. Cost change
    b. Risk change
    c. Contract administration
    d. Both a and b
    e. Answers a, b, and c

18. To maintain performance measurement baseline integrity, changes should be thoroughly documented and records maintained. This project management process is known as:
    a. Record retention
    b. Lessons learned
    c. Configuration management
    d. Line of balance
    e. Change control

19. Inputs to project planning include historical information, organizational policies, constraints, and assumptions. Outputs include:
    a. Project charter and supporting detail
    b. Project plan and capability maturity model
    c. Work breakdown structure and supporting detail
    d. Project charter and project plan
    e. Gantt charts and PERT diagrams
20. Although corrective action is an output of the project control process, it is also sometimes considered an input because it:
    a. Completes the feedback loop
    b. Identifies subject matter experts
    c. Drives the business model
    d. Creates histograms
    e. All of the above

Appendix D

Sample Questions from Multi-Rater Project Manager Competency Evaluation

Key Result Area (KRA) #1: Understands, Defines, and Articulates Scope in Project Charter

1. Validates business case; answers question: "Why are we pursuing this?"
2. Demonstrates awareness of the big picture — can integrate internal and external systems
3. Anticipates project impact (both positive and negative)
4. Identifies key stakeholders; creates an effective communication distribution list of key stakeholders

KRA #2: Develops Project Plan with Project Team

KRA #2-a: Identifies Project Team and Shares Project Scope with Team:

1. Identifies project team (both internal and external) with the appropriate skill sets
2. Secures project team staff
3. Communicates scope of work, timeline, expectations, and deliverables to project team

KRA #2-b: With Team, Solicits, and Integrates Business Requirements into Project Plan:

1. Solicits and articulates the business requirements of the project
2. Applies methodology of the organization
3. Helps to influence the business requirements of the project
4. Supports the marketing function of the project

KRA #2-c: With Team, Establishes Metrics of Success and Creates Plan to Track Them:

1. Establishes criteria or metrics of project success
2. Identifies potential obstacles to project success (constraints, budget, time, risk, organization)
3. Creates a plan to track metrics or criteria of success

KRA #2-d: With Team, Develops Risk Management Plan:

1. Identifies project risks
2. Develops a risk mitigation plan for each project risk

KRA #2-e: With Team, Creates Draft of Project Plan:

1. Identifies novel solutions in planning and delivery
2. Incorporates previous "lessons learned" into project approach
3. Determines project resources (e.g., workspace, team room, computers, other infrastructure items) needed to address project deliverables

4. Establishes a cost, time schedule, and technical baseline
5. Demonstrates "systems thinking" awareness of other projects that are also going on; establishes and manages the links
6. Identifies post-project support/maintenance needs and articulates these needs to the appropriate parties
7. Establishes quality, cost, resources, and time baselines
8. Documents, with project team and business sponsor, a complete work breakdown structure (WBS), which organizes project work, quality, costs, resources, timeline, and deliverables, according to the agreed-upon scope

Appendix E

PM Solutions Career Planning and Development Program Artifacts

Professional Skills Inventory

Company Knowledge

■ Knowledge of company business (mission, vision, etc.) ■ Demonstrates keen business sense ■ Understands corporate priorities ■ Interest in company dynamics ■ Understands full range of PM Solutions capabilities ■ Knowledge of corporate organization structure	■ Understands corporate business targets ■ Supports company direction ■ Supports company policies and procedures ■ Stays abreast of industry trends and recommends new best practices and services for PM Solutions to focus on

Technical Knowledge

■ Strong knowledge of functional field ■ Utilized as a resource to peers in functional area of expertise ■ Acknowledged as strong resource throughout the organization ■ Strong experience base ■ Ability to ensure that the project satisfies the client's needs ■ Understands fees and financial arrangements and the ability to apply each ■ Can negotiate vendor contract and determine critical success factors ■ Demonstrates understanding of project processes for planning, controlling, and closing projects, and the tools associated with each process	■ Continuously updates knowledge ■ Willingly shares knowledge ■ Strong consulting skills ■ Good command of MS project ■ Good budgeting skills — allocates the overall budget to individual activities ■ Demonstrates general understanding of current technology in order to clearly follow the work of the project team ■ Has PMP® certification ■ Has Master's certificate in Project Management

Communication Skills

■ Strong presentation skills ■ Strong written and verbal skills ■ Communicates effectively and efficiently ■ Ensures client has accurate understanding of the project and project status ■ Maintains excellent communications about client with Account Manager and PM Solutions Management ■ Prepares thoroughly for client meetings ■ Collecting and disseminating performance information (i.e., status reports, progress measurement, and forecasting) ■ Active listening skills ■ Effective e-mail communication	■ Uses appropriate tone for all correspondence ■ Identifies client needs and communicates to team members ■ Maintains ongoing relationship with key client contacts ■ Actively works to build reputation of PM Solutions and client ■ Making needed information available to project stakeholders ■ Demonstrates an ability to decipher and send the appropriate project information to the appropriate project audience in a form that is understandable

Analytical Skills

▪ Good PC skills (i.e., Excel) ▪ Understands "financials" ▪ Detail oriented ▪ Develops and executes project plan by measuring and evaluating performance throughout project life cycle ▪ Continually uses best practices, and contributes to their involvement	▪ Thinks systematically ▪ Can budget and plan ▪ Understands the analysis phase of Systems Development Life Cycle ▪ Good command of MS Project ▪ Completes projects within approved budgets

Problem Solving/Decision Making

▪ Decisive ▪ Does not get bogged down in details ▪ Zeros in on core issues ▪ Analyzes all facets of an issue ▪ Effectively manages the effect of change on a project ▪ Can make key decisions for different projects at different times in their life cycle; key decisions might include allocation of resources, the costs of performance and schedule trade-offs, and changing the scope	▪ Can handle subjective inputs ▪ Rational/logical ▪ When pressed by time, can make good decision without all the facts ▪ Exhibits sound business management skills ▪ Good understanding of project risk ▪ Objective

Results Orientation

▪ Prides self in getting results ▪ Moves/acts responsively ▪ Has "can do" attitude ▪ Strives to grow the business ▪ Manages the overall project budget against results ▪ Overcomes obstacles	▪ "Hands-on" when necessary ▪ Shows initiative ▪ Creative ▪ Deals promptly with client requests ▪ Has MBA or other graduate degree

Self-Management Skills

■ Appropriate level of professionalism ■ Conducts self in professional manner ■ Exhibits integrity in all business dealings ■ Acts appropriately to the situation	■ Seen as "organized" ■ Prioritizes well ■ Exhibits self-control ■ Adaptable

Interpersonal Skills

■ Approachable ■ Team player ■ Does not talk down to people ■ Understands situation and takes appropriate action	■ Relates well to associates at every level ■ Does not compromise a confidence ■ Active listening skills ■ Manages vendor relationships effectively

Leadership

■ Leads by example ■ High expectations ■ Respected by peers and subordinates ■ Empowers people ■ Action oriented ■ Delegates well ■ Demonstrates the ability to solve conflicts as they arise, guides diverse workforce, and motivates those not directly under his or her authority	■ Effective coaching/counseling skills ■ Gets the best from subordinates ■ Creates "right" professional environment ■ Encourages creativity ■ Has vision ■ Is assertive and does not defer to the client ■ Creates a supportive environment where client and project team members can work together and not against each other

People (Personnel) Development Skills

■ Sets development plans ■ Sets aside time to discuss development issues ■ Emphasizes "learning organization" concept ■ Manages group process, facilitates team member participation, conflict resolution, consensus building, and providing performance feedback to other staff contributing to project	■ Encourages self-development ■ Supports those who seek development ■ Getting the right people assigned to the project ■ Developing individual and group skills to enhance project effectiveness ■ Pushes associates to get further certifications

Notes to Skills Matrix

Skills Definitions

1. **Basic:** Associate should be aware of the self-development required to meet expectation, as defined in the associates' development plan.
2. **Development:** The associates' competencies in its primary development phase. Development is supported by the identification of specific training and activities, as defined by the associate's development plan. The employee is expected to display significant progress in the basic knowledge of the competency.
3. **Proficient:** The associate demonstrates the competency in a skillful and consistent manner. The associate confidently takes on the opportunities to exhibit or use the skill. The associate should progress to the mastery stage with additional time and experience.
4. **Mastery:** The employee demonstrates the competency in a highly proficient and consistent manner. The employee exhibits mastery of the competency in a wide variety of situations and circumstances. PM Solutions management, other employees, and clients regard the employee as an authority in the competency area.
5. **Expert/Teacher:** The associate demonstrates the competency with a high degree of knowledge. The associate exhibits mastery of the competency in a wide variety of complex situations and circumstances. PM Solutions management, other employees, and clients regard the associate as an expert in this area. The associate is capable of leading client, regional, and national activities, which provide the associate with an opportunity to teach or mentor others.

Questions and Answers — Career Development

1. Isn't performance different than skills? Can't someone have skills and not perform, and vice versa?

   A: If an associate has the skills but is not performing, it will be reflected in the skills session (i.e., results orientation, self-management, leadership, etc.). Likewise, if someone is performing well with limited skills, the skills exhibited will be noted as well as the need for new skills. In PM Solutions, it is assumed that associates will be giving their best effort.

2. Why change from our current system?

   A: Performance appraisals tend to be negatively perceived by those receiving them and giving them. This is supported by research on the topic. A career development program is a more constructive approach, focusing on career development feedback, which is better received and is a more collaborative and positive approach for a supervisor. This approach is particularly appropriate for consultants, who may not have performance goals per se. With our Career Development Program, associates will have meetings twice a year (as opposed to once) to discuss their future goals.

3. Will my supervisor only rely on his or her observations?

   A: To have a fair and high quality discussion, supervisors will solicit input from various sources, including the associate's peers, subordinates, clients, senior managers, etc.

4. Some positions do not require some of the ten skill sets on the worksheet. How can someone be rated fairly?

   A: The skill sets apply to every position, to some degree. The ten skill sets are critical to professional development. Every associate, to develop long term as a professional, at some point will need to obtain skills in each area. Shorter term, if a position is nonsupervisory, certain skills may not be a key focus area, but still must be considered.

5. How are merit increases tabulated using this approach?

   A: The merit review is separate from the Career Development Program and takes place on the anniversary date. This is not a formal review and will be based on client satisfaction, supervisor/peer/management team input, ability to garner a certain level of fees for consultants, position in salary structure, skill improvement, company profitability, cost of living, competitive salary information, etc.

6. How will we know what the positions are that we can aspire to?

   A: The positions and how they fit into the new structure will be communicated to each department head so he or she can communicate to his or her respective associates.

7. Will we know what the salary ranges are?

   A: Research has indicated that most companies do not publish salary ranges. It is felt that publishing this information can cause problems and be counterproductive. We have chosen to keep this information confidential.

8. Will salary ranges be reviewed?

   A: Yes, annually.

9. How will Career and Development discussions be handled if someone is promoted to a new area or position?

   A: The discussions will continue as scheduled on the twice a year schedule. The new supervisor will meet with the associates and discuss career development based on their new position and possible new career direction. The personnel file should also be referred to by the new supervisor to review the past career development discussions of the associate.

10. How are the Professional Skills Inventory and Competency Matrix used? Are the attributes listed under each major skill area the only areas to consider?

    A: No. The Professional Skills Inventory and Matrix is only a guide to assist the supervisor in the discussion. Other attributes can certainly be included. In fact, different positions may require different attributes. The Skills Inventory lists some of the more common attributes.

11. When will the résumé be updated under this system?

    A: Résumés will be updated at the time of the merit review.

12. What about the skills form and résumé updating?

    A: Around the merit review date, associates need to update their skills form in the HR skills database and, as noted, update their résumés.

Professional Development Profile

(Confidential When Filled In)

Education Code

11 - 11 Years or Less
12 - High School Diploma
13 - 1 Year College
14 - AA Degree
15 - 3 Years College
16 - Bachelor's Degree
17 - Master's Degree
18 - Doctor's Degree

Performance

Performance	Trend
7 Outstanding	5 Increasing
6 Very Good	4
5 Exceeds Expectations	3 Remaining constant
4 Good	2
3 Meets all objectives	1 Decreasing
2 Fair	
1 Poor	

Management Skills

For each column, evaluate the employee according to the scale below. Enter one number in each column.

1-2	3-4-5	6-7
Low	Average	High

Columns:
- 1, 2 Business Knowledge — Tech. / Co.
- 3 Comm. Skills
- 4 Analytical Skills
- 5 Prob. Solving Dec. Making
- 6 Results Orientation
- 7 Self-Management Skills
- 8 Interpersonal Skills
- 9 Leadership Skills
- 10 Person. Devel. Skills

Short-Term Potential (0–12 Mos.)

Action Codes
PR Promote
TR Transfer
KP Keep in Position

Long-Term Potential (1–5 yrs)

Long-Term Probability Code
T Too soon to determine
1 Probably unable to remain in present position
2 Able to handle present position; some growth possible
3 Promotable to higher levels in our own or other area
4 High potential for top-level corporate or gen. management

Career Ambition

- Actively seeks to increase responsibility with current position
- States desire for specific type of advancement
- Demonstrates enterprise

1	2	3	4	5
Very Low				Very High

Comments on Long-Term Potential

Data entry columns:

Name (Last, First)

Time in Position

Education Level

Performance — Current / Trend

Business Knowledge — Tech. / Co.

Management Skills — 1 · 2 · 3 · 4 · 5 · 6 · 7 · 8 · 9 · 10

Short-Term Potential — Action Code / Take Action When / Position

Long-Term Potential — Action Code / Position / Highest Attainable Position / Long-Term Promotability / Career Ambition Code / Career Discussion Occurred Y – Yes N – No

Job Title

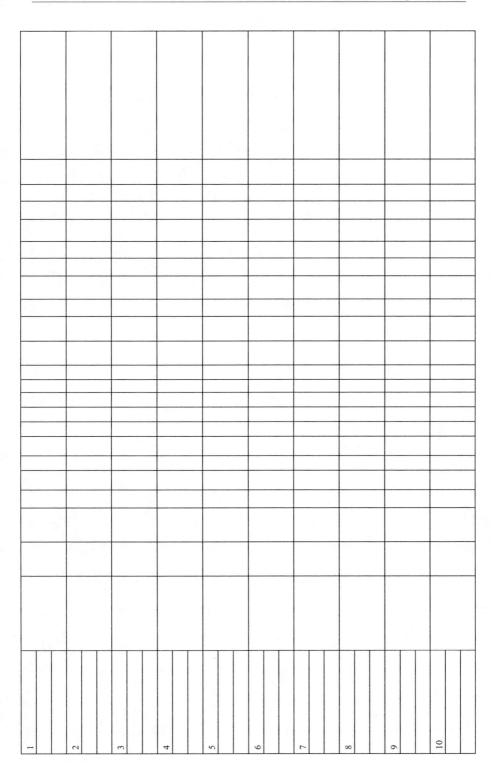

Appendix F

Value of Project Management Training Research Study Results

This survey on the value of project management training was developed by the Center for Business Practices to better understand a variety of issues of importance to project management practitioners. The survey provides benchmark data on the following topics:

- How many employees receive project management training
- How many hours of project management training are conducted
- What training methods are used
- What specific types of project management training are delivered
- Who delivers the project management training and what the criteria are for selecting those sources
- How organizations approach project manager certification
- How organizations evaluate project management training
- What value organizations have shown in implementing project management training, including participant satisfaction, knowledge and skill improvement, on-the-job performance improvement, and improvement in overall business results
- What barriers exist to the use of knowledge and skills gained from the project management training
- What the project management training cost

Members of the Center for Business Practices Survey Research Network were invited to participate in this Web-based Value of Project Management Training survey. The CBP Survey Research Network is a benchmarking group with knowledge of their organizations' project management practices and their organizations' business results. E-mails were sent to 1305 project management practitioners, inviting them to participate in the survey; 423 of those e-mails bounced, 385 were opened, 62 responses were received, and 53 were found useable for benchmarking purposes.

Survey participants reported on PM training delivered to their organizations. "Organization" can be the enterprise as a whole or a subunit within the enterprise. Those reporting on subunits represented 62 percent of the responses, and 26 percent of the responses represented the project management subunits within the company (e.g., project office, project management department, center of excellence).

Composition of Organization

The median number of employees involved in projects (defined as those eligible for PM training) was 40 (the average was 264, skewed significantly by the responses of several very large organizations). The number of employees involved in projects is about 10 percent of the total number of employees in the organization. The median number of PM training hours per eligible employee is 13.

PM Training Practices

The most used training delivery method is the on-site classroom (40 percent of the time) followed by off-site classroom (22 percent of the time). E-learning (both instructor-led and self-directed) also accounts for a significant amount of PM training time (27 percent combined).

The types of PM training were fairly evenly spread, with the largest number of organizations offering PM basics (74 percent), followed by advanced PM skill development (55 percent) and PM software tool training (55 percent). Those percentages are expected to change somewhat in 2004: PM basics (60 percent), advanced PM skill development (62 percent), and PM software tool training (58 percent).

The three major sources of PM training were from private training or consulting companies (for 57 percent of organizations), in-house trainers (43 percent), and independent training instructors (34 percent). The criteria for selecting these sources, ranked in order of importance, are: (1) quality,

(2) cost, (3) organizational requirements, (4) convenience, (5) customer service, and (6) reputation.

Most organizations do not require their project managers to take PM training (47 percent), but a significant number of organizations require their project managers to take more than 50 hours of PM training per year (21 percent).

A significant number of organizations have a formal PM professional development program (36 percent). A majority have not addressed the idea of project manager certification (57 percent), but 34 percent formally recognize the PMP® certification offered by the Project Management Institute.

PM Training Value

Organizations use most types of evaluation methods to measure the value of PM training, including participants' satisfaction with training (44 percent), informal observations by supervisors (24 percent), improvement in knowledge or skill (17 percent), improvement in performance (13 percent), and improvement in business results (11 percent). Organizations show moderate to extreme improvement due to the PM training initiatives in all areas measured:

- 96 Percent show moderate to extreme satisfaction with PM training
- 81 Percent show moderate to extreme improvement in the participant's knowledge or skills
- 91 Percent show moderate to extreme improvement in the participant's on-the-job performance
- 46 Percent show moderate to extreme improvement in cost performance
- 75 Percent show moderate to extreme improvement in schedule performance
- 67 Percent show moderate to extreme improvement in requirements performance
- 62 Percent show moderate to extreme improvement in quality
- 63 Percent show moderate to extreme improvement in productivity
- 66 Percent show moderate to extreme improvement in cycle time
- 78 Percent show moderate to extreme improvement in employee satisfaction
- 69 Percent show moderate to extreme improvement in customer satisfaction

The most significant barriers preventing the use of new knowledge and skills gained through PM training include cultural resistance to change (in 62 percent of organizations), the value of the training not perceived (42 percent), not enough time to apply the knowledge and skills (38 percent), a work environment that does not support the use of the new knowledge and skills (34 percent), and no opportunity to use the new knowledge and skills (32 percent).

Cost of PM Training

Organizations spent an average of $142,306 (median = $25,000) on PM training in 2003. This amounted to $1734 per project management employee (eligible to receive PM training) at $109 per hour of training.

Most organizations expect their PM training expenses to remain the same (45 percent of organizations) or to increase (45 percent) in 2004. Those who expect it to increase expect a 77 percent increase in expenses.

Most organizations also expect their expenses to outside training companies for PM training to remain the same (49 percent) or increase (44 percent) in 2004. Those who expect it to increase expect a 94 percent increase in expenses.

Respondent Profile

Most of the responses came from project/program managers (47 percent), followed by directors of project/program management (17 percent) and project/program office managers (15 percent). The size of their company and their industry was similar to other studies we have done, with all size organizations represented and manufacturing companies most represented (19 percent), followed by information (15 percent) and professional, scientific, and technical services (13 percent). More than 45 percent of the companies had annual sales of $1 billion, and 36 percent had annual sales less than $50 million.

SUMMARY RESULTS (53 TOTAL RESPONSES)

Respondent Profile Mean

Percentage of respondents with the following job title:

C-Level (CEO, CIO, CFO, etc.)	6 percent
VP or Director-Level Business Management	2 percent
Director, Project/Program Management	17 percent
Project/Program Office Manager	15 percent
Project/Program Manager	47 percent
Other	13 percent

Percentage of companies with the following sales revenue:

<$10 million	23 percent
$10 million–$50 million	13 percent
$50 million–$100 million	4 percent
$100 million–$500 million	9 percent
$500 million–$1 billion	6 percent
$1 billion–$3 billion	11 percent
>$3 billion	34 percent

Percentage of companies in the following industries:

Accommodation and Food Services	0 percent
Agriculture, Forestry, Fishing and Hunting	0 percent
Arts, Entertainment, and Recreation	0 percent
Construction	9 percent
Educational Services	6 percent
Finance and Insurance	6 percent
Health Care and Social Assistance	4 percent
Information	15 percent
Mgt. of Companies and Enterprises	2 percent
Manufacturing	19 percent
Mining	0 percent
Other Services (except Public Admin.)	4 percent
Professional, Scientific, and Tech Services	13 percent
Public Administration	4 percent
Real Estate and Rental and Leasing	0 percent
Retail Trade	2 percent

Transportation and Warehousing	8 percent
Utilities	8 percent
Waste Mgt. and Remediation Services	0 percent
Wholesale Trade	2 percent

Percentage of companies reporting on their enterprise or subunit only (and which subunits):

Enterprise	38 percent
Subunit only	62 percent
Project management	26 percent
IT	17 percent
Engineering, construction, capital projects	11 percent
New product development	0 percent
Other	8 percent

Percentage of companies reporting on the following period:

Calendar Year 2003	98 percent
Other	2 percent

Composition of Organization   Median–Mean

Total number of employees in organization	400–2465
Total number of employees involved in projects (eligible for PM training)	40–264

PM Training in Organization

Total number of hours of formal PM training received by employees involved in projects	380–1,387
Number of training hours per employee involved in projects	13–5

Percentage of PM training time using following delivery methods:

	Mean
Non-classroom (instructor-led E-learning)	10 percent
Non-classroom (self-directed E-learning)	17 percent
Non-classroom (CD-ROM or other technology-delivered)	6 percent
On-site Classroom (instructor-led or technology-delivered)	40 percent
Off-site Classroom (instructor-led or technology-delivered)	22 percent
Other	3 percent

Percentage of organizations where employees engaged in the following types of PM training:

PM basics	74 percent
Advanced PM skill development	55 percent
PMP preparation	0 percent
PM software tool training	55 percent
PM certificate or degree program	26 percent
Soft-skills training (e.g., teambuilding)	45 percent
Leadership training	47 percent
Other (please specify)	8 percent
None of the above	0 percent

Percentage of organizations where employees expect to engage in the following types of PM training in 2004:

Number of in-house PM trainers	3.4
PM basics	60 percent
Advanced PM skill development	62 percent
PMP preparation	34 percent
PM software tool training	58 percent
PM certificate or degree program	23 percent
Soft-skills training (e.g., teambuilding)	51 percent
Leadership training	47 percent
Other (please specify)	8 percent
None of the above	2 percent

Percentage of organizations that provided the following sources of PM training:

In-house corporate university	17 percent
Other in-house trainers	43 percent
Four-year colleges and universities	23 percent
Community and junior colleges	4 percent
Technical and vocational institutions	15 percent
Product suppliers	21 percent
Independent training instructors	34 percent
Private training or consulting companies	57 percent
Unions, trade, or professional associations	11 percent
Federal, state, or local government organizations	4 percent
Other (please specify)	9 percent
None of the above	8 percent

Ranking of criteria for selecting PM training sources in order of importance:

1. Quality
2. Cost
3. Organization Requirements
4. Convenience
5. Customer Service
6. Reputation

Percentage of organizations that require the following hours of PM training to serve as a project manager:

0 hours	47 percent
1–8 hours	9 percent
9–24 hours	11 percent
25–40 hours	11 percent
More than 50 hours	21 percent

Percentage of organizations with a formal PM professional development program:

36 percent

Percentage of organizations that have taken the following approaches to project manager certification:

Not formally addressed project manager certification   57 percent
Formally recognize the PMP certification offered by PMI®   34 percent
Formally recognize a certification other than PMP   6 percent
Developed an internal certification program   4 percent

Percentage of PM training activities that received the following types of evaluation:

Reaction (participants' satisfaction with training)   44 percent
Learning (improvement in participants' knowledge or skill)   17 percent
Behavior (improvement in participants' performance)   13 percent
Results (impact of training on business results)   11 percent
Observation (informal observations by supervisor or others)   24 percent
Focus groups (facilitator-led groups discussing results
  of training)   5 percent
Return on expectation (perceived value versus stakeholder
expectation)   6 percent
Other   3 percent

Percentage of organizations reporting the following participant satisfaction with PM training (Reaction):

None   0 percent
Slight   5 percent
Moderate   39 percent
Large   41 percent
Extreme   16 percent
Percentage of organizations that track this measure   *88 percent*

Percentage of organizations reporting the following improvement in training participants' knowledge or skill (Learning):

None   5 percent
Slight   14 percent
Moderate   38 percent
Large   38 percent
Extreme   5 percent
Percentage of organizations that track this measure   *84 percent*

Percentage of organizations reporting the following improvement in training participants' on-the-job performance (Behavior):

None	8 percent
Slight	3 percent
Moderate	58 percent
Large	30 percent
Extreme	3 percent
Percentage of organizations that track this measure	*80 percent*

Percentage of organizations reporting the following improvement in cost performance (Results):

None	21 percent
Slight	32 percent
Moderate	35 percent
Large	9 percent
Extreme	3 percent
Percentage of organizations that track this measure	*67 percent*

Percentage of organizations reporting the following improvement in schedule performance (Results):

None	8 percent
Slight	17 percent
Moderate	36 percent
Large	36 percent
Extreme	3 percent
Percentage of organizations that track this measure	*71 percent*

Percentage of organizations reporting the following improvement in requirements performance (Results):

None	17 percent
Slight	17 percent
Moderate	33 percent
Large	28 percent
Extreme	6 percent
Percentage of organizations that track this measure	*71 percent*

Percentage of organizations reporting the following improvement in quality (Results):

None	11 percent
Slight	27 percent
Moderate	24 percent
Large	27 percent
Extreme	11 percent
Percentage of organizations that track this measure	*73 percent*

Percentage of organizations reporting the following improvement in productivity (Results):

None	11 percent
Slight	22 percent
Moderate	27 percent
Large	32 percent
Extreme	8 percent
Percentage of organizations that track this measure	*73 percent*

Percentage of organizations reporting the following improvement in cycle time (Results):

None	24 percent
Slight	9 percent
Moderate	39 percent
Large	24 percent
Extreme	3 percent
Percentage of organizations that track this measure	*76 percent*

Percentage of organizations reporting the following improvement in employee satisfaction (Results):

None	12 percent
Slight	9 percent
Moderate	39 percent
Large	24 percent
Extreme	15 percent
Percentage of organizations that track this measure	*67 percent*

Percentage of organizations reporting the following improvement in customer satisfaction (Results):

None	14 percent
Slight	17 percent
Moderate	26 percent
Large	26 percent
Extreme	17 percent
Percentage of organizations that track this measure	*69 percent*

Percentage of organizations reporting the following barriers preventing the training participants' use of new knowledge and skills gained in the training:

No opportunity to use the knowledge/skills	32 percent
Cultural resistance to change	62 percent
Not enough time to apply the knowledge/skills	38 percent
Work environment does not support use of new knowledge/skills	34 percent
Value not perceived	42 percent
Senior management does not support project management	16 percent
Training did not apply to job situation	18 percent
Other	12 percent

Cost of PM Training   Median–Mean

Average amount organizations that had the following expenses spent on them:

In-house trainer salaries	$20,000–$53,624
Outside training expenses	$20,000–$96,125
Tuition for PM courses	$10,000–$93,600
Technology expenses	$2,500–$53,657
Other expenses	$1,200–$10,700
Cost of training ($/organization)	$25,000–$142,306
Cost of training ($/hour)	$80–$109
Cost of training ($/PM employee)	$571–$1,734

Percentage of organizations expecting change in PM training expense from 2003 to 2004:

Increase	45 percent
About the same	45 percent
Decrease	11 percent

Amount of expected change in expense:

Increase	77 percent
Decrease	54 percent

Appendix G

Project Manager
Support Survey*

A project manager support survey is used to find out what learning and skill development is important to your project managers. The focus is on determining what subjects project managers think will help them and their team members achieve better results on their current projects, then asking them how they would like to learn about those subjects (training courses, self-study, brown-bag seminars, books, etc.). This survey gives project managers a chance to voice what they need *right now*, and ties it directly to helping their projects be successful, so that when you plan training and other forms of learning for your PMs, you give high priority to subjects they can put to use right away. And you provide the learning in a form they will be receptive to using.

Edit the following template to add or change items to be most applicable to your organization and projects. Distribute it to project managers/ leaders, and if you wish, to related functional managers and team members. They can return it anonymously if that makes them more comfortable. Tally the results and use that to feed your planning for bringing training and other forms of learning into your group.

---

* Source: © Copyright 2001 Emprend Inc. Accessed from ProjectConnections.com, http://www.projectconnections.com/knowhow/template_list/index.html. Used by permission.

Project Manager Support Survey
(DUE BY: _____)

Your efforts are critical to the company: what additional support can we offer you in your project leader role? Speak up! (anonymously if you wish)

SECTION 1: Learning/Training

Which of the following subjects do you want you, your project team, and/or managers to learn more about? For each, fill in A, B, or C, where

    A = High interest, would greatly help my project go better
    B = Moderate interest, would somewhat help my project go better
    C = Low interest, is not really needed to help my project

Note that "training" in these subjects might take many forms, as shown in Section 2.

	Subjects	You (Project Manager)	Your Team Members	Functional Managers	Comments
1	Leadership and team-building				
2	Meeting management: status meetings				
3	Techniques for design reviews, code reviews, etc.				
4	Conflict resolution, dealing with difficult people				
5	Time management				
6	Delegating				
7	Presentation and communication skills				
8	Product vision process and trade-off negotiating				
9	Problem-solving techniques for groups				

	Subjects	You (Project Manager)	Your Team Members	Functional Managers	Comments
10	Project scheduling techniques: development models, using our life-cycle work breakdown structures, etc.				
11	Estimating techniques for accurate schedules				
12	Project schedule progress tracking				
13	Techniques for status reports, meeting minutes				
14	Risk analysis, decision making, risk management				
15	Using project management software; scheduling basics such as Gantt and PERT charts				
16	Business case creation, ROI analysis				
17	System engineering, product architecture				
18	Writing functional and implementation specs				
19	Hardware design methodologies				
20	Software design methodologies				
21	How to apply our PM methodology to different sizes and types of projects				
22	Design for manufacturability				
23	Product cost estimation (unit cost, life-cycle costs)				

	Subjects	You (Project Manager)	Your Team Members	Functional Managers	Comments
24	Test planning and execution: development test				
25	Test planning and execution: SQA, alpha, beta				
26	How to run effective beta tests				
27	Other:				
28	Other:				
29	Other:				

Other comments

_____

_____

_____

SECTION 2: Ways for getting the information you want

How do you like to get information about the above topics to help you and your team learn new skills?

__ Day-long classes with case studies, exercises

__ 1- or 2-hr lunch-time classes with food provided, focused on a particular topic

__ Articles from trade journals that talk about how other companies do things

__ Self-study courses (online courses, video, CD-ROM, or just books and workbooks)

__ After-hours classes such as university extension (continuing education) courses

__ Coaching from and questions answered by a more experienced project manager

__ Project facilitation help (meetings, design reviews, etc.) to learn by watching

__ Online resources such as documents created on other projects, how-to materials, and outside online services

__ Other (Explain) _____

Comment specifically on anything you'd like to receive private coaching on from another PM or an internal/external consultant; and areas you want some facilitation help on your project.

_____
_____
_____
_____
_____
_____
_____
_____

SECTION 3: Tools

What tools do you wish you had? Check all that apply:

- ☐ Detailed checklists for design reviews
- ☐ More design simulation tools
- ☐ Test tools
- ☐ Schedule estimating tools
- ☐ Project management software
- ☐ Template documents
- ☐ Access to docs from other projects.

Discuss the above, or list any other tools ideas here:

_____
_____
_____
_____
_____

SECTION 4: Other feedback

What do you see as the three biggest roadblocks to doing your job as project leader?

1. _____

2. _____

3. _____

Does your team make adequate use of "hoopla" and rewards, or do you need additional support in this area?

_____

Any other comments:

_____
_____
_____

NAME (optional): _____

Department (optional): _____

Source: © Copyright 2001 Emprend Inc. Accessed from ProjectConnections.com, http://www.projectconnections.com/knowhow/template_list/index.html. Used by permission.

Appendix H

Project Management Mentor's Competency Scorecard*

Rate your mentor and yourself on each competency and skill, and then establish a personal development plan for improving low-scoring areas.

COMPETENCIES	Needs Improvement			Excellent	
	1	2	3	4	5
Integrator	—	—	—	—	—
Educator	—	—	—	—	—
Expeditor	—	—	—	—	—
Coach	—	—	—	—	—
Problem Solver	—	—	—	—	—
Quality Manager	—	—	—	—	—
Risk Taker/Risk Manager	—	—	—	—	—
Conflict Manager	—	—	—	—	—
Partnering	—	—	—	—	—
Visionary	—	—	—	—	—
Information Powerful	—	—	—	—	—
Flexible	—	—	—	—	—

---

* From Project Management Solutions, Inc., *Mentoring Guide,* 1999. Used with permission.

	Needs Improvement			Excellent	
SKILLS	1	2	3	4	5
Facilitation	—	—	—	—	—
Listening	—	—	—	—	—
Team Building	—	—	—	—	—
Negotiation	—	—	—	—	—
Coaching	—	—	—	—	—
Presentation	—	—	—	—	—
Interpersonal	—	—	—	—	—
Communication	—	—	—	—	—
Conflict Management	—	—	—	—	—

Rate your mentor using these questions; or, rate your own performance as a mentor by asking yourself what your mentee's response would be if asked these questions.

Does your project mentor:	1	2	3	4	5
Seek out your requirements, priorities, and expectations?	—	—	—	—	—
Effectively support your project and/or program?	—	—	—	—	—
Treat you with respect and understand your situation?	—	—	—	—	—
Solicit, listen to, and resolve your concerns?	—	—	—	—	—
Provide timely advice?	—	—	—	—	—
Deliver quality information and guidance?	—	—	—	—	—
Display flexibility in responding to your needs?	—	—	—	—	—
Keep you informed?	—	—	—	—	—
Would you select this mentor for future projects?	—	—	—	—	—

Rate your mentor (or self) on the following:	1	2	3	4	5
Project Management	—	—	—	—	—
Project Planning	—	—	—	—	—
Project Scheduling	—	—	—	—	—
Communication Skills	—	—	—	—	—
Interpersonal Skills	—	—	—	—	—
Judgment	—	—	—	—	—
Team Participation	—	—	—	—	—

PM Coaching Guidelines: Assisting Project Managers and Their Projects

What: Guidelines for setting up and carrying out a coaching arrangement, where a more experienced project manager coaches a less experienced project manager during a project.

Why: Provides the PM with direct hands-on guidance and mentoring during a project. The Coach mentors the PM in understanding project management principles and how to apply them in this company and on this project. The coaching can provide practical nuts-and-bolts learning about key elements necessary for successful projects, including cross-functional involvement; overcoming technical and team obstacles; determining deliverables the team will create; proper management involvement; etc. Coaching is especially useful in organizations where PMs are created "overnight" (e.g., by designating a capable technical lead to take on a PM role with no or little prior management training).

How: Your project organization can set up a coaching program to make sure project managers get hands-on practical support as they take on new challenges. The program can be very visible and formal, a requirement for all new PMs; or it can be informal and on an as-needed basis. In some organizations, the coaches are full-time internal "consultants," part of a Project Management Office or a Project Support Group. In others, more senior PMs allocate some of their time to coach, spending the rest managing the projects themselves.

This document provides guidelines for how a coaching relationship can work — how often the PM and coach meet, what subjects get covered, what expert advice and oversight the coach can provide, etc. It discusses:

- Possible levels of coaching, depending upon PM skills and experience
- Typical coaching involvement during a project
- How to get the coaching started
- Subjects to cover in a one-on-one coaching meeting
- Coach's checklist items for helping keep a project on track
- Project Summary Sheet for use during PM coaching

Levels of Coaching Recommended, Depending upon PM Skills and Experience

The following table provides ideas for deciding what level of coaching to provide to a PM based on experience and abilities.

Type	Definition	When Needed
A	**Total coaching.** Attend most or all team meetings, reviews. Meet with project manager off-line to give detailed guidance about what should be done next. Review all deliverables.	Project Manager who has never before led a project. Project manager who has trouble with the following: leading the team with appropriate sense of urgency; operational issues such as running effective meetings or resolving scope/schedule/cost issues, or handling people issues.

Type	Definition	When Needed
B	**Mid-range coaching.** Meet with project manager once per week off-line to ask questions about risks, state of project, and make detailed recommendations if needed. Do not necessarily review all deliverables.	Project managers who are new to the company but nevertheless have enough experience or natural ability with people and project management skills that they do not need close coaching. Project manager who is showing signs of not having enough time to do the job properly.
C	**Periodic check-in/audit.** Do not review all deliverables.	Project leader is relatively strong; just want to check in periodically to make sure nothing important is forgotten, look for holes, offer encouragement to not be in denial about severity of particular problems.

Typical PM Coach Involvement during a Project

1. Meet with project manager one-on-one once a week.
2. Attend team meetings once a month or more frequently, depending on maturity of project manager and team.
3. Attend all major design reviews or review results of them.
4. Review phase deliverables lists for your process. At beginning of a project phase, agree on which ones will be done. At or near the end of the phase, make sure they were done with high quality. Depending on the experience level of the project manager, may decide to have the coach review drafts of deliverables.
5. Have more interaction with project manager as each major phase completion is approached.
6. Keep in touch with project managers for their perspective on the project and progress.
7. Help the project managers learn from the coaching process how to be self-assessing of project/milestone performance, team performance, and their own effectiveness.

How to get coaching going: Coach makes contact with project manager, sets up an initial meeting.

Note: it is not uncommon to start coaching *during* a project rather than at the beginning. The coach has a unique opportunity to assess the state of the project to help determine the best focus for the coaching going forward, including the chance to help course-correct the project.

1. Talk with the project manager about the purpose of coaching.

This is very critical for setting up a good working relationship. Some PMs take the idea of coaching as an affront to their abilities, a statement that they are not good enough or something is wrong with them. They may be afraid of being micromanaged, or having you report back to management. Talk with them about the goal being to help them be as successful as possible on the project; answer questions about how the organization does things; give pointers and ideas from past project experience; save them time; give them a sounding board for tough decisions; give them someone to talk to privately about touchy team issues; etc.

Some groups do this initial meeting with the project manager, the designated coach, and the responsible director or functional executive to make sure everyone agrees on the scope and goals of the coaching and to emphasize that the executives feel this is an important activity.

2. Talk about the state of the project.

a. What phase is it in? Has the project gone well so far, or not? Discuss how the team is doing meeting cost, quality, schedule, and scope goals thus far.
b. Have the project manager identify any specific concerns about the project's chances for success.
c. If you are starting the coaching after the project is well underway, check to see whether a Project Vision or Charter was created, whether the team has committed to a set of milestones, and whether design reviews have been held.

3. Assess project manager's current experience and skills.

a. Has he (she) led a project in this company before? Anywhere? How was his (her) effectiveness on that project? Where does he (she) feel he (she) excelled, and what areas does he (she) see as opportunities for learning?

b. What is his (her) attitude toward project management principles, and any defined process the company uses?
c. If he (she) is a technical professional, does he (she) understand that his (her) role is to manage the entire cross-functional team, including other functions? Is he (she) comfortable with leading a cross-functional team?
d. What training in project manager skills has he (she) had thus far?

4. Agree with project manager as to what your coaching interaction and project involvement will be.

Subjects to cover in one-on-one coaching meetings include:

a. Discuss the state of the project. Probe for risks and team issues. Review milestone progress.
b. Have the project manager identify problems and discuss possible resolutions. Help the project manager talk through options for solving the problem. He (She) may have good ideas already but lack confidence.
c. Encourage the PM to discuss any interpersonal team issues. Many PMs are new to having to get a group of disparate people to work together on a cross-functional team and may find this to be the biggest challenge, but may also feel awkward talking about it, especially if their team includes peers.
d. Discuss elements of the company's project management or product development process that are important to the current project activities. Answer any questions the project manager has.
e. Discuss upcoming major decisions such as release for hardware builds and make sure proper testing and reviews are done first.
f. Review contingency plans to ensure risks are being adequately addressed.
g. Provide comments on project deliverables as needed.

Coach's Checklist Items for Helping Keep a Project on Track

1. Help the PM set an initial target for completion of investigation and planning. Watch for team getting dragged down by product feature/schedule negotiation issues and facilitate resolution. Requirements churning on the front end has delayed many a project, and newer project managers may be less comfortable bringing the team to tough decisions.

2. Make sure the project manager follows best practices such as recording action items and reviewing them weekly.
3. Make sure all functions have a representative on the team during early investigation and planning.
4. Make sure everyone is available enough to contribute to the design and schedule work.
5. Identify any critical dependencies that should be started early in the project because of lead times: tools? training? more staff?
6. Attend and facilitate project vision/charter meetings — meetings where the team discusses and documents the high-level objectives of the project.
7. Review schedules for the following:
   a. Timeline is reasonable. Is the project under undue pressure for early delivery?
   b. Dependencies between groups are shown explicitly (e.g., development hand-offs to publications groups or manufacturing).
   c. Ample time is included for design reviews, especially for complex projects that will require multiple long meetings or iterative review cycles.
   d. Time and milestones for prototyping and testing are shown.
   e. Specific risk mitigation work is scheduled.
   f. Major design reviews are included.
   g. Integration time is not cut short.
   h. Adequate time for meaningful beta testing with customers is scheduled.
   i. Project manager checks with common groups such as manufacturing, SQA, etc., for overuse of resources that are shared across teams.
8. Make sure critical risks, issues, and milestones stay visible and are referenced weekly by the team.
9. Watch for schedule impacts from outside projects and crises, and make sure project manager and team do not immediately accept them as "normal", then let the schedule slip without giving anyone very direct, specific warning. Teach them to raise it to executives and make sure those executives are making a *conscious choice* to let the schedule slip because something else is higher priority.
10. Review test plans for completeness and definable exit criteria.
11. Make sure support groups get involved to start getting ready to support the new product/software/etc., after its release.

Add your own company and project-specific checklist items here. Think back to issues on previous projects, especially those run by new project managers — what items tended to cause problems? How would you watch for signs of them when coaching a new project manager?

Project Summary Sheet for Use during PM Coaching

The next two pages are simply a form that a coach can use to make notes on a project during coaching sessions. Our staff has found it especially useful when an internal "consultant" in a PM support group is coaching multiple projects weekly, and needs a concise way to keep track of where each project is, what coaching is done, and what is coming next.

Project Name: _____

Project Leader: _____

Meeting Date/Time: _____

**Consulting Activities
This Week:** _____
(team meeting, project leader
coaching, document review) _____

Current Project Phase: _____

Docs Reviewed This Period: _____
_____
_____
_____

**Current Critical Issues,
Actions Discussed, Steps
To Be Taken:** _____
_____
_____
_____

Current Milestone Status: _____
_____
_____

**Important Upcoming Activities
(what, when, prep required):**
_____
_____
_____
_____

Project Summary Sheet for Use during PM Coaching

Project Name: _____

Project Leader Coaching Notes: (Skills issues discussed, advice given, training decisions made, further coaching requested, etc.)

_____
_____
_____
_____
_____
_____
_____
_____

Notes:

_____
_____
_____
_____
_____
_____
_____
_____

Appendix J

Project Management Performance Appraisal Form*

This template can be used to promote recognition of project performance as part of someone's normal performance appraisal each year, as an additional input to an existing review process, rather than a replacement of it. It addresses both individual team members and project leaders. A common complaint by project managers is that individual team members are rewarded by the company for their performance in their functional area, such as engineering or marketing or manufacturing. Their review often does not take into account whether they contribute well to a project.

Process and Form for Project Leader Performance Appraisal Input

- When a person is about to leave the project, he (she) will fill out a form on the project leader. The form can be anonymous.
- The person will give the form to the project leader's functional manager.

---

* Source: Accessed from ProjectConnections.com at www.projectconnections.com/knowhow/template_list/index.html <http://www.projectconnections.com/knowhow/template_list/index.html>. Copyright Global Brain®Inc. and Orion Kopelman from *Projects at Warp-Speed™ with QRPD®): The Definitive Guide to Quality Rapid Product Development, 9th Edition.* Used by permission.

- The functional manager will review the form with the project leader. (The functional manager will be responsible for protecting the anonymity of the team member.)
- The project leader will sign, indicating that he (she) reviewed the form, and it will be filed for the next performance review.

Project Leader Being Appraised: _____

Team Member (optional): _____

Project: _____ Date: _____

Introduction: The purpose of this form is to solicit your feedback for this individual's annual performance appraisal. Please rate and comment upon his (her) work on the above project. Provide enough detail to allow the person's functional manager to commend the individual on strengths and accomplishments, and to point out specific areas for improvement in the next year. Note: The intent is for you to spend only 5 to 10 minutes doing this basic assessment.

	Poor	*Fair*	*Good*	*Very Good*	*Excellent*	*N/A or no opinion*	*Comment specifically on strengths/ accomplishments, or weaknesses/ shortcomings in this area.*
Project results: degree to which product vision, schedule, and costs were met	—	—	—	—	—	—	_____
Leadership of a synergistic team:	—	—	—	—	—	—	_____
Effective use of the company's project life cycle; continuous improvement of technical/team processes	—	—	—	—	—	—	_____
Success at obtaining adequate cross-functional participation	—	—	—	—	—	—	_____
"People skills" demonstrated in working with individuals and motivating the team	—	—	—	—	—	—	_____

	Poor	Fair	Good	Very Good	Excellent	N/A or no opinion	Comment specifically on strengths/ accomplishments, or weaknesses/ shortcomings in this area.
Ability to apply technical skills and other knowledge to make right project decisions	—	—	—	—	—	—	_____
Management skills:							
Accurate and thorough planning, scheduling	—	—	—	—	—	—	_____
Ability to keep the project on course	—	—	—	—	—	—	_____
Open, accurate, and timely communication of objectives, progress, status, issues	—	—	—	—	—	—	_____
Ability to run effective meetings	—	—	—	—	—	—	_____
Overall performance as Project Leader	—	—	—	—	—	—	_____

Particularly commendable contributions/strengths:

_____

_____

_____

Major dissatisfactions (major areas for improvement):

_____

_____

Other comments:

_____

_____

Process and Form for Team Member Performance Appraisal Input

- These forms will be filled out, not necessarily at the very end of the project, but when the particular team member is leaving the team. Performance will therefore be fresh in the project leader's mind.
- The expectation will be set with functional managers that they must incorporate feedback from project leaders in people's annual review.
- They would have these forms on file for already-completed projects in the past year.
- They would be expected to solicit some kind of input from project leaders of current projects the person is on (but does not have to be the form).
- All those designated as team members on the team roles list should be reviewed, even if they are part-time members. Any appropriate notes about their amount of involvement can be included on the form.
- When the person is about to leave the project, the project leader will fill out the form.
- The project leader will then give a copy to the person and give him (her) the option to schedule time to discuss it. (If it is negative, it is assumed that they will discuss it.) The discussion could be a three-way meeting with the functional manager and project leader.
- The person will sign to indicate that he or she has seen the form and had a chance to review it (or selected not to review it) with the project leader.
- The project leader will give a copy of the signed form to the functional manager to be filed for the person's next review (and for any current issues to be addressed in the near term).

Team Member Being Appraised: _____

Project Leader: _____

Project: _____ Date: _____

Introduction: The purpose of this form is to solicit your feedback for this individual's annual performance appraisal. Please rate and comment upon his (her) work on the above project. Please provide enough detail to allow the person's functional manager to commend the individual on strengths and accomplishments, and to point out specific areas for improvement in the next year. You may leave an item blank if you do not have an opinion. Note: The intent is for you to spend only 5 to 10 minutes doing this basic assessment.

	Poor	Fair	Good	Very Good	Excellent	N/A or no opinion	Comment specifically on strengths/ accomplishments, or weaknesses/ shortcomings in this area.
Quality of work performed on project	—	—	—	—	—	—	_____
Timeliness of project task completion	—	—	—	—	—	—	_____
Timeliness of action item completion	—	—	—	—	—	—	_____
Contribution to meeting product cost and project budget targets (may be not applicable — N/A — for all software projects)	—	—	—	—	—	—	_____
Participation as a synergistic team member (rate each subcategory)	—	—	—	—	—	—	_____
Cooperation with other team members	—	—	—	—	—	—	_____
Communication of progress, status, issues	—	—	—	—	—	—	_____
Communication on technical matters	—	—	—	—	—	—	_____
Contribution to continuous improvement of development, technical, team processes	—	—	—	—	—	—	_____
Overall performance on project	—	—	—	—	—	—	_____

Particularly commendable contributions/strengths:

_____

_____

_____

Major dissatisfactions (major areas for improvement):

_____

_____

_____

Other comments:

_____

_____

_____

Appendix K

Service Level Agreement Tips for Better Outsourcing Relationships*

This document identifies the agreed-upon type, quality, and quantity of services that will be provided to an organization by a service supplier. Each Service Level Agreement (SLA) is unique to the type of service being purchased and there literally is no way to design a "boilerplate." There are, however, common things to look for when reviewing an SLA, regardless of the format chosen, to make sure it is crafted to meet your needs. The following is a list of 12 questions to ask yourself as you review an SLA document as well as areas that deserve your special attention.

---

* Created by Joe Santana for Tech Republic.com. Reprinted with permission.

Question to Ask Yourself	What to Look For
1. Does the document clearly state the type, quality, and quantity of services I will receive?	Your SLA document should clearly state the services the supplier will provide, as well as levels of performance or quality in the *scope of work* section (e.g., calls to the help desk will be answered on the second ring and either resolved or escalated within a 12-minute timeframe).
2. Would variations in quantities be better addressed in the pricing structure rather than as a service performance level measurement?	If there is not a definite quantity of services identifiable at the outset, it is better to establish a flexible pricing schedule to accommodate variations in quantity. Pricing for the various quantifiable levels is then locked in and the service provider is capable of offering discounts for higher quantities up front, while customers have the information they need to help plan for the amount of services they can afford.
3. Are the desired outcomes clearly defined and documented?	Clearly documenting what the outcome needs to be assists the service provider in determining what needs to be done to provide higher-level services. Additionally, it eliminates the problem of having the SLA "reinterpreted" if there are changes in management. Make sure you get a clear definition of what suppliers mean when they use phrases such as 99% uptime or 99.99% closure of tickets or any other similar terms. In many cases, these (for example, 99% uptime) do not include scheduled maintenance.
4. Are the performance levels that are being measured clear and quantifiable?	If performance levels are quantifiable, they are normally also adjustable or scalable. Additionally, quantification minimizes the difficulties associated with interpretation if management changes. The *Service Measures* section documents procedures and standards around collecting information and calculations used to produce the different measurements associated with the delivery of the services. This section should include: Definitions of each specific measurement Collection processes and sources for each measurement Calculation rules for each measurement How, when, and to whom metrics will be reported

Question to Ask Yourself	What to Look For
5. Are the roles and responsibilities clearly outlined for both the client and the supplier?	The *Roles and Responsibilities* section should outline specific roles and responsibilities associated with the delivery of these services. These include: Client management and business user roles and responsibilities Supplier team roles and responsibilities Baseline ongoing support for core applications Requirements gathering, analysis, and prioritization for additional applications or upgrades Project management for all IT projects and initiatives: work plans, sequencing/dependencies, deliverables, timing Management of internal development disciplines: development, test, production environments, source code management, change management, system documentation, etc. IT vendor interface: manage vendor relationship, selection and negotiation, pursuit of service issues All desktop support activities In summary: all current MIS, technical development, and other IT support activities will be outsourced to and managed by the supplier
6. Are you properly allocating levels of service based on a clear set of priorities relative to what is important to you?	Of the things you would like the service provider to accomplish, which are most urgent? Which are most important? The *service request or services requested section* of your agreement should contain assigned severity and priority levels for each specific type of service request.
7. Is the cost of achieving the higher performance level supported by the improved outcome?	The "nice to haves" are often far more expensive than the benefits they generate. Be wary of asking for levels of perfection that will result in inordinately more expensive performance if perfection is not needed for success.

Question to Ask Yourself	What to Look For
8. Do penalties for underperformance need to be established to balance the incentives for achieving higher levels of performance?	Many contracts permit termination or cancellation for outright failures to perform. However, in SLAs, if there are multiple performance areas being measured, the incentives to exceed performance levels in one area may lead to reduced performance in other areas. A general rule is to establish penalties for falling below an acceptable level for any requirement that permits incentives for exceeding performance standards.
9. How will performance be reported? How frequently and with whom will the SLA performance be reviewed?	The SLA should spell out whether biweekly, monthly, or quarterly meetings will be held to review performance against the SLA. It should also spell out who will collect and present the data as well as to whom they will present it. Make sure you agree with the metrics and the means the service provider will use to track and report performance.
10. Is there an opportunity to add, delete, or change performance areas?	Throughout the life of a contract there is a natural progression that would necessitate a refocus of what is important to encourage higher levels of performance. Permitting additions, deletions or changes to the defined areas of performance measurement as negotiated between the parties encourages a process of continuous quality improvement throughout the evolution of the contract.
11. Is there a well-defined process for presenting, reviewing, and making changes?	A well-defined change process identifies the events that trigger a change, as well as who is involved, and their roles and responsibilities, including: The steps they will take to process the change (submit, review, approve/reject/modify, table or implement) The criteria that trigger a change (for example, a change in the number of seats may trigger a change for a per-seat help desk engagement)

Question to Ask Yourself	What to Look For
12. What are some of the reasons for voiding the agreement? What will the supplier do when the contract comes to an end?	You want the supplier to spell out at what level of underperformance you have the right to end the deal. Make sure this is very specific and not open to interpretation. You also want the supplier to spell out the exact steps for disengagement and the role the supplier will play in disengagement (whether disengagement results from a loss of contract due to failure to meet terms or simply the natural conclusion of the arrangement). Perhaps you want the supplier to phase out over a 90-day period, while transferring control of the services to your in-house staff or another supplier? Make sure this is included as a required service.

Contract Tip

In connection with the terms and conditions that are placed on the contract document, the best recommendation is to engage the advice of legal counsel that has specific experience in the field of outsourcing contracts.

INDEX

Index